Contents

Results Series

Sandra Nelson and June Garcia
for the Public Library Association

AMERICAN LIBRARY ASSOCIATION
Chicago 2003

Sandra Nelson is a consultant, speaker, trainer, and writer specializing in public library planning and management issues. She has worked in both large and small public libraries and in state library agencies, and has presented hundreds of training programs in more than thirty-five states during the past two decades. She chaired the Public Library Association committee that developed the PLA planning process, *Planning for Results: A Public Library Transformation Process* (1998) and is co-author of *Wired for the Future: Developing Your Library Technology Plan* (1999) and *Managing for Results: Effective Resource Allocation for Public Libraries* (2000), all published by ALA.

June M. Garcia is managing partner with Dubberly Garcia, a consulting firm that advises on a broad range of library projects including planning, facilities, and executive recruiting. She has been active with the Public Library Association to develop processes for public librarians to effectively plan, measure, and evaluate public library service. Garcia was the president of the Public Library Association from 1991 to 1992 and a member of the ALA Council. Her awards include the Librarian of the Year Award (1986) and the President's Award from the Arizona State Library Association.

Composition by the dotted i in Stempel Schneidler and Univers using QuarkXPress 4.01 on a Macintosh

Printed on 50-pound white offset, a pH-neutral stock, and bound in 10-point coated cover stock by Sheridan Books

The paper used in this publication meets the minimum requirements of American National Standard for Information Sciences—Permanence of Paper for Printed Library Materials, ANSI Z39.48-1992. ♾

Library of Congress Cataloging-in-Publication Data

Nelson, Sandra S.
Creating policies for results : from chaos to clarity / Sandra Nelson, June Garcia for the Public Library Association.
p. cm. — (PLA results series)
Includes bibliographical references and index.
ISBN 0-8389-3535-4 (alk. paper)
1. Public libraries—Administration. 2. Library rules and regulations. 3. Public libraries—United States—Administration. 4. Library rules and regulations—United States. I. Garcia, June. II. Public Library Association. III. Title. IV. Series.
Z678.N445 2003
025.1'974—dc21 2003006971

Printed in the United States of America.

07 06 05 04 03 5 4 3 2 1

Figures

Acknowledgment

The authors would like to thank Greta Southard, Executive Director of the Public Library Association, for her ongoing support of the PLA Results Series. She has a clear vision of how this series can assist library managers, staff, and trustees to improve library services, and she has shared that vision with the members of the PLA boards over the past six years. The strength of the series lies not in any single title, but rather in the consistent themes and messages that occur in every book. It is Greta's commitment to the series that has ensured that the messages remain consistent throughout multiple titles written by a variety of authors.

Introduction

Managing a public library has always been hard work, and it is becoming even more difficult under the twin pressures of restricted public funding and rapid change. The Public Library Association (PLA) plays a major role in providing the tools and training required "to enhance the development and effectiveness of public librarians and public library services."[1] During the past six years, PLA has provided support for the development of a family of management publications that are being used by library managers, staff, and boards around the country to manage the libraries in their communities more effectively. The four publications that are currently available are

The New Planning for Results: A Streamlined Approach[2]

Managing for Results: Effective Resource Allocation for Public Libraries[3]

Staffing for Results: A Guide to Working Smarter[4]

Creating Policies for Results: From Chaos to Clarity

All of these publications provide a fully integrated approach to planning and resource allocation, an approach that is focused on creating change—on *results*. The underlying assumptions in all the books in the PLA Results Series are the same:

Excellence must be defined locally. It is a result of providing library services that match community needs, interests, and priorities.

Excellence does not require unlimited resources. It occurs when available resources are allocated in ways that support library priorities.

Excellence is a moving target. The best decision-making model is to estimate, implement, check, and adjust—and then to estimate, implement, plan, and adjust again.

The PLA Results Series

All of the books in the PLA Results Series are intended to be used with *The New Planning for Results: A Streamlined Approach.* That book describes a library planning process that is focused on creating an actual blueprint for change rather than a beautifully printed plan for your office shelf. As you can see in the Planning for Results Model in figure 1, the process starts by looking at the community the library serves to identify what needs to happen to improve the quality of life for all of the community's residents. Once the community needs have been established, library planners look for ways the library can collaborate with other government services and non-profit agencies to help meet those needs. That, in turn, provides the information required to establish the library's service priorities.

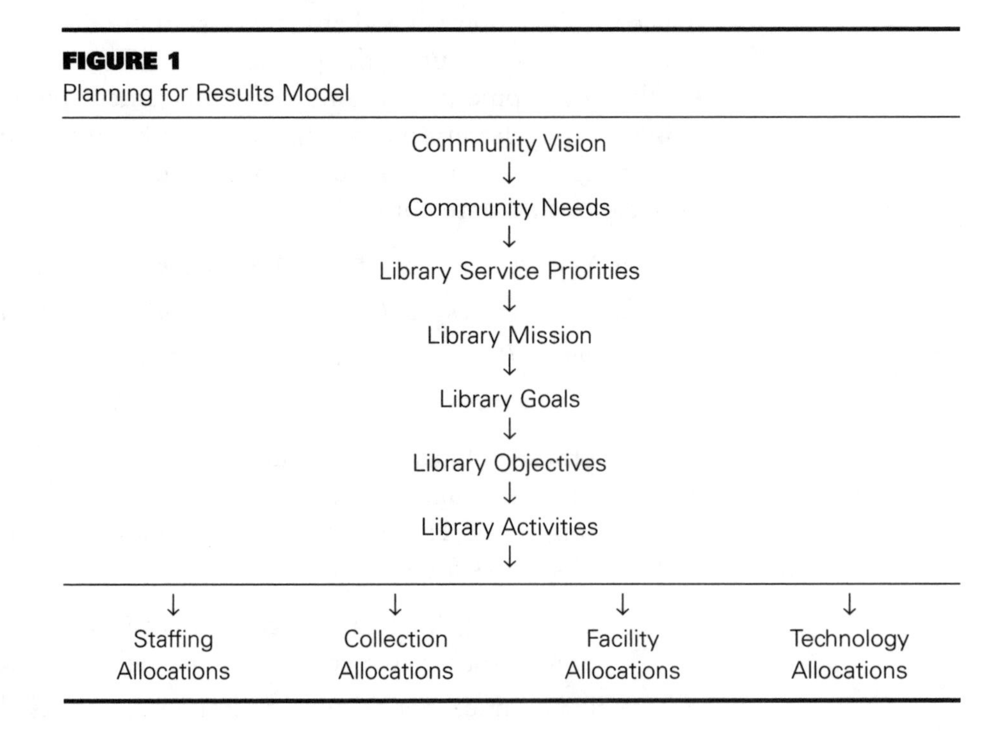

FIGURE 1
Planning for Results Model

The planning process includes significant participation by community residents who represent all of the constituencies served by the library: parents and children, working adults and seniors, businesspeople and civic leaders, students and educators, the various ethnic and religious groups in your community, government and non-profit leaders, and all of the other groups that together create your unique community. By involving all of these groups in your planning process you ensure that the services you provide are really what community residents want—and not what you or your staff or board think (or wish) that they want.

Because *The New Planning for Results* is focused on identifying and implementing the activities that will help library managers and staff to accomplish community-based goals and objectives, the decisions that are made are sure to affect every part of library operations. Every library manager, every library staff member, and every library board member is going to have to become used to the idea of continuously evaluating all of the services and programs the library provides and all of the policies that support those services in the context of the library's identified priorities—and then be willing to make any changes that are necessary. Changes don't happen because we want them to or hope they will. Changes happen only when we do things differently.

A library's policies are almost always affected by changes in the library's priorities. In fact, in many cases library policies have to be changed in order to actually implement new programs and services that support the new priorities. *Creating Policies for Results* provides a detailed series of tasks and steps that will help library managers and staff members to inventory, review, revise, and develop policy statements, regulations, procedures, and guidelines that support the library's priorities and ensure that library users receive equitable and consistent services.

Some Basic Definitions

Before you begin to read this book and use it to make policy decisions, it will be helpful if you understand how some basic terms have been used. Every public library is a little different. Staff in one library talk about "branches," in another library the term is "agencies," and in a third staff refer to both branches and departments as "units." Some libraries have "central" libraries, others have "main" libraries. There are libraries that report to authority boards and libraries that are units of the government entity that funds them, which may or not have advisory boards. Such differences can cause confusion because each reader expects to see his or her reality reflected in the terms and examples used. A list of terms and their meanings *in this book* follows:

Branch A separate facility.

Central Library The largest library facility, usually in a downtown area; referred to as the main library in some places.

Department A unit within a single facility that is normally a central library.

Library The entire organizational entity and its units.

Manager A generic term that refers to the staff member or staff members who are responsible for resource allocation in a particular area; in some libraries the "manager" is actually a team of staff members.

Team A group of staff members brought together to work on a specific project or program; often includes members from different departments and with different job classifications.

Unit A term used to refer to individual library departments and branches, if any.

The Anytown Public Library and the Tree County Public Library

The Anytown Public Library was introduced in the original *Planning for Results* and has appeared in most other titles in the PLA Results Series. Anytown is a mythical community somewhere in the United States and is one of two libraries used in case studies throughout this book. The Anytown Public Library serves a countywide population of 100,000 people and has an authority board. The library operates from a single facility with no branches and provides bookmobile services throughout the county.

The Tree County Public Library was introduced in *Staffing for Results* and is also used in some of the case studies in this book. Tree County is a mythical county somewhere in the United States with a countywide population of 400,000 people. The library serves the residents of Tree County with seven branches and has a governing board.

Using the Materials in This Book Effectively

Creating Policies for Results is intended to help library managers and boards to develop policies that reflect and support their library's priorities. That clearly implies that before managers and board members can use this book effectively, they must have a clear understanding of what they are trying to accomplish. This book is a part of the PLA Results Series, so there are references throughout to library planning documents developed using the *New Planning for Results* process. However, that certainly is not the only process that libraries use to identify priorities. Some libraries have participated in city or county strategic planning processes. Other libraries choose to develop annual goals and objectives for the library as a whole rather than to develop a multiyear plan. Yet others develop goals and objectives for individual units or for specific programs or services.

What should you do if your library has no current plan? Must you complete a whole planning process before you can use any of the tools in this book? Absolutely not. *Creating Policies for Results* can be used to develop new policies regardless of your environment. However, it is worth repeating that this book is about developing policies that reflect and support the library's priorities and not about determining what those priorities should be. *Before you can decide whether or not your current policies are effective and comprehensive, you must know what you want to accomplish.* Any process used to determine your library's desired outcomes can serve as the starting point for the processes described in this book.

NOTES

1. Public Library Association Mission Statement. Available: http://www.pla.org/factsheet.html on 9/7/01.
2. Sandra Nelson, *The New Planning for Results: A Streamlined Approach* (Chicago: American Library Association, 2001).
3. Sandra Nelson, Ellen Altman, and Diane Mayo, *Managing for Results: Effective Resource Allocation for Public Libraries* (Chicago: American Library Association, 2000).
4. Diane Mayo and Jeanne Goodrich, *Staffing for Results: A Guide to Working Smarter* (Chicago: American Library Association, 2002).

Chapter 1

Issues

MILESTONES

By the time you finish this chapter you will know how to

- explain to staff and board why the library needs formally adopted policies
- recognize the difference between library practices and library policies
- identify the elements of a library policy
- define the terms *policy statement, regulation, procedure,* and *guideline*
- explain why it important that policy statements, regulations, procedures, and guidelines are complete and current
- deal with the challenges you will face when reviewing, revising, or developing policy statements, regulations, procedures, and guidelines

Virtually every public library in this country has some sort of policy manual and most managers and board members understand the need for such manuals. It would be hard for them not to. Students in graduate school attend library management courses that discuss the importance of having library policies. Staff from state library agencies and library systems have been encouraging library managers and boards to develop policies for decades. Library management books start with the assumption that libraries have policies. Periodically, there are programs on policy development at state, regional, and national library conferences. The need for clear policies has been underscored recently as library managers grapple with such thorny problems as Internet use and filtering.

Although most people involved with libraries agree that it is important to have good library policies, the term *good* is clearly subjective. In an effort to illustrate what *good* policies look like, staff from a number of state libraries and library systems have developed or collected sample policies intended to provide a starting point for discussion or an actual outline for those charged with policy development. Human nature being what it is, many library managers and boards have simply made cosmetic changes in the sample policies under review and adopted them with little or no discussion—a sort of one-size-fits-all approach to policy development. Even this approach has become more complicated in the past several years because the Internet has expanded the number of policies available for review. In 2003, a Google search for "public library policies" resulted in 1,500,000 hits, which is more samples than any of us will ever be able—or want—to review.

Given all of the attention that has been focused on developing library policies for decades, it would seem that a book on library policies wouldn't have much of an audience. However, formal and informal discussions with library staff members, library managers, and library board members have made it clear that while most libraries have policy manuals, very few of the people who work in libraries are satisfied with those manuals or with the ways in which library policies are being developed or implemented. People identify a number of problems with library policies and the way they are developed:

Policies are not accurate reflections of current practice.

Policies are not accurate reflections of the library's priorities.

Policies are not updated regularly.

Policies do not address all of the issues that need to be addressed.

Policy manuals are often written in a narrative format that makes it difficult to separate policy statements, regulations, procedures, and guidelines.

Policy manuals may be poorly written and hard to understand.

It can be difficult for staff to get access to the policy manuals.

Policies are being developed by people who do not understand the concerns of the staff who will be charged with implementing those policies.

Policy statements or regulations conflict with local, state, or federal regulations.

The distinctions among policy statements, regulations, procedures, and guidelines are unclear.

Policy statements, regulations, procedures, and guidelines contradict each other.

These concerns make it clear that there is a big difference between having a policy manual and having an *effective* and *efficient* policy manual. Every book in the PLA Results Series has discussed efficiency and effectiveness. The difference between the two is simple:

Effectiveness = doing the right thing
Efficiency = doing the thing right

Those concepts certainly apply to the development of library policy statements, regulations, procedures, and guidelines. Policies and regulations are intended to ensure that the library operates in ways that are consistent with the organization's mission, goals, and objectives—*doing the right things.* Procedures and guidelines, on the other hand, are much more concerned with efficiency—*doing those things right.*

In fact, as you can see in figure 2, it is possible to define an effective policy manual by restating the problems listed above. This chapter will look at some of the issues you need to consider when deciding whether or not to update your library's policy manual.

Definitions

There are a variety of terms that are used when discussing policies: *guideline, policy, policy element, policy manual, policy statement, practice, regulation,* and *procedure.* These terms are open to almost as many inter-

FIGURE 2

Characteristics of Effective Policy Manuals

Effective policy manuals define current practice.

Effective policy manuals reflect the library's priorities.

Effective policy manuals are current, comprehensive, and consistent.

Effective policy manuals can be accessed easily by all staff and are user-friendly.

Effective policy manuals are in compliance with all local, state, and federal regulations.

Effective policy manuals are developed and reviewed by all staff who will be affected by the policy statements, regulations, procedures, and guidelines.

pretations as the terms *goal, objective,* and *activity.* There is no way you can have any meaningful discussions about the library's policy manual with your staff or the members of your governing body unless you all have a common understanding of the terms relating to policies. The following definitions have been used throughout this book:

Guideline A description of best practice that provides suggestions for staff on the most efficient ways to implement policy statements, regulations, and procedures. Guidelines are more philosophical than policy statements, regulations, or procedures and often are developed by staff committees. Guidelines are always approved by the library director but are rarely reviewed by the library's governing authority. Typical guidelines include reference guidelines and guidelines for serving people with special needs.

Policy The generic term used for the policy statement, regulations, procedures, and guidelines (if any) that apply to a specific issue.

Policy Element One of the four components of a policy: a policy statement, regulation, procedure, or guideline.

Policy Manual A collection of library policy statements. Policy manuals may include regulations, procedures, and guidelines. Policy manuals are normally available in print format and may be available electronically as well.

Policy Statement A brief, written statement that describes *why* the library does something. Policy statements are written from the customer's point of view and approved by the library's governing authority. See figure 3 for a sample policy statement.

Practice The way things are actually done in your library. Practice may or may not be supported by policy statements, regulations, and procedures. Practice is generally conveyed via oral tradition as a part of a new staff member's orientation, and it can become very subjective.

Procedure A written, step-by-step description of *how* the staff will carry out a policy and regulations. Procedures are more flexible than regulations and will change as the tools available to staff change. Frontline staff may be allowed to modify procedures in certain circumstances. Procedures are developed by staff and approved by library managers. They are not reviewed by or approved by the library's governing authority.

Regulation A specific, written rule that further defines a policy, describing *what* must be done to support the policy. Regulations are normally approved by the library's governing authority. See figure 3 for a list of sample regulations.

Figure 3 provides an example of the Tree County Public Library *policy statement* concerning staff borrowing privileges and the *regulations*

FIGURE 3

Sample Policy Statement and Regulations

BORROWING MATERIALS BY STAFF

Policy Statement

To ensure equitable access for all library users, the borrowing rights, privileges, and obligations of the Tree County Public Library staff are the same as those extended to the general public.

Regulations

1. A new staff member who lives within the county limits and does not have a library card will be issued one by the circulation supervisor on his or her first day of work.
2. A staff member who lives outside the county may purchase a nonresident library card for a fee of $50 per year, the same fee paid by other nonresidents.
3. A staff member who wishes to borrow library materials must have a valid Tree County Public Library card.
4. A staff member who lives outside the library's service area and does not have a personal Tree County Public Library card may use the unit card assigned to his or her department to borrow materials associated with a work assignment.
5. Circulation services staff are responsible for checking out and checking in the materials borrowed by library staff members. Library staff are not to check out the materials they wish to borrow or check in the materials they are returning.
6. Staff members will observe the same loan periods and loan limits that are observed by the general public.
7. Staff members are responsible for paying the same fines and fees that the general public is charged as described in the Fees and Fines policy. Fees and fines should be paid at the circulation desk by presenting the amount owed to a member of circulation services staff. Library staff are not to clear their own fees and fines from their borrower's records.
8. A staff member who wishes to borrow an item that is not currently available should place a reserve on the item.
9. New books and other new library materials should be made available to the public within 24 hours of their receipt from technical services. Staff members may borrow any of these items once they have been shelved in the public area.
10. A staff member who is aware that another staff member is violating the Borrowing Materials by Staff policy must inform his or her immediate supervisor.
11. Unit supervisors are authorized to waive these regulations for a member of their staff if so doing is essential to the completion of a work-related assignment.

that support that policy. The *procedures* have not been included in this example because the actual circulation procedures in each library are driven by the type of circulation system being used. However, an example of appropriate procedures might include the steps in the process of issuing a staff library card. There are no *guidelines* that apply to this particular policy, and the only way to determine the Tree County Public Library *practice* would be to visit each branch and unit and observe the staff.

Practice and Policy

Staff in many libraries operate in a gray area that falls somewhere between the formally adopted policies of the library and the staff's informal understanding of "how we do business here." In some libraries the differences between the formal policies and the informal practices are minor. In others there is no real relation between what the library policies say and what the staff do. It is the informal understanding of the way we do business in this library that defines the decisions made by staff rather than the formal policies that have been adopted by the library's governing authority.

There are a variety of reasons for the gaps between practice and policy. The most common reasons are that the library has no policy on a specific issue, that the library policies are outdated, or that staff resist a specific policy.

No Policy

Sometimes the gap between practice and policy occurs because the library management team has not developed policies in certain areas. In the mid-1990s many libraries began offering public access to the Internet before developing policy statements and regulations to govern that access or procedures for staff to follow when providing that access. As we all know, this led to a variety of problems and—ultimately—to the adoption of Internet access policies by virtually every public library in the United States. In another example, when library staff move to a new facility that has multiple meeting rooms from an old building that had no public meeting space, it may take awhile before the staff recognize the need for policies relating to public use of meeting space.

Outdated Policy

The gap between policy and practice can also occur because the existing policies are so outdated they no longer make sense in the current environment. There are numerous examples of this kind of dichotomy. In many libraries, the first policies addressing the circulation of video materials were developed at least 20 years ago and most prohibited the circulation of videos to minors. At that time videos were expensive and seen as peripheral to the core collection. In the intervening years lots of libraries have purchased automated circulation systems and staff have had to set the circulation parameters for each type of material the library circulates. Videos are now considerably less expensive and staff attitudes have changed as well. Many staff now see videos as an integral part of the library's collection. Therefore, it is not uncommon for libraries to establish circulation parameters in the library automation system that allow users with juvenile cards to check out videos even though the original—and outdated—video policy is still in place. Most of the circulation staff will allow kids to check out videos because the automation system allows them to do so. However, there will probably be a few members of the circulation staff who don't think the library should have videos for children (or adults) and who will continue to enforce the old policy.

Another example of this problem can be seen in older reference policies. It is not uncommon for a library's reference policy to state that the library staff will provide reference service to users on-site or by telephone. Some libraries have updated their policies to include faxes, but others have not. More and more libraries are offering e-mail and web-based reference service, and many of those same libraries haven't given any thought to updating the policies that in theory define the library's services in this area.

Staff Resistance to a Policy

Occasionally, staff members who feel strongly that a policy decision by library management is wrong may knowingly ignore the policy—or the parts of the policy they don't like. This can be a particular problem if the staff member is in a management position. Look again at the example in figure 3. As you review the policy and regulations relating to staff borrowing privileges in the Tree County Public Library, consider how the practice in the library or some branches within the library might differ from the official rules governing staff use of materials. Unless all of the managers in Tree County Public Library actively support the policy and monitor the regulations, this is an area in which practice may well differ widely from unit to unit.

Staff resistance to policy decisions can occur in large, multibranch systems because the various units serve such diverse clients. One such system recently developed a policy that required that all library users have their cards with them to check out any items. The regulations stated that if users did not have their cards they could be issued replacement cards but would have to pay a $10 replacement card fee. Several branch managers felt the policy and regulations were unfair and virtually impossible to enforce, particularly in small neighborhood branches where the staff knew most users by name. Therefore, the branch managers ignored the policy and encouraged their circulation staff to continue to allow checkouts to regular users whether they had their cards or not.

Functions of Library Policies

Libraries in which there is a significant gap between practice and policy face a number of potentially serious problems. The disparity may well create both formal and informal impediments to the successful implementation of the library's service priorities. Certainly any kind of variance between practice and policy may lead to confusion and frustration for both library staff and managers and for the public. Libraries in which practice takes precedence over policy often discover that different branches or units approach the provision of even basic services with different assumptions, which can lead to inequities in the services provided to the public. These in turn can create legal issues for both library staff and the members of the library's governing authority. The four primary functions of library policies are listed in figure 4.

Priorities and Values

Library policies define what a library values. That means that they have to be integrally connected to the library's priorities, mission, goals, and objectives. When the priorities, mission, goals, and objectives change, it is probable that the policies will have to be revised as well. That should go without saying but often doesn't. There are at least two different ways that libraries end up with conflicting priorities and policies.

In some cases library managers identify a procedural problem—or, even worse, a desired procedural outcome—and then write a policy that supports the procedural solution even if that policy does not support the library's mission or goals. For example, the process of placing reserves on materials was once both cumbersome and staff-intensive. As a result, many libraries had policies prohibiting reserves or limiting the number of items a user could have on reserve at any one time. A surprising number of libraries kept those restrictions in place after converting to an automated circulation system. Over the course of time, some of those libraries altered policies to allow staff to place reserves for library users. However, by the time they had decided to allow staff to place reserves, the automation software had advanced to the point

FIGURE 4
Functions of Policies

Policies

1. provide a mechanism for library managers and staff to translate the library's service priorities into actions
2. serve as the primary tool for ensuring that all staff have the information they need to do their jobs effectively
3. provide a way to ensure that all members of the public know what they can expect from the library and that they are treated equitably
4. provide support for the library staff and members of the library's governing body in the event of legal action

of allowing library users to place their own reserves on items. At the time that this book is being written—many years after the introduction of user-placed holds—there are still libraries in which user-placed holds are not allowed because of concerns about increased staff workload.

On the surface that concern may seem appropriate, but on closer examination it becomes clear that the policies restricting holds were written to make things easy for staff and not to provide quality services to the public. This was a particular challenge for both the staff and the public in libraries in which planners had selected "popular materials library" as a role or "current topics and titles" as a service response or that had phrases like "provide residents with the materials they want in a timely manner" in the mission statement. It is hard to give people what they want when they want it if you refuse to allow them to place holds on high-demand items because of the work it causes for staff.

Sometimes the gap between policy and priority occurs when the library priorities change. A planning process that results in shifts of priorities is almost always time-consuming and challenging. The process ends with the identification of activities that support the new goals and objectives and with the allocation or reallocation of resources required to accomplish those activities. Realistically, that means that most new activities are supported by the reallocation of resources.

Virtually every activity in a strategic plan will require some staff action to be implemented. However, library staff are fully occupied—some would say overoccupied—with current tasks. Changing staff assignments is always challenging. So is the process of reallocating collection resources. Many staff have proprietary feelings about the library collection and regard any possible changes in emphasis as a personal affront. If facilities resources need to be reallocated, there are often territorial issues to be resolved. It's not surprising that library managers get so involved in the process of reallocating resources that they simply forget to look at the existing policy structure. However, if there are conflicts between current policies and the new priorities, these can lead to real problems for library managers, staff, and for the public they serve. Part 1 of the Anytown Public Library Policies case study illustrates the issues that can arise.

CASE STUDY

ANYTOWN PUBLIC LIBRARY POLICIES

Part 1
Reflecting Priorities

The Anytown Public Library[1] recently completed a new strategic plan using the process described in *The New Planning for Results (NPFR)*.[2] At the conclusion of the planning process, the library planners had identified several new priorities, including "Commons." *NPFR* defines Commons by stating, "A library that provides a Commons environment helps address the need of people to meet and interact with others in their community and to participate in public discourse about community issues."[3]

The Anytown Public Library has four meeting spaces. There is a large meeting room that has a seating capacity of 100, a smaller room with a seating capacity of 25, and two rooms currently being used as study rooms that each has a seating capacity of 12. The library has traditionally used the two larger meeting spaces for library-sponsored programming. The meeting room policy is ten years old and restricts use of the library's meeting spaces to library or city employees only.

Clearly that policy will have to be revised to support the new priorities, but there are a variety of other policy issues that will need to be reviewed as well. The current customer service policy states that there can be no food or drink in the library. The existing policy on use of audiovisual equipment states that only staff can use library-owned equipment. The policy of posting materials to the library bulletin boards restricts the types of materials that outside groups can post. The policy on library hours makes no provision for use of the meeting room spaces when the library is closed. Each of these policy statements, and the regulations and procedures that support them, will have to be reviewed and revised before the library staff can begin to provide services that support a Commons environment.

Library staff may also discover the shift in priorities will require that they develop new policy statements or regulations. For instance, the Anytown Public Library has limited parking. If the revised meeting regulations allow community groups to meet before the library opens, it is likely that the meeting participants will use all of the available parking. Is that acceptable to the library managers and members of the library's governing authority, or would they prefer to ask meeting participants to park in a nearby city parking garage? This is a regulation decision that someone will need to address. You will hear more about the Anytown Public Library staff and board as they address these issues in later sections of this case study.

Internal Communication

As most library managers know, it is hard to keep all staff members fully informed about everything they need to know. One of the primary functions of internal communication is to clarify job duties, yet one of the most consistent complaints that staff make is that they don't have the information they need to do their jobs. There is also a pervasive feeling in some organizations that "everyone else knows more about what is going on than I do." This mild paranoia is becoming more prevalent as the pace of change in libraries accelerates. Library procedures are typically the most specific source of information about job duties available to staff. However, too often the procedures are outdated or not easily accessible. There is no question that the process of issuing updated procedures can be cumbersome. However, the Intranet technology that is available in most libraries now can provide an easy means to issue procedures updates and to provide key word access to those procedures to all staff.

A second function of internal communication is to define the library's values and norms. As stated in the previous section, library policy statements should reflect the library's priorities and values. Library regulations describe the expected service norms. Library managers can use the process of developing policy statements and regulations to build consensus about the library's priorities and values and to create a broad understanding of the organizational norms. Part 1 of the Tree County Public Library Policies case study illustrates how the staff in one library approached this process.

CASE STUDY

TREE COUNTY PUBLIC LIBRARY POLICIES

Part 1
Building Consensus

The Tree County Public Library[4] Board has just approved the new library strategic plan. The plan was developed using *The New Planning for Results*[5] and all staff members were given the opportunity to be involved in discussions about the library's service priorities. The potential service priority that raised the most questions was "Information Literacy." *NPFR* defines Information Literacy by stating, "A library that provides Information Literacy service helps address the need for skills related to finding, evaluating, and using information effectively."[6]

The planning committee members had agreed that it was critical that library staff take the lead in helping the growing number of seniors in the community to become more proficient at using computers in general and the Internet in particular. During the staff discussions about the potential effect that the selection of Information Literacy as a priority might have, staff members expressed a number of concerns.

- The library system doesn't have enough public access terminals to meet current demand.
- The public access terminals that are available are not spread equitably throughout the branches.
- Many staff members do not have the skills they need to help others to become proficient on computers.
- Many staff members feel that they do not have the skills they need to help others to find, evaluate, and use information on the Internet.
- Some staff members believed that this focus on technology will take needed resources from more important library services.
- Some staff said that if the public knew they were available to help with the Internet and other technology-related issues, staff would have no time for anything else.

The members of the planning committee and the members of the library's governing authority considered the staff concerns carefully but ultimately decided that the Information Literacy priority was critical for the community. Once the priority had been approved by the library board, library managers had the responsibility of making sure that the staff had the tools they needed to effectively provide this service.

The first task was to review the concerns that staff raised during the earlier discussions about Information Literacy. During the review, the managers realized that the staff concerns were a combination of resource issues and policy issues, and even the resource issues had policy or regulation implications. The managers identified the following policy and regulation issues to be resolved:

- acceptable use of public access terminals
- equity of access to public access terminals
- level of services to be provided by staff in support of general computer skills

- level of services to be provided by staff to assist users to find, evaluate, and use information on the Internet
- staff training policy statements and regulations

The managers decided that these policy issues affected all of the staff in the library in one way or another and that it would be important to provide a mechanism for all staff to be involved in the policy- and regulation-setting process. This meant the policy development process was going to take several months. That in turn meant that they would have to wait for at least six months—and possibly longer—to initiate most of the new services and programs that would support the Information Literacy priority. The trade-off of a six-month delay for a smoother transition seemed reasonable to most managers and was approved by the library director. You will hear more about the Tree County Public Library Board and staff as they address these issues in later sections of this case study.

Equitable Public Services

Libraries are publicly funded organizations and they are facing increasing scrutiny by unhappy taxpayers and budget-conscious politicians. It is important that members of the public believe that the services we provide are fair and equitable. To accomplish that, every library staff member must have access to, review, understand, and abide by the library's policies.

The first issue here is to be sure that all staff have access to the library's policies. Staff can't follow policies they don't know about. Most managers assume that all employees know where the policy manuals are located in each of the library's units. Like many other assumptions, that is often not the case, particularly if the policy manual is in print format in a three-ring binder. The binder is usually stored in the unit manager's office along with dozens of other binders and not readily accessible to staff for review. Furthermore, unless the policy manual is discussed and displayed during new-employee orientations, some staff members may not even know that it exists.

The second requirement for equitable public service is that all staff members actually read and understand the policy statements, regulations, procedures, and guidelines that are included in the library's policy manual, particularly those that relate to each staff member's job responsibilities. For example, circulation staff don't need to know all of the details of the library's reference policy, but they need to be very familiar with all of the policies relating to circulation functions.

The final requirement for providing equitable public service is to be sure that all staff members are following the library's policies. Both managers and frontline staff need to understand why it is so important that all members of the public be treated equitably. Managers need to monitor compliance and there must be consequences if certain units or specific staff members routinely ignore the library's policies. There are few things more frustrating for a staff member than explaining a library policy to a library user and then having the user respond, "The staff at the Elm Branch always let me do this." However, asking a library user if you can help him and having him reply, "No thanks, I'll wait for Mary Sue" comes close, particularly if you know that Mary Sue routinely bends the rules for certain people and that the branch manager lets her get away with it. It is unreasonable to expect staff to treat the public equitably if the staff believe that they themselves are being treated unfairly.

Legal Support

Library policies provide a legal framework for the delivery of services to the public. Public library policies are enforceable only if the policies are in writing and have been adopted formally by the library's governing authority in an open meeting. In addition, these policies will be valid only if they meet the four tests of legality, reasonableness, nondiscriminatory application, and measurability. Policies that do not meet those tests could be ruled invalid if challenged in court. Once adopted by the board, the policies should be made available to staff, the public, and the press.

The Library of Michigan has developed four tests for a locally enforceable policy that are appropriate for all public libraries in the country:

1. Does the policy conform to current law? Changes in the law often precipitate policy review. Remember the changes in many public policies after the passage of the Americans with Disabilities Act? Sometimes the answer to this question is not straightforward because the status of the law in a certain area is still being developed. Just think of the uncertainty surrounding the whole area of Internet access. Legislators at both the state and the federal levels are still examining the issues related to this technology. The courts are just beginning to hear cases that challenge various efforts to formulate public policy in this area. Competent legal counsel is a necessary expense when writing policy.
2. Is the policy reasonable? Many policies, although legal on the surface, could be successfully challenged if they are unreasonable. Most libraries have policies that establish consequences for the nonreturn of borrowed materials. Restrictions on borrowing additional materials, payment for replacement of lost materials, or fines are typical consequences. It would be reasonable to suspend borrowing privileges until materials are returned; it would probably be unreasonable to banish offending patrons from the library for the rest of their lives.

3. Can the policy be enforced in a nondiscriminatory manner? Policies must be applied fairly to all patrons. Circulation policies, for example, should be the same for all; board members or volunteers should not get special treatment. Giggling adolescents should not be treated more harshly than loud-speaking adults. A policy, no matter how reasonable or legal, might be challenged if it is not applied equally to all.
4. Is the enforcement of the policy measurable? It is difficult to enforce a policy fairly if the behavior specified or prohibited by the policy is not quantifiable. Most libraries, for example, have circulation policies that limit the number of items any one patron may borrow at any one time. A library is inviting a challenge if the policy states that the number of items borrowed must be "reasonable" and kept for a "reasonable period of time." Staff then determine what "reasonable" means on a case-by-case basis. Charges of favoritism or discrimination would soon follow. A good circulation policy would state a definite number of items loaned for a specific period of time.[7]

Challenges

It would seem clear that current, effective library policies play a critical role in providing quality library services. However, it is equally clear that lots of libraries have neither current nor effective library policies. This is rare because the library managers and members of the library's governing authority don't understand the importance of library policies. Most of them understand all too well. In fact, many library managers and board members feel a certain level of "policy guilt." It is sort of like the "attic guilt," "basement guilt," or "garage guilt" that many of us deal with at home. We know that the attic, basement, or garage is a mess and that it is getting worse every day. We know there are things stored there that we really need but that they are buried in junk and not very accessible, and we know that there are other things that should be thrown away. We just don't seem to be able to find the time, energy, or motivation to do anything about it.

Those same issues—time, energy, and motivation—play a role in policy guilt, but there are other problems that make it difficult to deal with policies as well. They include lack of staff or board support, the absence of a clear process for the development of policies, the complexity of the issues under review, reluctance to make hard or unpopular decisions, the difficulty in building consensus for certain policy statements or regulations, and the problems with disseminating and enforcing new policy statements, regulations, and procedures.

Time and Energy

In a recent survey of more than 2,500 men and women sponsored by Norelco, 94 percent of the people surveyed said they didn't have enough time to do everything they wanted and needed to do.[8] This is not exactly a news flash for a lot of us. Most library managers say they feel that they have less control of their time than they did five years ago and many say that they are overwhelmed by the sheer volume of things that need to be done.

A part of the problem is that we are all so busy with the things that are urgent that we have little or no time to do the things that are important. There is a big difference between urgent and important. According to *Merriam-Webster's Collegiate Dictionary*,[9]

urgent means "calling for immediate attention"

important means "marked by or indicative of significant worth or consequence; valuable in content or relationship"

In other words, urgent tasks are things that demand a reaction from us—often an immediate reaction. Important tasks, on the other hand, usually require us to be proactive and initiate action in an area in which there is no perceived immediate crisis but rather a long-term benefit.

There is no question that a comprehensive, current policy manual is "of significant worth" and "valuable in content." The challenge that you and other managers face is finding the time to address this and other important tasks in your library. There are no easy answers to this challenge, nor is there a single solution that works for everyone. However, effective library managers find ways to accomplish the important tasks in their organizations.

Motivation

One of the things that make it hard to tackle important but not urgent projects is that the important projects tend to get lost in the minutia of the day-to-day operation of the library. It can be useful to have a management retreat that is focused not on the crisis du jour but rather on the overall organizational health and well-being of the library. During this retreat, take the time to think about the underlying causes of the endless stream of crises you spend your time resolving. You will probably discover that many of the crises are caused by the lack of clear policies or by conflicting or outdated policies. That in turn can provide the motivation needed to begin to review and revise the library's policies. It is easier to commit to an important project if you believe that the results of the project will be of real benefit to you and your organization.

Belief is the first task in self-motivation. The second is action. This is normally where the process breaks down. Visualization is a tool that has proved effective in helping people move from belief to action. Start by visualizing the problems that are being caused by the lack of comprehensive and current policies. Be as specific as you can. You might visualize an angry library user complaining to you that another user received preferential treatment. Then you might see a staff member who doesn't know how to resolve a user problem because she doesn't know and can't find the applicable procedure. Perhaps you see a city council member who is angry because he wants the library board to name a new branch after an affluent constituent and the board refuses—although there is no policy on the subject. Then visualize the changes that will occur when you have completed the review and revision of all of the library's policy manual. Again be specific. You might see the circulation staff meeting to discuss how to implement new changes throughout the system or managers having the tools they need to resolve small problems before they become urgent. The process of visualization will help you stay focused on the benefits of action.

Staff and Board Support

You can't review and revise the library's policy manual by yourself. You need the input and involvement of the management team, the frontline staff, and the members of your governing authority. That means you have to persuade a lot of people that the project is important and worth their efforts.

Just as belief is the first task in self-motivation, it is also the first task in selling an idea to someone else. People won't buy something they don't believe they need. Your job will be to explain the benefits of creating a current, comprehensive policy manual in terms that make sense to the various constituencies that need to be involved. As you think about how you will sell the idea of reviewing and revising your policy manual to managers, frontline staff, and the members of your governing authority, remember two things. You can't sell something you don't understand and you can't sell something you don't believe in.

It is probable that you will have to make different presentations to managers, frontline staff, and the members of your governing authority. Each group has a unique point of view. The members of your governing authority may be most responsive to the suggestion that a good policy manual will provide legal protection for the library and serve as an overall framework for decision making. Library managers, on the other hand, are more likely to be influenced by the thought that a clear and comprehensive policy manual will make it easier to train new staff and to resolve problems with library users in an equitable manner. Frontline staff want the tools they need to do their jobs well. No one likes to be put in a position of appearing stupid or incompetent in front of a library user. Clear policy statements, regulations, procedures, and guidelines that are easily accessible can provide staff with the answers they need when they need them.

Be prepared to deal with people's concerns and objections during your discussions. While the members of your governing authority are likely to be very open about their concerns, managers and frontline staff might be more hesitant about expressing their feelings. It is dangerous to assume that a lack of questions or objections means that everyone agrees with you. Passive-aggressive behavior is not unusual in any library—and it is a way of life in some libraries. Even if people aren't saying anything, you can be sure that some of them are thinking "yes, but. . . ." The best way to deal with the "yes, but . . ." reaction is to identify the most likely concerns and objections and to acknowledge and respond to them when you are discussing the project you are trying to sell. Sometimes people are afraid that if they bring up potential problems, they will put ideas in people's heads that were not there before. This is not likely. Most people are more than capable of thinking up potential problems on their own, with no help from anyone else. Ignoring their concerns certainly won't make them go away. It will simply persuade the members of your audience that you are so out of touch you don't even understand the problem.

Process Problems

As noted earlier, there is often a gap between belief and action. Sometimes that gap occurs because people truly don't know what steps will be required to accomplish a given task. The unknown is scary and can make a project seem much more difficult than it actually is. The purpose of this book is to provide you with a detailed outline of the tasks you need to perform to review and revise the library policy manual and with tools to simplify the process. The process has been divided in four tasks:

1. *Inventory—chapter 2:* In this chapter you will learn how to conduct a policy audit to determine what policy statements, regulations, procedures, and guidelines currently exist.
2. *Assessment—chapter 3:* In this chapter you will learn how to evaluate your current policy statements, regulations, procedures, and guidelines.
3. *Development—chapter 4:* In this chapter you will learn how to revise policy statements, regulations, procedures, and guidelines and to develop new ones.
4. *Implementation—chapter 5:* In this chapter you will learn how to disseminate and implement the library's policy statements, regulations, procedures, and guidelines.

Decisions, Decisions, Decisions

The decision to review and revise the library policy manual will inevitably lead to many more decisions that need to be made. Some people find the process of decision making to be difficult. The Latin word *decido* has two meanings. It can mean "to decide." It can also mean "to fall off" (plants are called deciduous if they shed their leaves in the fall). A fear of falling—and failing—can keep people from making decisions.[10] There are other personal issues that can make decision making difficult. Some managers want to please everyone and are very well aware of the fact that any decision, no matter how simple, is going to make someone angry. Others are overcautious and refuse to make a decision unless they absolutely, positively know that it is the right decision. Unfortunately, that degree of absolute certainly about any library-related decision is almost nonexistent. There are managers who refuse to make any decision that will lead to change because they are invested in maintaining the status quo at all costs. Then there are those managers who will make a decision, . . . and then revisit the decision and make it again, . . . and again. . . . This can be more disruptive to an organization than never making a decision at all.

For most of us, decision making is a learned skill rather than an innate ability. That means that we can improve our decision-making skills through study and practice. There are four tasks in making a decision: define the problem, collect data about the problem, identify and evaluate the options for resolving the problem, and select the most effective option.

The Problem

Decisions are choices that you make to resolve a specific problem or issue. You can't make a good decision until you understand the problem or issue to be resolved. To do that, you first have to define the problem or issue. In part 1 of the Tree County Public Library Policies case study, the staff expressed concerns about the selection of Information Literacy as one of the library's priorities. Among other things, staff said they didn't think the library had the technology resources that would be required, nor did they feel that they were qualified to provide the service. These are legitimate concerns that need to be addressed. However, before the Tree County Public Library managers can make valid decisions about how to address these concerns, they need to identify the problem or problems to be resolved. Consider the two sets of problem statements below. Which seems more likely to you?

PROBLEM STATEMENTS, SET 1

The staff really resent the increasing role of technology in the library.

The staff don't want any changes in their jobs.

The staff expect the library to provide enough terminals at every site so that no one ever has to wait.

PROBLEM STATEMENTS, SET 2

The staff see that there are usually people waiting to use the public-access terminals and want to know how they are going to accommodate the additional demands that this priority will create.

The staff feel that they don't have the training they need to successfully implement this priority.

Managers who believe the first set of statements define the situation will be identifying very different options to resolve the problem than will managers who believe the second set of statements reflect the issues to be addressed.

The Data

In most cases, the possible options for resolving a problem are not immediately apparent, nor are they intuitive. That means that before you can identify the options, you need to gather data about the problem. The data you need will vary with the problem under consideration. Some of the data will probably be readily available, but other data may need to be collected. For instance, the Tree County Public Library managers may have data indicating that the library's public-access terminals are in use an average of 74 percent of the time. However, before they can identify options for providing the terminals needed to implement the Information Literacy priority, they will need to identify the use patterns—when the terminals are in use and when they are free. They will also need to review terminal use in each of the library's units. There is a good chance that the use patterns vary by site. The most important thing to remember when gathering data is the old acronym GIGO (garbage in—garbage out). You can't make good decisions based on bad data.

The Options

When you are through collecting data, you are ready to identify possible options. At first glance, it would seem that identifying options would be fairly easy. However, that is not always true. It can be surprisingly difficult to identify creative options, particularly if the problem has been around for a while. We all have preconceived ideas about things. We "just know" that something won't work based on experiences we had ten or fifteen years ago or something a colleague from another library once told us. The library environment has changed a lot in the past decade and things that didn't work at one time might well be worth considering again. There is also a tendency to think that there is only one right answer to every question. Many library managers were once reference librarians who spent their days finding *the* answer. Some managers find it hard to shift from that perspective and to begin thinking about multiple answers, any one of which might work, depending on the circumstance.

The Decision

Ultimately all decision making comes down to making a choice. You have to use the data you have collected and your knowledge of the library to evaluate each of the options you have identified and select the best one. The best option is probably not going to be the perfect solution to the problem. There is no perfect solution to some problems. The perfect solution to other problems may require more resources than you have or may be impossible to implement because of governance issues or union contracts. However, if you have defined the right problem, gathered accurate and relevant data, and identified a wide range of options, the decision you make will have a positive effect on the library. On the other hand, ignoring issues and refusing to resolve problems will inevitably have a negative effect on the library and the services it offers.

Staff Consensus

Libraries are bureaucracies, not democracies. The majority does not rule. The library director and the library's governing authority do. We are in the business of providing the best possible services to our customers and that means that the public's needs take precedence over staff desires. It is important for any discussion about building staff consensus to begin with this reality check. However, it is equally important to acknowledge that staff members who understand and support the library's policies will provide much better customer service than will staff members who do not.

Consensus building is a process by which group members seek a mutually acceptable resolution to the issue under discussion. Note that consensus does not mean that everyone agrees that the solution is the best of all possible answers. A group has reached consensus when everyone can and will support the decision. People are more likely to support a decision that they have been involved in making. The converse is true as well. Staff will resist most strongly decisions that appear arbitrary and capricious, sudden decisions, and decisions that are expected to be implemented immediately with no discussion. Chapters 4 and 5 include a variety of ways that you can involve staff in the policy development process and build consensus in your organization.

Dissemination and Enforcement

It would be nice if the policies you create were an end in themselves and your work was done when the last decision was made. Instead, your real work is just beginning. It doesn't do any good to have policies that no one knows about, cares about, or follows. The whole point of the process is to create a library environment in which staff members are fully aware of their duties and have the information they need to complete those duties and in which every library user is treated equitably. For this to occur, you have to disseminate the policies to the staff, train staff to be sure that they understand the policies, and then monitor implementation. You will need to be sure that the public is aware of the policies, understands why the policies exist, and believes that the policies are being applied equitably. These issues are discussed in detail in chapter 5.

Key Points to Remember

1. There is a difference between policy and practice. In libraries that offer excellent services the differences between the two are minimal. In libraries that offer mediocre or poor services the differences are often significant.
2. Policies are among the most effective tools library managers have for ensuring that all staff members have the information they need to do their jobs effectively.
3. Policies are necessary for the provision of equitable public service.
4. The process of developing or revising policies provides an opportunity for building consensus within the library.
5. If you avoid making policy decisions about controversial or challenging issues, you are still making a decision—and it is a decision that is likely to have negative consequences.

NOTES

1. There is more information about the Anytown Public Library and the community of Anytown in the introduction to this book.
2. Sandra Nelson, *The New Planning for Results: A Streamlined Approach* (Chicago: American Library Association, 2001).
3. Ibid., 65.
4. There is more information about the Tree County Public Library and the demographics of Tree County in the introduction to this book.
5. Nelson.
6. Ibid., 65.
7. Available: http://www.libofmich.lib.mi.us/publications/trusteejuly00.html on 5/1/02. Used with permission.
8. "Got Time?" *Tennesseean,* April 8, 2000, D1.
9. Available: http://www.m-w.com/home.htm on 5/2/02.
10. Hossein Arsham, *Applied Management Science: Making Good Strategic Decisions.* Available: http://ubmail.ubalt.edu/~harsham/opre640/opre640.htm on 3/25/02.

Chapter 2

Inventory

MILESTONES

By the time you finish this chapter you will know how to

- understand the key elements in a policy audit
- explain to staff and members of your governing authority why it is important to complete a policy audit
- select the staff members who should be involved in the policy audit
- develop a plan of action for completing a policy audit
- collect all of the library's current policy statements, regulations, procedures, and guidelines
- deal with the challenges you will face while completing the inventory portion of the policy audit

It is one thing to say that virtually every public library has a variety of policy statements, regulations, procedures, and guidelines. It is quite another thing to ask the managers in those libraries to find and organize all of those documents. At first glance, this may not seem like a difficult request. Most managers can pull out a print copy of the "official" library policy manual. However, if the official library policy manual has been printed on three-ring punched paper and stored in a binder—and most are—the odds of any two managers having exactly the same manual are not good.

Shortly after moving to a new library, a library director wanted a copy of the policy manual from her previous library to use as a model for her current staff. She asked the head of public services in her former library to send her a copy. The copy arrived without a table of contents and did not appear to be complete. She asked the head of public services to fax the table of contents and discovered that the manual was indeed missing a number of revisions. She asked another manager to send copies of the missing documents and discovered that he didn't have all of them either. The second manager finally gathered a full copy of the manual and sent them to the director with a note saying, "My unit now has what is probably the only current and accurate set of policies in the organization."

It is easy to laugh and say, "Boy, things sure are a mess at the first library." However, it would be wise not to make hasty assumptions. Before you cast too many aspersions, it might be informative to do a spot check in your library. It is very likely that you will discover the same situation that the library director in the example did. The reasons vary but they are all perfectly understandable. At some point in time one manager probably forgot to file a revision to a policy. Another manager may have misfiled one or more revisions. Perhaps an employee needed to photocopy the part of the manual that addresses "claims returned" items to give to a library user and then forgot to refile the original in the binder. The longer it has been since a complete and comprehensive version of the policy manual has been issued to everyone, the more likely it is that there are significant discrepancies in the manuals in the various units.

However, that is just the first of the difficulties that managers will face when they begin to collect all of the library's policy statements, regulations, procedures, and guidelines. In some units you may find that there are well-defined procedures that do not include any explicit policy statements or regulations. In other units there may be guidelines for services that have no clear relation to policy statements, regulations, or procedures. Many circulation procedures are driven by the library's automation software and may be available only in the manuals provided by the software vendor. You may even have policy statements that were adopted by the board at some point in time but for which regulations and procedures have not been written. This chapter will give you the tools and information you need to find and organize the library's current policy statements, regulations, procedures, and guidelines.

Definitions

This chapter will introduce several terms that will be used throughout the remainder of the book. To ensure that everyone has the same understanding of those terms, they are defined below:

Approved By The person or board that formally approved the policy statement, regulation, procedure, or guideline. If someone with the authority to do so hasn't approved the policy statement, regulation, procedure, or guideline, it is simply a written description of a practice.

Master Category List A complete list of the policy categories within a given policy type and an enumeration of the specific policies included in each category. See figure 5 for an example of a master category list.

Policy Audit The methodical collection, examination, and review of the library's existing policy statements, regulations, procedures, and guidelines. Policy audits have two parts:

Inventory The process of identifying, collecting, and organizing the library's existing policy statements, regulations, procedures, and guidelines. This chapter will address inventory issues.

Assessment The process of evaluating the library's existing policy statements, regulations, procedures, and guidelines. Chapter 3 will address assessment issues.

Policy Category Subdivisions of types of policies. Six policy categories have been used in this book to classify public service policy statements and the regulations, procedures, and guidelines that support those policy statements. The categories are listed below and described in more detail in figure 5:

- governance and organizational structure
- management policies
- customer services
- circulation services
- information services
- group services

Policy Type General groupings of library policies. Public libraries typically have at least five policy types: public service, technical service, personnel, financial, and collection development.

Purpose of a Policy Audit

Most of us are too busy to spend a lot of time on process activities that do not appear to have a big payoff. There is a tendency among library managers to say, "OK, we need to do something about the library policy manual. Just tell us what policies we need to write and we'll do it."

There are two major problems with this approach. The first is that it assumes that every policy, regulation, and procedure the library has now is just fine the way it is. In this time of continuous change one of our mantras has become "if it ain't broke, don't fix it," and most of us have fallen into the habit of thinking that if there are no overt and immediate problems in a given area, then "it ain't broke." This is a dangerous assumption for any manager to make about her area of responsibility. As we have seen, it is certainly an inaccurate assumption in terms of library policies. There is no way for an organization to develop a complete and comprehensive policy manual without first doing a full inventory and review of existing policy statements, regulations, procedures, and guidelines.

The second problem is the assumption that someone outside of your organization can wave a magic wand and tell you what policies you need. Just stating that assumption out loud is enough to make most managers realize how unrealistic it is. The only way you can determine what you have is to complete a policy audit inventory. The only way to make an informed decision about what you need is to evaluate what you have.

Essentially, a policy audit is a needs assessment process, and it is similar to other such processes in which you have participated. There are two parts of every needs assessment. You have to determine where you are now and you have to decide where you want to be. Many of you are familiar with *The New Planning for Results (NPFR),* a companion volume to this book. That book describes a planning process for public libraries that includes a comprehensive needs assessment process. The most challenging and time-consuming part of the *NPFR* needs assessment process is determining where the library wants to be. In the policy audit you know before you begin what you are working toward: a current, comprehensive policy manual. The larger challenge is to determine where you are now. The policy audit provides you with the information you need to define your current conditions.

Design of a Policy Audit

Although the primary focus of this chapter is on the inventory component of a policy audit, this section will address the broader issues involved in designing the entire policy audit process. There are three things to consider when designing your policy audit: first, *what* is the scope of the project; then, *who* should be involved in the project; and finally, *when* will the project begin and how long will it take.

What

A policy audit is not automatically an all-or-nothing proposition. It is perfectly appropriate for library managers or members of the library's governing authority to decide that they want to do a policy audit of just one type of policy or one part of the library's operations. This book focuses on public service policies, so all of the examples, case studies, and development tools in appendix A are related to public services. However, you would use the same policy audit *process* to review collection development policies, technical services policies, personnel policies, or financial policies.

Even the choice to focus the policy audit on public service policies does not mean that you have to include *all* the public service policies in the library in the audit. Public service policies can be divided into a number of broad categories, and you and your colleagues may choose to restrict the policy audit to a single category. Figure 5 shows examples of six broad categories of public service policies and lists the common policy subjects that might be included under each category. Templates for developing these policies have been included in appendix A.

There are several factors to weigh when determining the scope of your policy audit. The most critical issue is staff time. Obviously, you can complete a policy audit of your circulation policies with fewer staff resources than would be required to complete an audit of all of the public service policies. It might make sense to focus on one category of policies at a time, which would allow the people you have involved in the process to develop their skills as they work through the library's policies. By the time you reach the last several categories, the whole process will probably be both easier and more effective because everyone will know what to expect.

There are other benefits to this approach as well. It creates an environment in which there is an expectation that the review and revision of policy statements, regulations, procedures, and guidelines will be an ongoing process. It also gives all staff members who are interested the opportunity to really think about the policies in a single category, rather than forcing them to divide their attentions among all of the library's public service policies.

Sometimes, the choice of which category or categories of your policy manual should be addressed first is driven by external considerations. If you are moving to a new automated circulation system vendor, you will probably have to do a full audit on your circulation policies. The procedures will almost certainly change, and even the policy statements and regulations should be reviewed and considered carefully. A

FIGURE 5

Public Service Policy Categories and Subjects

	GOVERNANCE AND ORGANIZATIONAL STRUCTURE
GOV-1	City/County Organization Chart
GOV-2	Locations and Hours of All Units
GOV-3	Library Board Bylaws
GOV-4	Library Board Standing Committees
GOV-5	Library Organization Chart
GOV-6	Staff Association Activities
	MANAGEMENT POLICIES
MNG-1	Confidentiality of Library Records
MNG-2	Statistics
MNG-3	Petty Cash
MNG-4	Fund-Raising and Donations
MNG-5	Reconsideration of Library Materials
MNG-6	Building Maintenance
MNG-7	Emergencies and Disasters
MNG-8	Meeting Room Use
MNG-9	Exhibits and Displays
MNG-10	Bulletin Boards
MNG-11	Distribution of Nonlibrary Materials
MNG-12	Staff Committees and Staff Task Forces
MNG-13	Inclement Weather and Closing
	CUSTOMER SERVICES
CUS-1	Customer Service
CUS-2	Customer Behavior
CUS-3	Unattended Children
	CIRCULATION SERVICES
CIR-1	Library Cards for Residents
CIR-2	Library Cards for Nonresidents
CIR-3	Loan Periods and Loan Limits
CIR-4	Renewals
CIR-5	Reserves
CIR-6	Claims Returned or Claims Never Had
CIR-7	Lost or Damaged Materials
CIR-8	Fines and Fees
CIR-9	Borrowing Materials by Staff
	INFORMATION SERVICES
INF-1	Priorities for Reference Service
INF-2	Interlibrary Loan
INF-3	Internet Use
INF-4	Use of Library-Provided Personal Computers
	GROUP SERVICES
GSV-1	Programs in the Library
GSV-2	Co-Sponsored Programs in the Library
GSV-3	Community Presentations
GSV-4	Special Events
GSV-5	Tours
GSV-6	Computer Training for the Public

lot of library policy statements and regulations were developed ten or twenty or even thirty years ago and the assumptions upon which the policies were based may no longer be valid.

Who

In most libraries, the library director does not have the authority to set policy—that is a function of the library's governing authority. Therefore, it is important to be sure that the members of the library's governing authority officially approve the policy audit. They are going to have to act on any recommended policy changes that result from the audit and they are likely to be more responsive if they have been involved in the policy review process from the beginning.

You will also need to decide who is going to be responsible for managing the policy audit. On first glance, it may seem easiest to assign the inventory part of the audit to one person and the assessment part of the process to another, but it normally works best if a single person is put in charge of the overall project. That ensures that someone is keeping an eye on the big picture, which is important in a project as detail-driven as a policy audit.

Policy Audit Project Manager

The person you select to manage the policy audit needs to have certain skills. First and foremost, the project manager should be someone with broad library knowledge and a clear understanding of the current operations of the library. It is equally important that the project manager be organized. The inventory part of the policy audit is going to produce a large amount of data in a variety of formats and you will need someone who knows how to manage effectively in that kind of environment.

During the assessment part of the audit, the project manager is going to have to work with staff throughout the library to review and classify existing policy statements, regulations, procedures, and guidelines. This is complex work and requires a person who is both logical and comfortable with details. In other words, this is probably not the job for the most creative person on your staff. On the other hand, the analytical person who loves databases, who can always put her hand on the memo that everyone else has lost, and who can spot a discrepancy in a procedure at a glance is just the person you are looking for.

Assistants to the Project Manager

The next decision that you have to make is whether or not to assign one or more staff members to assist the project manager. One option would be to ask one person to help the project manager with the inventory part of the process and a second to assist with the assessment part of the process. This decision will be based on the size of your library, the probable complexity of the policy audit, and the workload of the project manager. Generally, larger libraries with more outlets have more complex policy audit environments than smaller libraries, although this is not always true. A library housed in a single building that has had three directors in the past six years, each with very different ideas about the appropriate policies for the library, might well be a more complex policy audit environment than a multibranch library.

Consider, too, the workload of the project manager. If the library director decides to serve as the project manager, then it is imperative that additional staff be assigned to assist her. On the other hand, if you are fortunate enough to work in an organization that has a staff position that includes policy development in the job duties, you probably won't want to subdivide the responsibilities. In most libraries, the decision will not be as clear-cut as either of these examples, and the library director and project manager will have to consider local circumstances carefully when determining project staffing needs.

Policy Audit Advisory Committee

The third issue to consider when deciding whom to involve in the policy audit is whether or not you want to appoint a team of people from throughout the library to serve on a Policy Audit Advisory Committee. An advisory committee can serve several important functions throughout the audit and is usually the most efficient way to complete the process.

During the inventory part of the audit, the advisory group provides an excellent way to spread the word about the policy audit throughout the library. Committee members can also serve as conduits of information from the staff back to the person managing the policy audit. Staff members are often more comfortable talking about questions or concerns with their peers than with members of the management team.

During the assessment part of the audit, the advisory committee can take the lead in developing evaluation criteria and evaluating the quality and accuracy of the existing policy statements, regulations, procedures, and guidelines. Finally, the individual members of the advisory group may be asked to chair subcommittees assigned to revise or develop new policy statements, regulations, procedures, or guidelines.

It is evident from the possible functions of the advisory group that it will be important to select the members carefully. You will want to include staff representing all of the library units. As the audit moves into the assessment phase, you will want to be sure that you have members who have a good understanding of the various services the library offers as a well as practical hands-on knowledge of how things are done in the library.

When

The timeline for your policy audit will depend on the scope of the project and the amount of staff time available for the project. This is not the kind of project that you need to rush to finish. However, the project should not be open-ended either. All too often, a project that has no official deadline is never finished. It makes sense to consider the timeline in two parts: policy audit (inventory and assessment) and policy development.

The time required for the policy audit is fairly easy to estimate. The inventory part of the policy audit will probably take six or eight weeks to complete. That will allow enough time to inform the staff of the project; gather all of the existing policy statements, regulations, procedures, and guidelines; and organize all of the materials that are received. The assessment part of the policy audit should also be able to be completed in six or eight weeks.

That means that at the end of three or four months you will be ready to move on to the development phase of the policy review process. It is impossible to make a general estimate of how much time the development part of the process will take. It depends entirely on what you discover during the policy audit. If only minor revisions to a few procedures are needed, you can complete the work in weeks. If major revisions or lots of new policy statements, regulations, procedures, or guidelines are needed, you may well be looking at months or even years of work. There is more information in chapter 4 about estimating the time required to revise existing policies or develop new ones.

Policy Audit Inventory

The inventory part of the policy audit is a straightforward data collection process, with the data consisting of existing policy statements, regulations, procedures, and guidelines. The inventory has three tasks:

Task 1: *Identify* the specific categories (or subcategories) of the library's current policies to be included in the policy audit inventory.

Task 2: *Collect* all existing policy statements, regulations, procedures, and guidelines in the categories of policies identified in Task 1 above.

Task 3: *Organize* the policy statements, regulations, procedures, and guidelines that you collect so that you are ready to begin the policy audit assessment process (discussed in chapter 3).

These three tasks are each divided into three steps, which are listed at the beginning of the discussion of each task below. Figure 6 shows all of the tasks and steps in the policy audit inventory.

TASK 1: IDENTIFY

Step 1.1: Refine the scope of the inventory.

Step 1.2: Prepare a list of all official policy statements, regulations, procedures, and guidelines that fall within the scope of the inventory.

Step 1.3: Prepare a list of any other (unofficial or quasi-official) policy statements, regulations, procedures, and guidelines that fall within the scope of the inventory.

Step 1.1: Refine the Scope

The first step is to identify specifically what you intend to include in the policy audit. There was a discussion about determining the general scope of the policy audit earlier in this chapter. However, once the general scope is identified, someone will have to identify specifically what items are included within that scope. Let's say you and your colleagues decide to complete a policy audit of the library's public service policies. Even though figure 5 is a sample list of such policies, you can't just photocopy it and tell people to send you the items on the list. Each library is unique, and the staff and members of the governing authority of every library have created a different taxonomy for their policies and procedures. Look again at figure 5. It would be an amazing coincidence if any public library had a policy manual that used exactly the same organization and

---

FIGURE 6

Tasks and Steps in Policy Audit Inventory

Task 1: Identify

Step 1.1: Refine the scope of the inventory

Step 1.2: Prepare a list of all official policy statements, regulations, procedures, and guidelines that fall within the scope of the inventory

Step 1.3: Prepare a list of any other (unofficial or quasi-official) policy statements, regulations, procedures, and guidelines that fall within the scope of the inventory

Task 2: Collect

Step 2.1: Prepare instructions for the staff

Step 2.2: Inform staff and collect the documents

Step 2.3: Keep a log of documents collected

Task 3: Organize

Step 3.1: Identify the policy categories to be used to organize the documents you received

Step 3.2: Review and define each item received

Step 3.3: Group items by category and subject

---

terminology and had exactly the same policies as those presented in this sample.

In your library, you might have eight categories of policies—or four. You probably use different terms for at least some of the categories. In some libraries information services are called reference service. Group services may be referred to as programming services. In other libraries, information services and group services are combined under the single heading public services. Sometimes public programming and public computer training have been divided into two separate policy categories. The actual policies included in each category also will vary by library. Meeting room use has been included under management policies in figure 5. It might be included as a part of group services in your library. The total number of policies listed under each category will be different as well.

The policy manual illustrated in figure 5 consists of individual documents, each of which includes a policy statement and appropriate regulations, procedures, and guidelines (if there are any). That is the easiest model to write, use, and keep current, and it is the model that will be recommended later in this chapter and then discussed again in chapter 4. However, many libraries have policy manuals that were developed using different models. Some policy manuals have been written in a narrative style with policy statements, regulations, procedures, and guidelines intermingled. Other policy manuals include only policy statements and regulations. Procedures are developed and maintained by the unit or units affected by the procedures. The project manager will need to identify clearly and specifically what is being included in the policy audit.

Step 1.2: List Official Policy Statements, Regulations, Procedures, and Guidelines

The second step consists of compiling and disseminating a detailed list of the library's official policy statements, regulations, procedures, and guidelines that are included in the scope of your audit. This serves two important functions. First, it provides a clear illustration to the staff of the types of policy statements, regulations, procedures, and guidelines that are being included in the audit. Second, it limits the amount of paper that the project manager will receive and have to organize. There is little point in asking all the managers in the system to make copies of their current policy manuals and send the copies to the project manager. Instead, managers should be encouraged to review their copies of the manual to see if they differ in any way from the manual being used by the project manager. Managers will need to send the project manager only copies of things that are not included in the master manual.

The easiest way to do this is for the policy audit project manager to use Workform 1, Contents of the Library Policy Manual, to create a detailed summary of the contents of the most current library policy manual. You might wonder why you can't just use the actual table of contents of the policy manual instead of Workform 1. As you can see in figure 7, completed Workform 1 includes the policy category, the identifying number of the policy (if any), the subject of policy, the date the policy was issued or revised, and the person or group who approved it. This is more information than is normally found in a table of contents. It is also all the information you will need for the assessment process described in chapter 3, so it makes sense to gather it in a single place and have it available when you need it.

Completing Workform 1 is going to be fairly easy if the library's policy manual consists of individual policy statements along with the regulations, procedures, and guidelines that support them. It is going to be much more complicated if the policy manual is a narrative. In fact, if the current policy manual is a narrative document, the project manager may want to skip Workform 1 altogether. Unless revised pages of the narrative have been issued, it is highly probable that everyone has the same manual. If revised pages have been issued, the revisions can be listed on Workform 1 and staff can be asked to check that the list of revisions is complete and accurate.

FIGURE 7

Completed Example of Workform 1, Contents of the Library Policy Manual

Policy Category Public Programs

A. No.	B. Subject	C. Date Issued/Revised	D. Approved By
	Children's Programming	9/93	Board
	Adult Programming	9/93	Board
	Tours	9/93	Board
	Nonlibrary Programs	Revised 3/98	Board
	Use of Meeting Rooms	Revised 10/01	Board

Step 1.3: List Other Policy Statements, Regulations, Procedures, and Guidelines

The third step is to use Workform 2, Other Policy Statements, Regulations, Procedures, and Guidelines, to create a summary of any policy statements, regulations, procedures, or guidelines that the project director knows have been developed but have not been incorporated into the official policy manual. The key words in the preceding sentence are "that the project director knows have been developed."

It is very possible that the project director won't have a clue about policy statements, regulations, procedures, or guidelines other than those in the official library policy manual. In that case, a blank copy of Workform 2 will be sent to the staff. In the completed example of Workform 2 in figure 8, the project director was able to identify three items not in the official policy manual. Workform 2 includes the same data fields as Workform 1 plus two additional fields: the identification of the policy element (policy statement, regulation, procedure, or guideline) and the name of the unit that prepared the document.

TASK 2: COLLECT

Step 2.1: Prepare instructions for the staff.

Step 2.2: Inform staff and collect the documents.

Step 2.3: Keep a log of documents collected.

Step 2.1: Prepare Instructions

The first step in this task is to prepare instructions for the staff. Regardless of the decisions you make about who to involve in the design and implementation of the policy audit, virtually every professional and paraprofessional staff member will have be involved in the collection phase of the inventory. It is amazing how many policy statements, regulations, procedures, and guidelines exist in even a relatively small library. There are librarywide policies that—in theory at least—have been disseminated to every unit. However, it is possible that different versions of those policies are in use in different units. The probability of this happening increases each time the policy or a regulation or procedure that supports the policy is revised. There are section policy statements, regulations, procedures, and guidelines that apply only to the work of that section and that may or may not have been approved by the library director or the library's governing authority. Finally, there are all of the procedures and guidelines that have been written over the years by staff in specific jobs. These might include guidelines for story hours or procedures for using the library audiovisual equipment.

It would be very difficult for one person to track down all of these documents without help from the library staff. However, if staff members are going to be able to provide useful assistance, they will need

FIGURE 8

Completed Example of Workform 2, Other Policy Statements, Regulations, Procedures, and Guidelines

A. No.	B. Category	C. Element	D. Subject	E. Date Issued/ Revised	F. Unit	G. Approved By
	Reference	Guideline	Reference Guidelines	1999	Reference—Main	Head of Reference
	Circulation	Procedure	Circulation System Parameters	2002	Technology	Director
	Reference	Procedure	Maintaining Obituary Files of Local Citizens	1989	Local History	?

very specific instructions. The instructions should be written and include the following elements:

- a brief explanation of the policy audit process
- the category or categories of policies that will be covered in this policy audit
- the name of the person who will be responsible for the audit and any people who will be assisting him or her
- the names of the members of the policy audit advisory group (if there is such a group)
- specific instructions about what information is to be sent to the policy audit manager, which includes the definitions of policy statements, regulations, guidelines, and procedure (see chapter 1)
- the definition of *practice* (see chapter 1) and a reminder that you are not collecting information about practice at this time
- the date by which the information should be submitted

Step 2.2: Inform the Staff and Collect the Documents

When the policy audit instructions (see sample in figure 9) and Workforms 1 and 2 have been completed, they should be distributed to the library staff who will be involved in the policy audit. The memorandum in figure 9 is addressed to all staff. However, before it is sent, all library managers should be informed about the project and given the information needed to answer questions and help staff gather the requested documents. The most effective way to do this would be during one or more meetings with managers during which the project was described, the memorandum was distributed and discussed, and questions were answered.

FIGURE 9

Sample Policy Audit Instructions

MEMORANDUM

To: Library Staff

From: Library Director

Subject: Library Policy Review—Public Service Policies

Date: June 1, 20xx

Action Deadline: July 12, 20xx

Overview

As you know, we recently completed a strategic plan that identifies a number of new priorities for the library. Several of you have noticed areas in which our current policies do not support the new service priorities. Given the fact that it has been quite some time since our public service policy statements, regulations, procedures, and guidelines were fully reviewed and revised, the board has decided that this is an appropriate time to do so. We will be using the policy review and development process described in the new Public Library Association publication *Creating Policies for Results.* Copies of the book are available in my office if you would like to look at it.

Project Managers and Staff Committee

I have asked Josephine Lu to be responsible for managing the policy review process. George Fullerton and Susan Smith will be working with her. We also plan to appoint a Policy Audit Advisory Committee early next month. If you are interested in being considered to serve on that committee, please e-mail Josephine by June 24.

Your Task

The first step in the process will be a *policy inventory,* during which we will collect all existing written public service policies, regulations, procedures, and guidelines in use throughout the library. The definitions of those terms have been attached to this memo (attachment 1). We are not collecting information about current practice (informal, unwritten policies or procedures) at this time, but we will want to know more about how practice differs from the official policy statements, regulations, procedures, and guidelines later.

1. Official Documents

Josephine already has a copy of the 1995 Tree County Public Library Policies. She also has copies of the revisions to the circulation regulations and procedures that were completed and distributed to all units in 200x, when the library changed automation vendors. A detailed list of the contents of those documents can be found in attachment 2. Please compare your documents carefully with this list and send Josephine a copy of anything you have that is more recent than what is listed on attachment 2.

2. Other Documents

I know that the official policy manual is not comprehensive and that there are other regulations, procedures, and guidelines in use. I was looking at the reference guidelines in the main library reference department the other day and I know that several branches have created in-house procedures and guidelines as well. Josephine has prepared a list of the unofficial documents that she currently has and it is included as attachment 3. You will note that it is considerably less comprehensive than the official list in attachment 2. Please check your files and records and send Josephine copies of all written regulations, procedures, and guidelines that are in use in your unit but not included in the official library policy manual. Remember, we are looking at all of our public services—reference, circulation, programming, meeting room and bulletin board use, customer behavior, and so forth. We are not looking for policies relating to personnel or finance.

Deadline

The copies are to be sent to Josephine by *July 12*. Don't worry about duplication and don't assume someone else is going to submit a specific document. It is important that we have copies of everything that is currently in use before we begin the assessment part of this process. Besides, you all know that Josephine loves to create order out of chaos, so just think of it as giving her more to work with.

Thanks for your help with this important project. We'll keep you informed about the project as it progresses and you will certainly be asked for your input in early September when we begin to discuss revising the current policy statements, regulations, procedures, and guidelines or creating new ones. If you have questions, e-mail Josephine or me.

Step 2.3: Log Documents

The third step is to keep track of the documents that are received from the staff. This is going to take some preplanning or the policy audit project manager may be left with stacks of paper and no idea of what is in those stacks. The easiest way to keep track of what has been received is to give each item a tracking or log number when it is received and record the pertinent information about the item on Workform 3, Policy Audit Inventory Log. Be sure to check that each document is not a duplicate of something you have already received and logged. This will avoid unnecessary duplication.

After a document has been logged it has to be put someplace—and a stack in the corner of the room is not a good place. The easiest way to manage the paper is to three-hole punch each document when it is received, log the document as shown on sample Workform 3 in figure 10, write the log number on the first page of the document, and put the document in numerical order in a three-ring binder.

TASK 3: ORGANIZE

Step 3.1: Identify the policy categories to be used to organize the documents received.

Step 3.2: Review and define each item received.

Step 3.3: Group items by category and subject.

FIGURE 10
Completed Example of Workform 3, Policy Audit Inventory Log

A. Log No.	B. Received From	C. Element	D. Subject
101	AV	Procedure	Use of Library Equipment
102	Special Services	Guidelines	Serving People Who Are Hard of Hearing
103	Circulation	?	Serving People Who Don't Speak English If You Don't Speak the Language They Do Speak

Step 3.1: Identify Policy Categories

Policy manuals are useful only if the information they contain can be easily found and quickly updated. The most effective organization for any library policy manual is one that is divided into categories and subdivided by specific policies, each of which includes the appropriate policy statement regulations, procedures, and guidelines (if any). This organizational structure makes it easy for staff members to find everything they need to know about a particular issue. Most staff members don't care whether the fact that library users are responsible for items that they claim to have returned but that still show on their cards is a regulation or a procedure. What the staff members want is to be able to find the appropriate section of the policy quickly so that they can show it to the user.

There are at least two levels of organization to be considered in this type of taxonomy. The first is the master list of categories to be included in the manual. There is a natural tendency to shuffle the existing policies into some sort of order and use that to develop the master category list. This will work but it probably won't lead to the most logical or comprehensive category list possible. A more effective approach would be to gather a group (perhaps the Policy Audit Advisory Committee described previously) and spend some time brainstorming possible policy categories within each policy type. By starting from a theoretical point of view, you and your colleagues can discuss the categories of policies that are actually needed now and that are likely to be needed in the future rather than get bogged down trying to create a logical pattern from your old policies.

When you have created the master category list, you are ready to identify the policies that should be included under each category. Again, it will probably be more effective to work from a theoretical, best practice approach rather than to start with the current policies and then try to fill in the blanks. Depending on how long it has been since the library policy manual was completely updated and the sources of the information used to develop the original manual, you shouldn't be surprised to find that your library has policies it doesn't need anymore. These will be easier to identify if you and your colleagues start with the ideal and then compare the existing policies to that ideal.

Librarians have known for over a century that the easiest way to keep track of things is to assign a unique number to each of them. This certainly holds true with your policies. As you identify the policies to include in your master category list, assign a number to each. Use a numbering scheme that is simple and easy to understand. A scheme that works for many libraries is to assign one or more letters to each of the categories in the manual and a number to each of the policies included in that category. For example, you might decide to assign the letters INF to the information services category. The four policies included in that section would then be numbered like this:

INF Information Services

- INF-1 Priorities for Reference Service
- INF-2 Interlibrary Loan
- INF-3 Internet Use
- INF-4 Use of Library-Provided Personal Computers

Step 3.2: Review and Define

This is the most complex step in the entire policy audit inventory process, because it is here that the policy audit manager and those working with him or her will have to actually review all of the library's policies, regulations, guidelines, and procedures to determine if they are in fact what they are labeled to be. There is little question that a close review of all of the library's policy documents will show that some items currently labeled policies are really procedures and—even more frustrating—some things currently called procedures may well be policies or regulations. Before you can move on to assessing the *quality and scope* of the existing policy documents (discussed in the next chapter), you have to know exactly what you have.

You created a master category list in the preceding step. That, along with Workform 4, Policy Audit Inventory Results, will provide the framework for your review. Use a separate copy of Workform 4 to

FIGURE 11
Partially Completed Example of Workform 4, Policy Audit Inventory Results

Policy Category Information Services

Part 1: Documents in the Master Category

A. No.	B. Subject	C. Policy Statement		D. Regulations		E. Procedures		F. Guidelines	
		Yes	No	Yes	No	Yes	No	Yes	No
INF-1	Priorities for Reference Service								
INF-2	Interlibrary Loan								
INF-3	Internet Use								
INF-4	Use of Library-Provided Personal Computers								

Part 2: Other Documents in This Category

A. No.	B. Subject	C. Policy Statement		D. Regulations		E. Procedures		F. Guidelines	
		Yes	No	Yes	No	Yes	No	Yes	No

record the documents in each of the policy categories you identified in your master category list. Record all of the policies within each category of the master category list in the Subject column of Part 1 of Workform 4. The documents included in the Information Services category have been used in the partially completed example of Workform 4 in figure 11. When you have completed the Subject column for each of the policy categories under review, you will be ready to begin reviewing each of the library's existing policies, regulations, procedures, and guidelines.

If the current library policy manual is divided into categories and subdivided by specific policies, each of which includes the appropriate regulations, procedures, and guidelines, the process is fairly straightforward.

1. Collect all of the policies in the category under review from the manual.
2. Carefully review Workform 3, Policy Audit Inventory Log, and identify and collect any items in the log that apply to the category under review.

3. Analyze each document carefully to determine what elements it contains. Use the definitions of *policy statement, regulation, procedure,* and *guideline* from chapter 1 as the basis for your review and analysis.
4. As you make your decisions about the elements in each document, note them in the margin (for example, write "policy statement" by the part of the document that appears to be a policy statement, "regulation" by each regulation, "procedure" by each procedure, and so on. Remember, your decisions may differ from the current labels.)
5. Record your findings on Workform 4, as illustrated in figure 12.
6. If some documents appear to belong in this category but are not covered in the subject list developed in step 3.1 above, record them on Part 2 in the "Other Documents in This Category" section of Workform 4. (Chapter 3 will explain how to evaluate them further.) In the example in figure 12, the project manager thought that the guidelines for classroom collections belonged in the Information Services category, but they were not in the master category list. Therefore, she listed them separately.

As noted earlier, if the current library policy manual is a narrative document, the process is going to be more complex. Before any assessment can begin, the project manager is going to have to deconstruct the manual to determine exactly what it includes. There are two ways to do this. One is to make a photocopy of the manual and cut and paste each policy statement and the regulations, procedures, and guidelines that support the policy statement onto separate pages. It may be necessary to make more than one copy of the manual, because it is not uncommon to have a regulation or procedure that applies to more than one policy. The other option is to use an electronic version of the manual and do the cutting, pasting, and copying electronically.

In either case, the result will be a group of policy statements with the regulations, procedures, and guidelines that support them, plus some spare regulations, procedures, and guidelines that don't seem to apply to any policy. The narrative form of policy writing seems to encourage the inclusion of guideline statements—whether or not they apply to specific policy statements. When you have deconstructed the narrative manual and recorded your results on Workform 4, you will be ready to move on with the review and assessment process.

Step 3.3: Group Items

The final step in the inventory process is to gather all of the documents relating to a category together, three-hole punch them, and place them in a notebook along with a completed copy of Workform 4 for that category. This will serve as the starting point for the assessment process that will be discussed in the next chapter.

FIGURE 12
Completed Example of Workform 4, Policy Audit Inventory Results

Policy Category Information Services

Part 1: Documents in the Master Category

A. No.	B. Subject	C. Policy Statement		D. Regulations		E. Procedures		F. Guidelines	
		Yes	No	Yes	No	Yes	No	Yes	No
INF-1	Priorities for Reference Service	X		X			X	X	
INF-2	Interlibrary Loan		X		X		X		X
INF-3	Internet Use	X		X		X			X
INF-4	Use of Library-Provided Personal Computers	X		X		X			X

Part 2: Other Documents in This Category

A. No.	B. Subject	C. Policy Statement		D. Regulations		E. Procedures		F. Guidelines	
		Yes	No	Yes	No	Yes	No	Yes	No
	Classroom Collections							X	

Challenges

In some ways the inventory part of the policy audit is less complicated than the assessment portion of the audit or the development phase that follows the audit. It is almost always easier to gather and organize existing documents than it is to evaluate those documents or create new documents. However, the term *easier* is relative. It is important to acknowledge that there are very real challenges in the inventory process and to understand how to address those challenges.

The first and potentially most destructive challenge is the desire to shorten the inventory process—or to omit it all together. The second is in some ways the opposite of the first. If the inventory process isn't carefully structured and managed, the project manager runs the risk of being buried in paper. The third challenge is more subtle. Task 3 in the inventory process requires the project manager and others to define the elements of the various documents gathered during the inventory.

Unless those people are very careful, they may find themselves arguing about vocabulary and not content. The definitions in chapter 1 make the difference between a policy statement and a regulation perfectly clear. Applying those definitions to existing documents, however, is rarely as clear-cut.

Desire for Shortcuts

Most of the activities in the inventory part of the policy audit are process activities, and, as noted earlier, many people resist spending time on things that they don't think will result in concrete products. In fact, the whole concept of "planning to plan" strikes many people as redundant. However, there is no way you can develop an effective library policy manual until you and your colleagues have a clear understanding of the policy statements, regulations, procedures, and guidelines that exist now.

Some staff are going to want to start from the assumption that the official library policy manual is complete and accurate, but, as we have seen, that is not likely. Other staff members may say that there is no need for an inventory because you already know what you need. That normally means that those staff members have specific policies they want to have developed—and they aren't concerned about the possibility that other policies are needed as well.

Any process that includes reviewing or writing policies is going to take considerable time and energy. However, a carefully structured process that begins with an inventory and assessment of current policies is likely to take less time and energy in the long run than a process in which you just start writing policies, with no clear picture of the policy statements, regulations, procedures, and guidelines that exist now throughout the organization.

A sound understanding of where you are now and what policy statements, regulations, procedures, or guidelines are needed will be particularly important when you are ready to begin developing the needed documents. It is very unlikely that you will be able to create everything that needs to be developed simultaneously. Therefore you are going to have to decide which documents to develop first and which can wait. The priority-setting process you use to make those decisions will be based on the information you gathered during the policy audit.

There is one final thing to consider about the time invested in the policy inventory. It involves all staff from the beginning of the policy audit and development process. The policy inventory begins by explaining the process to all staff and then asks them to review the policy documents in their own units and submit any that are not included on the master lists. This early notification and involvement of staff will pay big dividends later in the process when you begin writing new policies and asking staff to review them.

Too Much Paper

While there is a danger in not completing the inventory or in taking shortcuts, there is also a danger that the inventory will become an end in itself and not simply the first activity in the policy audit and development process. The policy audit project manager is likely to receive a lot of paper from staff throughout the library. Even if the instructions make it crystal clear that staff are to send only things that are not on the lists in Workforms 1 and 2, some staff will send duplicate copies of documents. Others will dig up copies of 20- or 30-year-old policy manuals and send them in.

The project manager is going to have to be ready for this influx of paper and have a system prepared for keeping it organized and accessible. The audit inventory log in Workform 3 and the process described earlier in Step 2.3 will work—but only if they are used promptly and consistently. If the policy audit manager lets the documents stack up in the corner of her office until she has time to deal with them, with each passing day, as new documents are added to the stack, the job of logging and filing will become more difficult. Many of the documents in the stack will be duplicates, but there will be no way to tell that if they were not logged in as they arrived. If the project manager puts off organizing what she has received for too long, she may decide it is not worth the effort and stop the policy review and development process before it ever starts.

Vocabulary

Defining the various elements of a policy (policy statement, regulation, procedure, and guideline) will be a challenge during the inventory process and will continue to be a challenge throughout the audit and development processes. People are going to have trouble differentiating among the various elements, and there is a danger that you could end up arguing about words and not concepts.

Several things can be done to minimize this problem. The first is to photocopy the definitions from chapter 1 and make sure that everyone involved in reviewing, evaluating, or writing policies has a copy. The second is to spend some time discussing the terms and the differences among them with key staff before you begin the review process. You might want to use Workform 5, Defining Policy Elements, as a beginning point for your discussion. This workform provides sample statements from policies and asks people to define them. After people have completed the workform and you have gone through the responses, you should have a better idea of how clearly the participants understand the distinctions among the various policy elements. If most staff do well on the exercise in Workform 5, you will be ready to move forward. If they do not, you will need to continue your discussions. At that point, it might be useful to provide the staff with specific examples of each element from your own library policy manual.

Key Points to Remember

1. You can't assume that everyone in your organization is operating from the same set of policy statements, procedures, regulations, or guidelines. In fact, you probably should assume that the opposite is true.
2. The time spent organizing and defining the policy statements, regulations, procedures, and guidelines you have now is time well spent.
3. The policy audit project manager should be organized and efficient and have a broad knowledge of current library policy and practice.
4. It is important to inform all staff about the policy audit and to involve them in the inventory process.
5. Log and file documents as they are received during the inventory process. Discard duplicates.
6. Spend the time necessary to ensure that key staff (those who will be evaluating current policies or writing and revising policies) understand the terms *policy statement, regulation, procedure,* and *guideline.*

Chapter 3

Assessment

MILESTONES

By the time you finish this chapter you will know how to

- structure the assessment phase of the policy audit
- develop criteria to evaluate policy statements, regulations, procedures, and guidelines
- ensure that the people who will be evaluating the policies understand how to complete their evaluation assignments
- evaluate the library's existing policy statements, regulations, procedures, and guidelines
- identify any new policies that need to be developed
- deal with the challenges you will face while completing the assessment phase of the policy audit

When you have completed the inventory phase of the policy audit, you will probably have created a very impressive list of existing policy statements, regulations, procedures, and guidelines. It will be tempting to look at all of the information you have gathered and decide that all that is really needed is a little reorganization, some minor editing, and perhaps the creation of a couple of policy elements and the whole policy audit will be complete. However, a closer look at the results of your policy inventory will dispel this optimistic vision.

In the first place, it is likely that you are missing more than just a couple of elements from the various policies you have identified during the audit. Do a quick total of the number of times you put a check in one of the No columns on the final copy of Workform 4, Policy Audit Inventory Results. Each "no" represents an element of a policy that needs to be created by you and your colleagues. Even if this reality check results in the need to develop relatively few new elements, you are not home free yet. As noted earlier, the mere existence of a policy is no guarantee that the policy is either *effective* or *efficient.* A careful assessment is sure to indicate that some of your existing policies are out-of-date. Others will prove to be inconsistent with the library's goals and objectives, incomplete, unclear, or in need of revision for one of countless other reasons.

The assessment phase of the policy audit begins by deciding who will be involved in the assessment and what each person's responsibilities will be. The people involved will then develop the criteria that will be used to evaluate the various policy elements you identified on the final copy of Workform 4. Next, the criteria will be used to evaluate those policy elements. Finally you will review the policies you have and determine what additional policies need to be developed.

Definitions

This chapter will introduce two new terms that will be used throughout the remainder of the book. To ensure that everyone has the same understanding of those terms, they are defined below:

Degree of Revision A numeric indicator of the extent of the revision required to bring a policy element into compliance with the evaluation criteria for that element.

Evaluation Criteria The value-laden declarative statements that describe the characteristics of effective library policy statements, regulations, procedures, and guidelines. These criteria provide the framework for the assessment phase of the policy audit.

Policy Audit Assessment

The assessment part of the policy audit is an evaluative process consisting of three tasks.

Task 1: *Create* the evaluation criteria that will be used to assess the policy statements, regulations, procedures, and guidelines.

Task 2: *Evaluate* existing documents by comparing the policy statements, regulations, procedures, and guidelines of each policy to the criteria established in Task 1.

Task 3: *Conclude* the policy audit and prepare a final report with the audit findings.

These three tasks are each divided into a series of steps, which are listed at the beginning of the discussion of each task below. Figure 13 shows all of the tasks and steps in the assessment phase of the policy audit.

TASK 1: CREATE

Step 1.1: Assign responsibility for the assessment phase of the policy audit.

Step 1.2: Develop draft evaluation criteria for policy statements, regulations, procedures, and guidelines.

Step 1.3: Obtain approval of evaluation criteria.

Step 1.1: Assign Responsibility

During the *create* task of the assessment phase of the policy audit you will be developing the criteria that will be used to evaluate both your current policies (identified on your final copy of Workform 4) and any

FIGURE 13
Tasks and Steps in Policy Audit Assessment

Task 1: Create
- Step 1.1: Assign responsibility for the assessment phase of the policy audit
- Step 1.2: Develop draft evaluation criteria for policy statements, regulations, procedures, and guidelines
- Step 1.3: Obtain approval of evaluation criteria

Task 2: Evaluate
- Step 2.1: Design the review process
- Step 2.2: Learn how to use criteria to evaluate policies
- Step 2.3: Evaluate the policies
- Step 2.4: Discuss the evaluations with the Policy Audit Advisory Committee

Task 3: Conclude
- Step 3.1: Develop a list of all needed policies
- Step 3.2: Summarize the committee's recommendations
- Step 3.3: Thank the members of the Policy Audit Advisory Committee

new policies that are needed (identified during Step 3.1. later in this chapter). It is generally easier for a group of people to work together to develop criteria than it is for one or two people to try to do so. It is very helpful to have multiple points of view as you consider all of the possible criteria that might be used to evaluate your library's policies. This is exactly the kind of responsibility that the Policy Audit Advisory Committee was intended to deal with and they are the appropriate group to assume responsibility for the assessment process.

Step 1.2: Develop Draft Evaluation Criteria

There is no single list of evaluation criteria that can be applied to all of the policies in every public library. While it is possible to develop a core list of evaluation criteria for each of the four elements of a policy that can be used as a starting point, staff from most libraries will find that they have to modify and add to the core list of criteria to reflect local conditions. It takes only a few examples to illustrate the pitfalls of trying to use a single generic set of evaluation criteria to review policies in every library in your state or in the country.

Staff in one library might decide to rely on the online help provided by their automated system vendor in lieu of drafting and maintaining a current set of circulation procedures. Consequently, one of the evaluation criteria that staff would use to determine the efficiency and effectiveness of procedures in their library would be, "The online help provided by [the automation vendor] supplies sufficient detail to give staff the information they need to perform the required steps." If, when applying that criterion, staff decided that the online help was adequate, then the procedure portion of the policy would refer staff to the online help. If staff decided that the criterion was not met, then detailed procedures would have to be developed. On the other hand, staff in another library might decide that the online help provided by their automated vendor is generally insufficient. Therefore, the evaluation criteria they developed for circulation procedures would make no reference to the vendor-provided online help.

If a library is a city or county department and subject to city or county policy on certain matters, the library staff might develop an evaluation criterion for policy statements and regulations that states, "Appropriate policy statements and regulations from existing city [county] policies are used whenever they exist." The first step to take when applying that criterion would be to determine if a city or county policy exists. One common example of such a policy is closing because of inclement weather. If the city or county had such a policy, then the library policy and regulation would refer to the city or county policy. If the city or county did not have such a policy, then the library staff would have to draft a library-specific policy. In either case, the procedures would probably be unique to the library.

Although it is impossible to develop a comprehensive list of evaluation criteria that would apply to all of the elements of all of the policies of all public libraries, it is possible to identify a core list of criteria that are probably generally applicable to most libraries. These core criteria are derived from the definitions of the four elements of a policy. The easiest way to develop criteria from the definitions is to deconstruct each definition into a series of declarative sentences and insert a value-laden word such as *good* or *excellent* or *effective* into each sentence. For example, a policy statement was defined in chapter 1 as "a brief, written statement that describes *why* a library does something." The definition went on to say "policy statements are written from the customer's point of view and approved by the library's governing authority." When we deconstruct this definition and add value-laden words, we end up with the following criteria to apply when evaluating policy statements:

- An excellent policy statement is brief.
- An effective policy statement describes why the library does something.
- An excellent policy statement is written from the customer's point of view.
- An excellent policy statement has been approved by the library's governing authority.

Core criteria for each of the four elements of a policy have been included on Workform 6, Evaluation Criteria.

Members of the Policy Audit Advisory Committee should be encouraged to review the core criteria suggested in Workform 6 and to make any changes or modifications that are needed because of local conditions. The committee members will then move on to discuss the need to develop evaluation criteria specific to their own library. This part of the process is best managed by considering a series of questions about each of the four policy elements. Initial lists of questions to consider when developing criteria for each of the elements can be found in Workform 6. These lists are intended to help the committee members identify issues to be addressed in the criteria. They are certainly not to be considered all-inclusive. As the members work through the process, they will find that one question leads to another and that certain local conditions will trigger a whole new series of questions. That is appropriate and exactly the way the process should work. This is a somewhat intuitive process that requires discussion and judgment.

Step 1.3: Approval

The evaluation criteria that are identified for each of the elements of a policy will have a significant effect on the final policies that are developed. Therefore, it is important that the library management team members fully understand and support the criteria before they are actually used. Rather than asking the management team to review three or four separate sets of evaluation criteria, create a composite copy of Workform 6 that includes all of the recommended evaluation criteria for each policy element.

It is probable that the committee that developed the evaluation criteria found that the process became easier as they moved from policy statements to guidelines. The team members developed an understanding of the purpose, use, and structure of the evaluation criteria by working through the process several times. If you present the management team with all of the criteria at the same time, they will have the same opportunity to work through the criteria beginning with the policy statements and ending with procedures or guidelines. Although they will not spend as much time with the process as the members of the Policy Audit Advisory Committee did, the members of the management team will have the opportunity to get a sense of the structure of the criteria and to understand how the criteria interrelate.

In some libraries, the management team may prefer to read and comment on the written report. In others, the management team may meet with the committee that developed the evaluation criteria. Either way, or variations on one or the other, will work. The choice depends on your library and the typical approval processes within your library. What is important is that the management team be aware of, and have an opportunity to comment on, the evaluation criteria before they are applied. However, it is equally important that the criteria be reviewed in a timely manner so that the assessment process can stay on track. Select the simplest and quickest review process available.

Remember, the criteria are not ends in themselves. They are merely tools, albeit important tools, that will be used in subsequent steps of the process. Remember too that the evaluation criteria are not cast in stone once they have been approved. When you actually start to use the criteria, you can always ask to add additional criteria if you find that you overlooked something important. You can also recommend that some of the wording of the approved criteria be revised if you find that stating one or more criteria in a different way would make the meaning clearer.

When the evaluation criteria have been approved, use one or more photocopies of Workform 6 to develop a final copy of all of the criteria. As you will see in the next step, you will be evaluating all of the elements of a policy at the same time. Therefore, it makes sense to have all of the criteria to be used in a single document.

TASK 2: EVALUATE EXISTING DOCUMENTS

Step 2.1: Design the review process.

Step 2.2: Learn how to use criteria to evaluate policies.

Step 2.3: Evaluate the policies.

Step 2.4: Discuss the evaluations with the Policy Audit Advisory Committee.

Step 2.1: Design the Process

The questions to be answered when you develop this process are the standard ones: what, who, how, and when. The first thing to do is to decide *what* policies you intend to evaluate and the order in which you will evaluate them. In chapter 2 you identified the scope of the policy audit. At that time you decided whether you wanted to restrict the audit to one category of policies or to include all of the policies in the library. If you have already limited the audit to a single category of policies, all you have to do now is to decide the order in which you will review the policies.

If your library included more than one category of policies in your audit, then you will first have to select one category as the starting point for this step. In other words, will you first evaluate the circulation policies, then the information policies, then group services, or would it make more sense in your library to begin with group services and then move on to circulation and information? There is no right or wrong answer here. You will follow exactly the same evaluation process no matter which category you choose to do first and you will use exactly the same evaluation criteria for each category. The point is to select the category that makes the most sense in your particular library and your particular circumstances. One library might choose to begin with the policy category that appears from a review of Workform 4, Policy Audit Inventory Results, to be the most complete and that therefore will require the least amount of staff effort to revise and issue. Another library might have an immediate need for new policies in a specific category and might therefore choose to begin with that category.

As already noted, once you have decided the order in which you will evaluate the categories under review, you still have to determine the order in which you will evaluate the policies within each category. Again there are a variety of options. You could simply evaluate them in the order they are listed on Workform 4. If you just completed a strategic plan, you might want to start with the policies that are going to need significant revision to support the goals and objectives in that plan. Perhaps you will want to start with the policies that are creating the most questions from the staff or the public. The decisions pertaining to the order in which policies will be evaluated can be made by the library management team, the policy audit manager, or the members of the Policy Audit Advisory Committee. If the committee is charged with determining the evaluation order, their recommendations should be reviewed and approved by the management team.

Once you have established the order in which policies will be evaluated, you are ready to decide *who* should be involved in the review. It is at this point in the policy audit that the Policy Audit Advisory

Committee will be most useful. Someone—or some group—is going to have to examine every document that was identified in the policy audit inventory and recorded on Workform 4. Someone—or some group—is going to have to apply the evaluation criteria to each document and prepare a written summary indicating what, if anything, needs to be done to bring the policy statement, regulations, procedures, and guidelines (if any) into compliance with the library's criteria. That is a lot of work for some*one* but a reasonable workload spread among the six to ten people in the Policy Audit Advisory Committee.

There are a variety of approaches you can take when deciding *how* the committee will go about reviewing the policies. One way to proceed would be to assign each of the policies under review to one or two people on the committee. The major benefit of asking two people to work together to review each policy is that they will each bring a different point of view to the review process. That means that their recommendations may well be more complete than the recommendation made by a single reviewer. The obvious drawback to assigning two people to review each policy is, of course, time. It is harder and takes longer to get two people together to evaluate a policy than it does for one person to do it.

There are lots of different options for determining how the policies are assigned. The chairperson of the committee could make assignments based on his or her knowledge of the expertise of the group members. If all members of the advisory group are equally well informed about the policy subjects, the chairperson may decide to draw lots and let the member who drew 1 select the policy he or she wishes to evaluate, followed by the group member who drew 2, and so forth until all of the policies have been assigned to a group member. Select a method that works for your group. What is important is that every policy be assigned to someone.

One way to get the full benefit of spreading the workload among a number of individuals and still have the opportunity to get a variety of points of view about each policy is to ask the person or team who evaluated a policy to present their recommendations to the remainder of the committee for review and discussion. To do this each person or two-member team should be told *when* the evaluation of the assigned policies is to be completed. The chairperson of the Policy Audit Advisory Committee can then create and distribute agendas that identify what policies will be evaluated at each meeting so that all group members will have an opportunity to read the designated policies in advance and bring copies of them to the meetings.

Step 2.2: Learn How to Evaluate the Policies

The actual evaluation of the policies will begin during a preliminary meeting of the people who will be responsible for the evaluation. A sample agenda for that meeting has been provided in figure 14. As you

FIGURE 14
Sample Agenda for Preliminary Evaluation Meeting

Participants

Policy Audit Advisory Committee

Outcomes/Products

- Members will know how to evaluate the library's policies.
- Members will know what they are responsible for doing.
- Members will know when their assignments are due to be completed.

Handouts/Materials

- Policies to be reviewed
- Final copies of Workform 4, Policy Audit Inventory Results, for each policy under review
- Workform 6, Evaluation Criteria
- Evaluation assignments and deadlines
- Workform 7, Policy Element Review Summary (multiple copies for each member)

Agenda

2:00 Welcome
Distribute materials
Review and discuss final evaluation criteria (Workform 6)
Review and discuss evaluation assignments and deadlines
Distribute and review Workform 7, Policy Element Review Summary
Set date and time for next meeting
4:00 Adjourn

see on that agenda, each participant will receive a copy of the policies under review, a copy of the approved evaluation criteria (the final copy of Workform 6), a list of who will be responsible for the review of each policy along with the dates the reviews are to be completed, and multiple copies of figure 15, Workform 7, Policy Element Review Summary.

The chairperson should begin the meeting by reviewing the approved evaluation criteria on Workform 6 in detail with the members of the committee. It is important that all committee members have a common understanding of the general purpose of the evaluation criteria and of the reasons that each criterion was developed. Committee members will also need to know how to apply the criteria to the various elements of a policy. This discussion is particularly crucial if the people who will be responsible for evaluating the policies were not involved in developing the criteria or if the draft criteria were changed significantly by the management team during their review.

When everyone is comfortable with the criteria and understands how to apply them, the chairperson can move on to reviewing the assignments and deadlines. In most cases the chairperson will have assigned the policies to be reviewed to each committee member using one of the processes identified in Step 2.1. The deadlines were probably assigned in a more casual manner. It normally doesn't matter whether policy *X*

FIGURE 15
Sample Workform 7, Policy Element Review Summary

Policy Category ______________________________

Subject ______________________ **Evaluated by** ______________________

A. Element	**B. Revision Level Required***
1. Policy Statement *Observations:*	
2. Regulations *Observations:*	
3. Procedures *Observations:*	
4. Guidelines *Observations:*	

***Use the following scale to identify the level of revision required for each element of a policy:**

Level of Revision Required for an Element	
0	No revision needed to meet criteria
1	Minor revision needed to meet criteria
2	Moderate rewrite necessary to meet criteria
3	Total rewrite necessary to meet criteria
4	Does not exist—needs to be written
NA	Not applicable—refers only to guidelines

is reviewed before or after policy Y. The key is to be sure that both get reviewed in a timely manner. Therefore, the chairperson will want to ask people to check their deadlines to make sure they are realistic in the context of other projects that people might have. If two-person teams will be working on each policy, the chairperson will want to check with both members to be sure that deadlines are realistic.

The whole review process will flow more smoothly if everyone is encouraged to make whatever adjustments in deadlines are needed as early in the process as possible. One way to do this is for the chairperson to agree to make adjustments in deadlines for one week after the initial evaluation meeting and then to issue a final list of assignments and deadlines. Once the final list of deadlines is published, any changes will have to be made within the committee. A person or team that needs to extend a deadline will have to trade due dates with someone else on the committee. Be sure to make it clear that if dates are exchanged, it will be important to inform the chairperson so that he or she can inform the members of the committee. Committee members should receive a packet of all the completed copies of figure 15, Workform 7, that will be discussed at least one week prior to each meeting. This will ensure that there will be an even flow of work throughout the evaluation process.

When the committee members understand the evaluation criteria and have received their assignments, they are ready to discuss the actual evaluation process. This discussion will begin by reviewing figure 15, Workform 7. Committee members will complete a separate copy of Workform 7 for each policy they review and evaluate. The workform includes spaces to make comments about each of the elements of the policy under review as well as a place to indicate the extent of the revision required for each policy. A numeric ranking to be used to indicate the extent of revision required is included in the box at the bottom of the workform.

Most committee members will find that reviewing the actual documentation available and using the evaluation criteria to determine the extent of revision required for the various elements of the policy under review are a relatively straightforward process. The more difficult part of the review process will be deciding if the existing policy and each of the elements that make up the policy are complete. It is much easier to evaluate existing text than it is to identify any information that has been omitted.

The evaluation criteria will provide some guidance for committee members attempting to decide if a policy statement or regulation is complete. However, the information included in appendix A may be an even better resource for this purpose. Appendix A includes templates for 36 of the policy subjects listed in figure 5 in chapter 2. Each template in appendix A includes a list of questions to consider when evaluating, developing, or revising the policy statements and regulations for each of the 36 policy subjects. If appendix A includes a template for a policy that is being evaluated, committee members will want to incorporate the related questions into the review process.

One way to help everyone on the committee to understand the evaluation criteria, Workform 7, and the way to use the templates in appendix A would be to ask the members to review and discuss one policy as a group, completing the appropriate sections of the workform as they go. That will help ensure that everyone understands the process and knows how to complete the form.

Step 2.3: Evaluate the Policies

As noted above, the actual evaluation of the policies will be completed by the members of the Policy Audit Advisory Committee, working either alone or in teams. If teams of members will be working together to evaluate policies, their first step will be to decide if each team member should individually complete an initial evaluation before discussing the policy or if they will work through the entire evaluation as a team. Either approach works as long as everyone involved understands and agrees with the process.

The review itself begins with the policy statement. First reread the evaluation criteria for policy statements on Workform 6. Then check to see if appendix A includes a template for the policy under review. If it does, read the questions about policy statements in that document as well. Next read the policy statement carefully and compare it with the criteria and the questions in the appendix (if any). As you review the policy statement, consider both what is included and what is missing. The most obvious problem will be that the entire element is missing. When you completed Workform 4, you may have discovered that the library has a variety of procedures for which no policy statements have ever been developed. If that is the case in the policy under review, note the lack of a policy statement on Workform 7.

If the policy statement actually exists, compare it with the criteria. Are all of the suggested pieces of the policy statement present? For example, the criteria state that an effective policy statement describes why the library does something. If that part of the policy statement is missing, note the omission on Workform 7. Move through the evaluation criteria, noting items that need to be revised or edited. Be as specific as possible about the changes that are needed.

When you finish reviewing the policy statement, move on to the regulations, procedures, and guidelines. In each instance, note as specifically as possible on Workform 7 the ways in which the existing element does not meet the established criteria. For example, if the regulations for use of meeting rooms do not address the fees that are charged for meeting room usage, then you should so indicate in the "Comments" section under "Regulations." If the procedures on how to report petty cash usage are no longer accurate, then you should indicate that in the "Comments" section under "Procedures." The case study below provides a step-by-step illustration of the review process.

CASE STUDY

ANYTOWN PUBLIC LIBRARY POLICIES

Part 2
Policy Review

In part 1 of this case study, we learned that the Anytown Public Library had recently completed a planning process during which Commons was selected as one of the new library priorities. We also learned that the current Anytown Public Library Meeting Room Use policy was ten years old.

During the assessment phase of the policy audit, Gretchen Hummel was assigned the task of evaluating the Meeting Room Use policy. She first read the evaluation criteria that had been approved by library administration. Then she checked and found there was a Meeting Room Use template in appendix A that included a number of questions to consider when reviewing the policy statements and regulations of a meeting room policy. Gretchen used both of these documents during her review and evaluation process.

Gretchen began by reading the library's Meeting Room Use policy statement and comparing it to the evaluation criteria and the questions in the Meeting Room Use template in appendix A. She decided that the library's policy statement did not indicate how providing meeting room space supported the library's goals and objectives and she wrote that in the Policy Statement box on Workform 7.

Gretchen then reviewed the regulations portion of the policy. She found a number of issues that needed to be addressed and noted them in the Regulations box on Workform 7. They included the following items:

- Regulations need to be restated in specific terms.
- Regulations need to be rewritten as separate statements rather than as one long paragraph.
- New regulations need to be developed to address:
    1. What activities may occur in meeting room?
    2. What events or activities are prohibited in meeting room?
    3. Who may reserve meeting room?
    4. What is the fee schedule for each meeting room and when will refunds be made?
    5. When must fees be paid and when will fees be waived?
    6. How far in advance can the meeting rooms be reserved?
    7. Can room be used when library is closed?
    8. Can food or alcohol be served?
    9. Can library equipment be used?
    10. Can fees be charged to attend an event and can items be sold during an event?
    11. What statistics are to be kept?

Gretchen was very careful not to try to provide answers to the questions that she raised; she merely indicated what needed to be included in the regulations when they were rewritten.

Finally Gretchen reviewed the procedures and noted her comments in the Procedures box of Workform 7:

- Need to develop procedures that reflect regulations, including
    1. A meeting room agreement form to be completed by individuals or groups that want to use the meeting room
    2. Procedures for scheduling room for library events as well as events offered by others

There were no guidelines for this policy, so once Gretchen had recorded her comments for each of the other policy elements, she was ready to consider the extent of revision required for each of those elements. The policy statement needed only minor revision, so Gretchen entered the number 1 in the Revision Level Required box for Policy Statement. On the other hand, the regulations clearly needed to be completely rewritten, so Gretchen entered the number 3 in the appropriate Revision Level Required box. Gretchen reviewed her comments about the meeting room procedures and decided moderate rewriting was necessary, so she entered the number 2 in the appropriate box.

When Gretchen finished her review of each of the elements of the Meeting Room Use policy, she made one copy of completed Workform 7 for each member of the Policy Audit Advisory Committee and distributed the copies according the procedures established by the committee chairperson.

Step 2.4: Discuss the Evaluations

The process of reviewing existing policies based on criteria is not as cut-and-dried as it may seem at first. If the initial review is done by a two-person team, the partners will soon discover that a phrase that one person thinks is clear and concise seems confusing and contradictory to the other team member. Confusion can occur even if the original review is being done by an individual. The individual may well evaluate a policy in the context of what he or she already knows about the subject, unconsciously filling in the blanks when information is not provided or is ambiguous. The most effective way to deal with this issue is to have the reviewers share the drafts of their reviews with the full Policy Audit Advisory Committee. This will allow for a broader discussion of issues and will help correct the tendency we all have to read what we think something should say rather than what it actually does say.

During the meetings of the Policy Audit Advisory Committee in which the completed copies of Workform 7 are discussed, the chairperson will ask the designated evaluator (or one of the team of evaluators) to briefly review the findings and the rationale behind the recommendations. The evaluator should be able to identify the specific evaluation criteria that have not been met. If a part or all of an element is missing, the evaluator should be able to indicate how it was decided that the missing piece was needed.

Following the presentation of the evaluator, the committee members will discuss the evaluator's recommendations. They may accept the recommendations or suggest additions or changes. If changes are suggested, they should be discussed thoroughly. When the group has reached consensus on the changes and additions, Workform 7 should be revised to reflect the final recommendations of the Policy Audit Advisory Committee.

If the committee members are reviewing only the policies in a single category, their work is done when all of the policies in that category have been evaluated. If the committee members are reviewing policies in more than one category, they will repeat the process with the second policy category and so on until they have reviewed all of the existing documents on Workform 4. Depending on the number of policies under review, it may be necessary to schedule a series of committee meetings to provide adequate time to discuss the evaluations of each of the policies in the audit. It will probably take three to six weeks to complete this step. The exact time frame will be based on the number of policies to be reviewed.

TASK 3: CONCLUDE

Step 3.1: Develop a list of all needed policies.

Step 3.2: Summarize the committee's recommendations.

Step 3.3: Thank the members of the Policy Audit Advisory Committee.

Step 3.1: Develop a List of Needed Policies

Reviewing and evaluating all of the policies included within the scope of your policy audit are a big job and when the members of the Policy Audit Advisory Committee have completed their work they will have an excellent understanding of the issues surrounding the policies under consideration. There is one final step in the review process that will utilize this understanding and expertise. The committee members will work together to identify any new policies that need to be developed in the category or categories under review and to decide if any of the existing policies could be merged or deleted completely.

The members of the Policy Audit Advisory Committee first identified a list of all of the policies that the library needed during the policy audit inventory when they created a master category list as part of organizing the library's existing policies (see chapter 2, "Task 3: Organize"). A master category list was defined as "a complete list of the policy categories within a given type of policies and an enumeration of the specific policies included in each category." The committee members were encouraged to start from a theoretical, best-practices point of view when creating the ideal master category list rather than try to determine a pattern in the existing policies. The theoretical approach was far more likely to result in a logical list of policy categories and policy subjects that the library actually needed than was a reshuffling of existing documents. The result was the first draft of a master category list of the policies that the members of the committee thought were needed.

Now it is time to review that master category list in light of the learning that has taken place during the review process. Committee members will consider whether they still think it is necessary to have policies for all the subjects previously identified. They will also determine whether policies should be developed for subjects that are not currently on the master category list.

This step can be completed during a single meeting of the Policy Audit Advisory Committee (see figure 16 for a sample agenda). Prior to the meeting each member of the committee should receive a copy of the master category list that was previously approved and a copy of Workform 4, Policy Audit Inventory Results, for each policy category included in the audit. It is probable that all of the policies on the master category list in the categories that were included in the review are also listed on Workform 4. However, the committee members reviewed only policies for which one element or more had been identified during the policy audit inventory. There has been no previous discussion of policies that were included in the master category list but not yet created by the library. This discussion will focus on the big picture and look at both existing policies and those identified earlier as desirable but not yet written. Therefore, the committee members may find it helpful to have a single sheet of paper that shows the complete master list of all proposed categories and policy subjects. The committee members should be encouraged to review the contents of both documents and to make lists of what subjects should be deleted from the master category list and what subjects should be added to the master category list. All members should bring their lists to the meeting and thus be prepared to be active participants in the discussion.

FIGURE 16
Sample Agenda for Master Category List Review Meeting

Participants

Policy Audit Advisory Committee

Outcomes/Products

- Revised master category list

Handouts/Materials (to be distributed prior to the meeting)

- Master category list (from the policy audit inventory—see chapter 2)
- Workform 4, Policy Audit Inventory Results (one for each category being reviewed)

Agenda

2:00	Welcome
	Identify policies to be deleted from the master category list
	Identify policies to be added to the master category list
	Identify policies to be divided into shorter, less complex policies
	Review recommendations
4:00	Adjourn

The meeting should begin by looking at the subjects that committee members think should be deleted from the master category list or combined with another subject. To make sure each category is covered thoroughly, focus the discussion on one policy category at a time and avoid jumping back and forth among categories. This will be easy to do if you use Workform 4 as the framework for your discussion, because a separate copy of Workform 4 was created for each category under review.

The members of the committee will have become very familiar with all of the policies within the categories under review. That puts them in an excellent position to decide if all of the subjects identified in the original master category list really need to be developed as new policies. There are several other options. The committee might decide the subject is already adequately treated in another policy. If that is not the case, committee members may recommend that the subject be covered by including it in an existing policy rather than creating a new policy. For example, when the master category list was originally developed, the committee may have decided to develop a new policy that dealt with study rooms. Now during the discussion of whether a policy should be developed for each subject on the master category list, committee members may decide that a separate study room policy is not needed and that the Meeting Room Use policy should be expanded to cover study rooms as well. Once that decision is made, it is important to revise the completed Workform 7 for the Meeting Room Use policy to indicate that it needs to be expanded to address study rooms as well. The master category list will also have to be revised as changes are made.

When the committee members have decided what subjects should be deleted from the master category list, they should begin brainstorming what subjects might be added to the list. Begin the process by asking committee members to identify any issues that the staff are currently discussing that do not seem to be included in the master category list. If the group identifies any such issues, discuss whether each subject could be covered by revising an existing policy or if a new policy will be required. If the group decides to address an issue in an existing policy, revise the appropriate copy of Workform 7. If a new policy is needed on the subject, add the subject to the master category list and create a copy of Workform 7 for the policy. The new workform will simply list the title of the policy and indicate that the extent of revision required is 4 for each element (level 4 revision means that nothing exists and that the entire element needs to be written).

Another way to identify areas that are not covered in the master category list is to ask whether any events or activities will be occurring in the near future that will raise issues that current policies do not address. For example, the library might be planning for a bond election next year to provide funds to build two new branches. If so, consider whether the policies in place address subjects such as site selection for new facilities, architect selection, naming branch libraries, and donor recognition. If not, you may want to add some or all of the subjects to the master category list and create a copy of Workform 7 for each.

The final question to consider is whether any of the existing policies are so long or complex that they should be divided into multiple policies to make them easier to understand and use. For example, perhaps it would be better to break the policy on library cards for residents into a series of policies—one that addresses business cards, another that addresses teacher cards, another that addresses cards for homebound users, and so forth—rather than to attempt to cover all the unique regulations and procedures for each borrower type in a single policy. Again, remember to revise the master category list to reflect the decisions the committee makes, to make notations on the Workform 7 of any existing policy affected by those decisions, and to create a copy of Workform 7 for each new policy.

At the end of the meeting take a few minutes to review the recommendations that the committee members made one final time to be sure that everyone has the same understanding. This review will also serve as a way for the person who was responsible for editing the master category list as changes were made to verify those changes.

When the Tree County Public Library Policy Audit Advisory Committee had their meeting to review the master category list, the members identified several issues that needed to be addressed. Their meeting is described in part 2 of the Tree County Public Library Policies case study below.

CASE STUDY

TREE COUNTY PUBLIC LIBRARY POLICIES

Part 2
Identifying Needed Policies

In part 1 of this case study we learned that the Tree County Public Library had selected Information Literacy as a new service priority and that the library staff had expressed a number of concerns about the new priority. The staff concerns made it clear that the following policy and regulation issues needed to be resolved before the library began offering enhanced Information Literacy services:

- acceptable use of public access terminals
- equity of access to public access terminals
- level of services to be provided by staff in support of general computer skills
- level of services to be provided by staff to assist users to find, evaluate, and use information on the Internet
- staff training policies and regulations

When the members of the Tree County Public Library Policy Audit Advisory Committee developed the master category list early in the policy review process they used the master category list in figure 5 (chapter 2) as their model. They included Information Services as a policy category and had two subjects within that category that addressed electronic services: Internet Use and PC Use. The Priorities for Reference Service policy was also in that category, and members intended to include some information on use of electronic resources in that policy. In addition, there was a policy on Computer Training for the Public under the Group Services category.

The Tree County Public Library had existing policies on Internet Use, PC Use, and Computer Training for the Public. There were guidelines that addressed some issues relating to reference service but no policy for that area. The members of the committee had reviewed the policies on Internet Use, PC Use, and Computer Training for the Public, using their evaluation criteria and the templates from appendix A. They had noted that there were no existing policy statements, regulations, or procedures that addressed Priorities for Reference Service. All of the discussions during the review process were driven by the evaluation criteria and the questions from appendix A.

During the committee meeting to revise the master category list, one of the committee members reminded the others of the staff concerns about the selection of the Information Literacy service priority and distributed the list of policy issues that the staff thought needed to be addressed. Members compared the issues on the list with the master category list and created the following table:

Staff Issue	**Policy in Master Category List**	**Issues Not Addressed**
Acceptable use of public access terminals	PC Use, Internet Use	All issues covered
Equity of access to public access terminals	PC Use	Policies do not address distribution of PCs in units throughout system
Services that support general computer skills	Computer Training for the Public	Staff services that support individual users' needs are not addressed
Services that support ability to find, evaluate, and use information on the Internet	Computer Training for the Public	Staff services that support individual users' needs are not addressed
Staff training policies and regulations	In personnel policies	None of these issues were addressed in this review

The committee members felt that the PC Use and Internet Use policies covered the acceptable use of public access terminals. However, the issue of distribution of PCs throughout the system was not addressed in either policy. After some discussion, the group agreed this was a resource allocation issue and not a policy issue and therefore should not be included in the public service policies.

The questions surrounding the staff provision of services to individuals looking for assistance with general computer use or with finding, evaluating, and using information on the Internet were more complex. The members of the committee identified a number of ways to deal with these issues. Some members wanted to include everything in the Priorities for Reference Service policy. Others wanted to create a new policy on Priorities for Assistance with Electronic Services. Still others thought there should be separate policies on Staff Assistance with General Computer Needs and Staff Assistance with Internet Use. One person recommended that the levels of staff support available should be included in the PC Use and Internet Use policies.

The chairperson of the committee allowed all of the committee members to make their recommendations and recorded the suggestions on a flip chart. He then asked the members to consider the pros and cons of each suggestion. It became clear very quickly that most members felt that lumping all of the information together in the Priorities for Reference Service policy would lead to a very long, complex policy that would be difficult to use. That option was removed from consideration. There was more interest in including the levels of staff support in the PC Use and Internet Use policies, but ultimately the group agreed that those policies were already long enough and had a different focus. That left two choices: a single policy on staff assistance with electronic services or two separate policies, with one addressing assistance with PC use and the other addressing assistance with Internet use. Ultimately, the group recommended that a single policy be developed to address staff assistance with electronic services. They added that policy to the master category list under Information Services and created a copy of Workform 7, Policy Element Review Summary, for the policy. They also made a note on the copy of Workform 7 for Priorities for Reference Service that electronic services would be addressed in a separate policy.

Finally, they asked the committee chairperson to send a memo to the library director indicating that they had reviewed the staff concerns about the Information Literacy service priority and incorporated those concerns into the master category list when appropriate. The chairperson was also asked to make two recommendations from the committee:

1. The need for equitable distribution of PCs throughout the system should be addressed in budget process.
2. A committee should be appointed to review the library's personnel policies and develop one or more policies relating to staff training.

Step 3.2: Summarize the Committee's Recommendations

When the Policy Audit Advisory Committee has completed the review and revision of the master category list, the chairperson of the committee will have all of the information needed to create the final report from the committee. The final report will consist of the completed copies of Workform 7 for each of the policies that were reviewed (including the policies that were added during the review process) and a revised copy of the master category list.

The easiest way to present the revised master category list for each category is to complete columns A (policy number) and B (policy subject) on Workform 8, Policy Revision and Development Summary (see figure 17). This workform will be used in chapter 4 to record the level of effort required to complete each policy, the priority for the completion of each policy, the name of the person(s) assigned to review or develop the elements of the policy, and the date their work is due. The final master category list will have to be transcribed onto copies of Workform 8 at some point. It makes sense to do it now and cut out one step in the process later.

When the master category list was originally created you developed a numbering scheme for the policies. However, it is very rare for a Policy Audit Advisory Committee to go through the entire inventory and assessment process without revising the draft master category list

FIGURE 17

Sample Workform 8, Policy Revision and Development Summary

Policy Category Information Services

A. No.	B. Subject	C. Level of Effort	D. Priority	E. Assigned To		F. Due Date
				Policy/Regulations		
				Procedures		
				Guidelines		
				Policy/Regulations		
				Procedures		
				Guidelines		
				Policy/Regulations		
				Procedures		
				Guidelines		

developed during the inventory. Policies will have been added to the list, policies will have been combined, and policies will have been subdivided into two or more separate policies.

If this happened during your policy audit, it means that the order in which you expected your policies to occur within each of the categories in the policy manual and the corresponding numbering scheme will need to be reviewed and revised. This is a relatively simple process that can be handled by the chairperson of the Policy Audit Advisory Committee and recorded in column A of Workform 8. Once the final versions of Workform 8 for each policy category have been prepared, the Policy Audit Advisory Committee has completed its assignment.

Step 3.3: Thank the Committee

Over the past few months, the members of the Policy Audit Advisory Committee have put a great deal of effort into a challenging assignment that required knowledge of library operations, attention to detail, judgment, and perseverance. In most cases the work they did as committee members was in addition to their regular job duties, which means that many of them had to do at least some of the committee work on their own time in the evening or on weekends. It is vital that their hard work be acknowledged and that they be thanked for that work. There are a variety of ways to recognize such significant contributions to the organization. The library director might present each committee member with a certificate of appreciation or send each a letter of thanks. The members of the management team might decide to host a small reception for the committee to show their appreciation. The methods used to recognize the committee members' contributions will differ from library to library—what matters is that each person receives a personal commendation for his or her hard work.

Challenges

The assessment portion of the policy audit is important, but it is not an end in itself. The development of evaluation criteria and the subsequent evaluation of each policy are necessary precursors to actually revising or developing policies. The steps in the assessment phase should be completed in a thoughtful but expeditious manner.

There are several challenges that the members of the Policy Audit Advisory Committee will face as they work through the assessment process. Finding the balance between global thinking and excessive attention to detail may be difficult, particularly early in the assessment process, when members are developing evaluation criteria. Then, as the process moves to actually evaluating existing policies, some members of the committee are going to have a problem focusing their attention on identifying what needs to be changed rather than on describing what those changes should look like. The final and potentially most serious challenge is that the assessment process will drag on and on and never actually conclude at all. Staff in more than one library have become so bogged down in trying to evaluate what they have that they have never reached the point of actually revising or developing anything new.

Balancing Points of View

It is important that the members of the Policy Audit Advisory Committee include a mixture of those people who tend to look at the big picture and those who are more comfortable if they can examine every detail. Both points of view are important throughout the assessment process, but they are particularly critical during when the existing policy documents are being evaluated. During that process you need committee members who can see how any given policy or element of a policy fits into the overall library policy structure *and* you need staff members who can look at an existing policy element and say, "Yes, but what about . . . ?" and "Yes, but what does this *really* mean?"

The first part of this challenge is relatively easy to address. Simply be very sure that the people appointed to the Policy Audit Advisory Committee include both global thinkers and nitpickers. The real challenge will be for the committee chairperson to balance the needs of both types of personalities to ensure that each person's issues are heard and still ensure that the committee does not become paralyzed by excessive attention to detail. The most effective way to attain this balance is to discuss the issue during the preliminary evaluation meeting. The chairperson can point out that the committee includes two types of people, big picture people and detail people, and that each has a role to play in the evaluation. In most libraries, the members of the committee will be able to figure out fairly easily which committee members fall into each category. Once this initial discussion has taken place, the chairperson can refer to it as needed if one group or the other seems to be dominating the discussion. These gentle reminders may well become a running subtheme of the evaluation meetings and if the chair can inject a little humor into the reminders, so much the better. If the committee members can learn to laugh about the issue when it is raised, it is unlikely that the chairperson will have to deal with hurt feelings and misunderstandings.

Evaluation Only, Please

Most of the members of the Policy Audit Advisory Committee will be staff members who have worked at the library for a reasonable length time and have opinions about the appropriate content of the policies under review. This is a safe assumption to make because the average tenure in most libraries is long and virtually every library staff member seems to have strong opinions about how library business should be conducted. These two characteristics—an understanding of how the library operates and a commitment to certain types of services—will be valuable assets for the committee members during the assessment process if, and it is a big if, they remember that their sole responsibility is to identify areas in the policies under review that need to be changed. There will be a tendency on the part of the committee members, particularly the detail-oriented ones, to want to provide long lists of what needs to be included in the policy when it is revised or, even worse, to attempt to rewrite the policy during the evaluation phase. The committee members should be indicating the deficiencies of a policy, and it is critical that they stay on target and merely indicate the ways in which the policy element did not meet the appropriate evaluation criteria.

To combat this tendency, the chairperson must make it clear at the preliminary evaluation meeting that the committee charge is to identify problems with the policies under review. They are not responsible for problem resolution. During the meetings, when the actual evaluations are being presented and discussed, the chairperson will no doubt have to remind one or more people of the committee charge again. If some members continue to try to solve problems rather than identify them, the chairperson may want to schedule a private conversation to reinforce the committee charge.

Agonizing and Endless Debate

One of the challenges of the inventory part of the policy audit is that the people in charge of the inventory risk getting buried in paper. During the assessment process, there is an equal danger that the committee will become so involved in trying to reach consensus on evaluation criteria or on the changes needed in a policy that the members will lose sight of the underlying purpose of this part of the process. The only reason for completing a policy audit is to form a foundation for the revision of existing policies and identify needed new policies. The audit is not the end; it is just one of the means to the end.

As nice as it would be to have every member of the committee in total agreement on each topic, that is very unlikely to occur. It is important to provide an opportunity for all points of view to be heard, but the assessment process must be completed before the development phase can begin. At times it will be necessary for the chairperson to close discussion and announce that the majority point of view will prevail. If necessary, take a vote to determine what the majority of the advisory group believes should be done. There is more information on helping groups reach agreement in the "Groups: Reaching Agreement" section of the Tool Kit in *The New Planning for Results.*[1]

Key Points to Remember

1. Clearly defined evaluation criteria must be developed before library policies can be evaluated.
2. No global list of evaluation criteria can be applied to all of the policies for all public libraries. Each library needs to develop its own evaluation criteria.
3. Evaluation criteria should reflect local conditions and issues and should be approved by the library management team.
4. Members of the Policy Audit Advisory Committee should base all of their evaluations on the agreed-upon criteria. The prime purpose of the criteria is to ensure that each policy receives a fair and equitable review.
5. The members of the Policy Audit Advisory Committee are responsible for identifying areas that need to be revised, added, or deleted from each of the policy elements they review. They are *not* responsible for actually writing the revisions or additions or making the deletions.

6. The assessment process includes the responsibility for identifying new policies that need to be developed and outdated policies that need to be discarded.
7. It is essential to thank the Policy Audit Advisory Committee for their hard work.

NOTE

1. Sandra Nelson, *The New Planning for Results: A Streamlined Approach* (Chicago: American Library Association, 2001), 235–245.

Chapter 4

Development

MILESTONES

By the time you finish this chapter you will know how to

- determine the level of effort and assign a priority to each of the policies on the final master category list
- select the people to be involved in the development of new or revised policy statements, regulations, procedures, and guidelines
- identify current practice in your library and best practice in other libraries
- write policy statements, regulations, procedures, and guidelines
- select the appropriate review and approval process for each element of new or revised policies
- deal with the challenges that you will face while developing policies

We have finally reached the point when you are actually going to be writing policy statements, regulations, procedures, and guidelines. It has taken a significant amount of work to reach this part of the process, but as you will see, that work provides the foundation upon which you will build the library's new policy manual. If you had attempted to build a policy manual with no foundation, you would have ended up taking considerably more time than you have invested in the policy audit. Furthermore, the policies you would have created would have been much less effective and efficient than the policies you are now in a position to develop.

You will start the policy development process by reviewing the final report submitted by the Policy Audit Advisory Committee. That report includes a copy of Workform 8, Policy Revision and Development Summary, for each policy category that was included in the policy audit. The copies of Workform 8 are still mostly blank: the only data they contain are the policy subjects in the category and a unique number assigned to each policy. All of the copies of Workform 7, Policy Element Review Summary, that were completed during the review process have been divided by category and attached to the appropriate copies of Workform 8. A final draft of the policy master category list is also included in the committee's final report.

This final report contains all of the information that you need to move forward. The master category list will serve as a draft table of contents for your new policy manual. The copies of Workform 8 provide an overview of the work to be done, a place to record information about the level of effort required to complete each policy, the priority for the completion of the policy, and a mechanism for keeping track of assignments and deadlines. The copies of Workform 7 provide detailed information about what has to be done to revise or develop the elements of each policy to ensure that they meet the agreed-upon evaluation criteria.

Stop and think for a moment about how different the policy development process would be if you had simply started writing or revising policies without going through the policy audit inventory and assessment. It is unlikely that you would have even considered a new taxonomy for organizing the policy manual. You would simply have tweaked the old manual a bit and made do with what you had. Among other things, that would probably have meant that you would be spending most of your time revising existing policies instead of creating new policies. It was through the development and review of the master category list that you were able to look at the big picture and identify policies that were missing.

You would not have developed evaluation criteria for each of the elements of a policy. That would have meant that each person or team assigned to develop or revise a policy would have been using personal, subjective, and largely unstated criteria to determine what needed to be done. It would also have made it hard to judge the effectiveness and efficiency of any revised or new policies. You would not have any criteria upon which to determine the priority of the policies to be developed, nor would you have any idea of how long it would take to revise or write each policy, which would make scheduling very difficult. Finally, you would have missed the opportunity to involve the staff early in the policy development process and that would make it more difficult to get staff buy-in for new or revised policies.

Clearly, the work of the Policy Audit Advisory Committee has set the stage for the successful conclusion of the policy development process. However, there is one issue that remains to be addressed before we can move forward. The copies of Workform 8 that the committee completed include a mix of existing policies that need to be revised or rewritten and new policies that need to be developed. At first glance, it might seem that you would use one process to revise existing policies and a different process to develop new policies. However, a careful comparison of what actually has to be done to revise a policy with what has to be done to create a policy makes it clear that the processes are virtually identical. In each case, someone has to identify who should be involved in the process, someone has to identify current practice in your library and best practice in other libraries in the area under consideration, someone has to write or rewrite the policy or elements within the policy, and there has to be a process in place to review, revise, and approve the final policy. There is probably going to be more work involved in creating a new policy than in making minor revisions in an existing policy, but the tasks and steps required to do the work will be the same. Therefore, the tasks and steps in this chapter are arranged by policy element and not by whether the policy is new or needs revision.

Definitions

This chapter includes three terms that have specific meanings in the context of policy development. To ensure that everyone has the same understanding of those terms, they are defined below:

Best Practice Management practices and work processes that produce highly effective and efficient library services.

Level of Effort The amount of staff time and energy required to develop a new policy or revise an existing policy.

Priority The relative importance of each policy being developed.

Policy Development

The process that you will use to develop or revise your policies has four tasks:

Task 1: *Schedule* the development of the policy statements, regulations, procedures, and guidelines based on the level of effort required to complete them and the priority of the subject matter.

Task 2: *Write the policy statement and regulations,* establish a review process, and obtain approval.

Task 3: *Write procedures,* establish a review process, and obtain approval.

Task 4: *Write guidelines (if needed),* establish a review process, and obtain approval.

These four tasks are each divided into a series of steps, which are listed at the beginning of the discussion of each task below. Figure 18 shows all of the tasks and steps associated with developing new policies.

FIGURE 18
Tasks and Steps in Policy Development

Task 1: Schedule

Step 1.1: Determine level of effort
Step 1.2: Determine priority
Step 1.3: Develop master schedule

Task 2: Write the policy statement and regulations

Step 2.1: Identify who needs to be involved
Step 2.2: Identify and evaluate current practice in your library and best practice in other libraries
Step 2.3: Write
Step 2.4: Review and revise
Step 2.5: Obtain approval

Task 3: Write procedures

Step 3.1: Identify who needs to be involved
Step 3.2: Identify and evaluate current practice in your library and best practice in other libraries
Step 3.3: Write
Step 3.4: Review and revise
Step 3.5: Obtain approval

Task 4: Write guidelines (if needed)

Step 4.1: Identify who needs to be involved
Step 4.2: Identify and evaluate current practice in your library and best practice in other libraries
Step 4.3: Write
Step 4.4: Review and revise
Step 4.5: Obtain approval

TASK 1: SCHEDULE

Step 1.1: Determine level of effort.

Step 1.2: Determine priority.

Step 1.3: Develop master schedule.

The Policy Audit Advisory Committee completed its work in chapter 3. That means that the process of actually writing policies will start with the library director or the director's designee. The three steps in Task 1 should probably be completed by one or more members of the management team. The management team will almost always be responsible for identifying who should be involved in the development of policy statements and regulations and will always appoint the groups that develop procedures and guidelines (Steps 2.1, 3.1, and 4.1). There is more information about selecting appropriate people in the discussion of each of those steps.

Step 1.1: Determine Level of Effort

Before you can assign a level of effort to each of the policies to be revised or developed you need to understand why such a designation is important. That question is particularly pertinent when you remember that the members of the Policy Audit Advisory Committee have already assigned and recorded the extent of revision required for each element of each policy on Workform 7 using a scale of 0 to 4 plus NA:

0 = No revision needed to meet criteria

1 = Minor revision needed to meet criteria

2 = Moderate rewrite necessary to meet criteria

3 = Total rewrite necessary to meet criteria

4 = Does not exist—needs to be written

NA = Not applicable—refers only to guidelines

While it might appear that the numeric indicator of extent of revision required provides all of the information needed to begin to develop the policies, a closer look indicates that is not the case. The members of the management team are going to have to make a series of decisions before the actual policy development begins, and most of the decisions will be affected by the level of effort required to complete each policy. Although there is some relationship between the extent of revision required and the level of effort, that relationship is not absolute. There are completely new policies that can be written fairly easily and quickly by a knowledgeable staff member. If, for instance, the Policy Audit Advisory Committee recommended that a new policy be developed to codify the existing loan periods for different types of material, one or two people could develop the needed policy statements, regulations, and procedures with minimal effort. On the other hand, if the Policy Audit Advisory Committee recommended that moderate changes be made in the regulations of the Internet policy, the revisions might take weeks or months and require the involvement of numerous staff members, the library's governing authority, and even the public.

As you can see, the extent of revision required provides the starting point for the discussion of the level of effort that will be required to write or revise the policy, but it is certainly not the only thing to consider. Other issues include

- *Board Action.* Any policy revision that includes new or revised policy statements or regulations will have to be approved by the library's governing authority. Preparing documents for the library board or any other governing authority can be time-consuming, and thus the level of effort is often higher for policies that require new or rewritten policy statements and regulations than it is for policies in which only the procedures or guidelines will be changed.
- *Interrelated Policies.* Occasionally one policy affects other policies, which may mean that changes will need to be made to those policies if changes are made to the original policy. This in turn may require coordination among the people responsible for revising or writing the various policies and therefore a higher level of effort than dealing with stand-alone policies.
- *Complexity.* Some policies are inherently more complex than others. A policy on Priorities for Assistance with Electronic Services is very likely to be more complex than a policy on Bulletin Boards. Complex policies require higher levels of effort.
- *Controversial Policies.* Revising or developing policies that might be controversial, such as implementing new service charges, raising fees, or Internet filtering, often requires a higher level of effort than dealing with less sensitive subjects. This is especially true if the governing authority decides to schedule presentations on the subject and provide time for public comment on the proposed changes prior to making any decisions.
- *Legal Issues.* Any policy that has to be reviewed by outside legal council will require a higher level of effort than policies that can be developed without such review.
- *Staff Time.* The number of staff that need to be involved during the process of developing and reviewing a policy affects the level of effort required. Policies that reflect current practice can be developed by one or two knowledgeable people. They require considerably less effort than policies that need to be developed by cross-functional teams who must gather considerable information about practices in other libraries before making any decisions.

- *Training.* Some new or revised policies reflect current practice that is clearly understood and supported by staff. These policies require less effort than policies that require staff to understand and adapt to changes in regulations or procedures. Anytime staff need to be trained to use any element of a policy, the level of effort increases significantly.

The six-point scale shown in figure 19, Levels of Effort Required for Policy Revision, can assist you in classifying the level of effort that will be required to revise a policy so it meets the established evaluation criteria. The scale uses a single number to indicate the amount of time it will take to revise the policy as well as the number of staff or others who will probably be involved in the revision.

The actual work of this step begins by deciding who will be responsible for determining the level of effort required to complete each policy. A small group of three or four managers is ideal. That includes enough people in the process to provide a variety of points of view but is still a small enough group to manage easily. The group should begin their work by reviewing and discussing the six-point scale in figure 19 and the completed copy of Workform 8, Policy Revision and Development Summary, for each category. The members of the group will then read Workform 7, Policy Element Review Summary, for each policy and discuss the issues surrounding the development of the policy. As the members of the group agree on the level of effort required to write or revise each policy, a recorder should write the appropriate number in column C of Workform 8. (Columns A and B were filled in earlier by the chairperson of the Policy Audit Advisory Committee.) In

FIGURE 19

Levels of Effort Required for Policy Revision

0 No revision necessary—policy meets or exceeds all criteria.

1 Very minimal effort—a knowledgeable staff member could quickly make the few minor changes needed to meet all criteria. Necessary changes are elaborations or clarifications and are noncontroversial.

2 Minimal effort—a knowledgeable staff member could make the changes needed to meet all criteria or create the new element. Subject is neither complex nor controversial.

3 Moderate effort—a few staff with expertise related to the subject could make the changes needed to meet all criteria or create the new element. Subject is noncontroversial but may be complex.

4 Significant effort—a staff task force is required to identify options and make recommendations. Subject is complex and affects other policies. May require governing authority to choose between proposed options related to policy statement or regulations.

5 Extensive effort—the library administration and library board are required to establish policy and regulations. Subject is potentially controversial, and proposed changes may require public comment or legal review.

the case study below, the management team of the Anytown Public Library goes through this process to determine the level of effort required to revise the library's Meeting Room Use policy.

CASE STUDY

ANYTOWN PUBLIC LIBRARY POLICIES

Part 3
Level of Effort

In part 2 of this case study, Gretchen Hummel reviewed the Anytown Public Library Meeting Room Use policy and recorded her comments and recommendations on Workform 7, Policy Element Review Summary. The members of the team responsible for determining the level of effort that will be required to revise the Meeting Room Use policy began by carefully reading Gretchen's recommendations. They noted that Gretchen had determined that the policy statement needed only minor (level 1) revision, that the regulations needed to be completely rewritten (level 3), and that the procedures needed moderate rewriting (level 2).

The team then considered the other issues that might affect the level of effort required to rewrite the Meeting Room Use policy. The library board was going to have to act upon the revisions of the policy statement and the regulations. Although the changes in the policy statement were going to be minor, the potential changes in the regulations could have an effect on other library policies, including Bulletin Board Posting, Parking, and Use of Library-Owned Equipment. The group did not think that the new regulations and procedures were going to be unduly complex, nor did they think they would be controversial with the public. However, the group was well aware of the fact that some members of the staff were very disturbed about sharing the meeting rooms with public groups. These staff members felt that the library's public programs would have to be reduced because of space constraints. Therefore, it was probably going to be necessary to spend time getting the staff to buy in to the policy statement, regulations, and procedures.

As the members of the group continued their discussion they realized that although the extent of revision required ranged from level 1 (minor) to level 3 (complete rewrite), the other issues surrounding the revision of the Meeting Room Use

A. No.	**B. Subject**	**C. Level of Effort**	**D. Priority**	**E. Assigned To**		**F. Due Date**
MNG-8	Meeting Room Use	4		Policy/Regulations		
				Procedures		
				Guidelines		
				Policy/Regulations		
				Procedures		
				Guidelines		

policy indicated that the level of effort required to complete the revision would be significant. Their decision was recorded by writing the number 4 in column C of Workform 8, Policy Revision and Development Summary.

Step 1.2: Determine Priority

There are two steps left before you and your colleagues can begin to develop or revise your policies and they are interconnected. In this step you will decide the relative priority of the policies to be developed. In Step 1.3 you will develop a master schedule based on these priorities.

The priority setting process is much like the triage process in an emergency room. When you go to an emergency room a nurse records all of the information about your condition. That information is used to assign you a treatment priority based on the emergency room's criteria of care. Generally, in an emergency room the most life-threatening cases are treated first while people with minor problems may have to wait for some time to see a physician.

In the case of policies the criteria that you will use to assign priorities are not as clear-cut as they are in an emergency room. There are at least three possible criteria to use when assigning priorities to the policies to be developed: urgency, importance, and momentum.

1. Urgency implies an immediate need and suggests that *time* is the critical element to consider when assigning a priority.
2. Importance is a measure of significance and suggests that *value* to the library is the critical element to consider when assigning a priority.
3. Momentum is a measure of movement and suggests that continuous *progress* on developing the policy manual is the critical element to consider when assigning a priority.

Figure 20 describes when it is appropriate to use each of these criteria and what to consider when assigning priorities based on each criterion.

Although the three criteria are not automatically mutually exclusive, the group responsible for determining priorities should come to agreement on a single criterion to use in most cases. If they don't, the priority setting process will be both confusing and difficult. Agreement on a single criterion to use when assigning priorities to most policies will still allow the group to decide that one of the other criteria might be more effective in the case of a specific policy. For instance, the Anytown Public Library group that is assigning priorities to the policies to be developed might agree that the most important issue in their library is that the staff be able to see continual progress in the policy development process. Therefore, they would identify momentum as the criterion they would use to assign priorities to most of the policies under review and give policies requiring a low level of effort higher priorities than

FIGURE 20
Criteria for Assigning Priorities

Criterion	When to Use	Examples	What to Consider
Urgency	• When there is a deadline approaching that will be affected by the policy under review • When there is an existing problem that is being affected by the policy under review • When there is an obvious issue that could cause serious problems for the library in the immediate future that is addressed by the policy under review	• There is no policy on site selection for a new branch and the library bond for a new branch just passed. • There is increasing use of Internet terminals for e-mail, which is against the old policy but will be allowed in the new policy. • The meeting room policy is vague at a time when nearby libraries have been dealing with a hate group that wants to use library space for a meeting.	• Immediacy of the problem • Potential seriousness of the problem
Importance	• When the library has a reasonably useful policy manual and the policies under review are additions intended to reflect current conditions • When new library priorities cannot be implemented until the policy under review has been completed	• The library has purchased a new automation system and the circulation procedures need to be updated. • The library has completed a new strategic plan and certain goals and objectives are adversely affected by existing policies.	• Effect of the policy on the ability of staff to do their jobs • Relative importance of the staff activities affected by the policy
Momentum	• When the library does not have a policy manual or has a manual that is so outdated that it is useless • When there has been a history of starting projects and not finishing them, resulting in staff skepticism about management's commitment to any long-term project	• The current library policy manual is a narrative document last updated in 1992. • The library management team started to revise the policy manual twice in the past and did not make any progress either time	• Level of effort required to complete the policy development process • Number of staff available to develop policies

policies requiring more effort. However, when the group considers the Meeting Room Use policy, they might decide that although the level of effort required to revise that policy is high, it is very important and should be added to the policies with the highest priorities.

You can use whatever scale you wish to designate priorities. One scale that is easy to use and clear to most people is to designate priorities in three tiers: high priority, moderate priority, and low priority. Another scale that some people use is A, B, C, and D. You could also use a numeric scale, although there are already two numeric scales in use in this process (extent of revision required and level of effort) and a third may well lead to confusion. Regardless of the scale that you choose, you probably won't want to designate more than three or four levels of priorities. That will provide enough differentiation to allow you to develop a master schedule without creating a situation in which some policies are given such a low priority that one might legitimately ask why they are being developed at all.

This step is completed by the same group of people who determined level of effort. They should be able assign a priority to the policies to be developed during the same meeting in which they determine the level of effort needed to complete each policy. First they will select a general criterion to use to assign priority to the policies under review and the scale to use to designate those priorities. When they have reached agreement on the general criterion and scale, they will discuss and assign a priority to each of the policies listed on the each of copies of Workform 8. A recorder will then write the priority in column D of Workform 8.

When the group has assigned priorities to all of the policies, it would be prudent to review the decisions that were made. If the group used a three-level scale to indicate priority, roughly a third of the policies under review should fall in each level. If they used a four-level scale, then roughly a quarter of the policies should fall in each level. Priority rankings do not have much meaning if everything is considered to be a high priority. If the group discovers that too many policies fall into the same level of priority, they will want to take another look at the policies in that level and make the adjustments needed to balance the number of policies in each priority level.

Step 1.3: Develop Master Schedule

Up to this point in the process, we have been reviewing and discussing each policy as a separate entity in each task and step. Starting with this step, we will begin to divide the work by element to be developed instead of looking at the total policy. The distinction between total policy and the elements within the policies is important to understand as you begin to create the master schedule for the development of your policies. Tasks 2, 3, and 4 in this chapter each address the specific elements of a policy and assume that you will complete the policy statement and regulations for a policy before moving on to procedures and then complete the procedures before considering guidelines (if any). This assumption obviously has an effect on the scheduling decisions you make.

There are several good reasons for dividing the remaining work by element. Policy statements and regulations have to be approved by the library's governing authority, so they should be completed before the development of procedures begins. Different people will be involved in creating or revising the various policy elements. Policy statements and regulations are commonly developed by library managers. Procedures and guidelines are often developed by the frontline staff who perform the functions described in the procedures and guidelines.

The master schedule is not intended to be so specific and rigid that it acts as a straightjacket. It simply provides a way to organize the work to be done in a logical manner and ensure that the work is distributed appropriately over a period of time. Earlier, it was stated that it would probably take the average library two or three months to complete the policy audit inventory and assessment processes. At the same time, it was noted that it is impossible to provide a general estimate of how much time it would take for libraries to develop the policies because each library would need a different number of policies, have a different number of staff available to do the work, and operate under different governance conditions. However, the fact that no general estimates can be provided does not mean that staff from each library going through this process cannot determine with relative accuracy the length of time necessary to complete all of the work to be done in their own environment. It is not only possible for them to make such a determination but also critical that they do so.

In Steps 1.1 and 1.2 of this task a group of library mangers read the final report from the Policy Audit Advisory Committee and determined the level of effort and the priority for each policy. As they reviewed policy after policy, it is probable that one or more members of the group said, "This is impossible! There is more to do here than we can ever get done. We might as well not even try." This is one of the most common reactions of librarians when faced with writing or rewriting dozens of library policies. It is also one of the reasons that most libraries continue to limp along with inadequate and incomplete policy manuals.

The truth is, of course, that anything can be done if you allow enough time and allocate enough resources to make it happen. The amount of time required to develop your policies will be directly affected by the level of staff resources available. If one or two people will be expected to do most of the work, then the process could take well over a year. If library management decides to involve teams of staff from all over the library, the process may be completed in six months to a year. It really doesn't matter how long the whole process takes as long as progress continues to be made. In fact, the review and revision of library policies should be a continuous effort in every library. This process is just the beginning of what will be an ongoing commitment.

The easiest and most effective way to schedule assignments and keep track of progress is to use a Gantt chart to develop your master schedule. A Gantt chart is a standard format for displaying a schedule graphically. It includes a column that lists the activities to be completed and then a series of columns that represent time periods. Arrows or bars are drawn across the time columns, beginning in the column during which the activity will start and ending in the column during which the activity is scheduled to be completed. The time period represented by the columns in a Gantt chart can vary depending on the project. Columns might represent days, weeks, months, or even years. For this process, the most efficient time period to use is months. Workform 9, Master Schedule, is a Gantt chart that you can use if you wish, although a Gantt chart is relatively simple to create and you might prefer to develop an electronic version that can be easily updated. A completed sample of Workform 9 can be seen in part 4 of the Anytown Public Library Policies case study later in this chapter.

There are five main things to consider when developing your master schedule. The first thing you will look at is the priority of the policy. Those policies in the highest priority group should be scheduled to be completed before policies in the second or third priority grouping.

The second thing to consider is the level of effort that will be required to complete the policy. Policies with a high level of effort will take longer than policies with a low level of effort. However, because you will be scheduling the elements of a policy and not the entire policy, you may have to go to back to the copy of Workform 7 for the policy being scheduled to refresh your memory about which elements require higher levels of effort. If the policy and regulations need minor changes, but the procedures are likely to take significant effort, you will want to reflect that in your scheduling.

The third thing to consider is the degree to which two or more policies are interconnected. You are going to have to take policy statements and regulations to your governing authority for approval. It will be easier for everyone if interconnected policies are presented at one time. That will allow board members to see the big picture and will reduce the chances of having the board adopt conflicting policies.

Fourth, you will need to consider whether or not you want to schedule the development of guidelines for any of the policies under review. One or more of the policies may already have guidelines, but most will not. In fact most policies don't even need guidelines. In chapter 1 a *guideline* was defined as "a description of best practice that provides suggestions for staff on the most efficient ways to implement policy statements, regulations, and procedures." The definition went on to note that guidelines are more philosophical than the other elements of a policy. You can choose to wait to develop all guidelines until you have completed the policy statements, regulations, and procedures for all the policies on your master category list, or you can choose to develop guidelines at the same time you develop the other elements of a policy that needs guidelines. If you intend to complete guidelines concurrently with the other elements of a policy, be sure to include the guidelines on the master schedule. If not, just cross out the word *guidelines* on Workform 9 or delete the Guidelines row when you create your electronic version of a Gantt chart.

Fifth, it will be important for you to be sensitive to the overall amount of work you expect to accomplish in a given time period. The staff who will be writing or revising the policy elements will be doing the work *in addition* to their regular duties. It is safe to assume that every staff member in your organization believes that he or she is already overloaded with work. You may be able to expect managers to deal with policy statements and regulations from two or three policies within the same time period, but it is likely that individual frontline staff will only be able to work with one set of procedures at a time. The Gantt chart provides a quick visual way to determine how many things are scheduled for each month, which should help you to balance the workload appropriately. The case study below illustrates how the members of the group developing the master schedule at the Anytown Public Library made some of their scheduling decisions.

CASE STUDY

ANYTOWN PUBLIC LIBRARY POLICIES

Part 4
Master Schedule

The Anytown Public Library management team had decided earlier in their discussions that they would defer the development of any guidelines until after the policy manual had been completed. Therefore, they crossed out the word *guidelines* on Workform 9, Master Schedule, and focused their energies on scheduling the development of policy statements, regulations, and procedures.

In part 3 of the Anytown Public Library case study, the management team agreed that the Meeting Room Use policy had a high priority. As a result it was the first policy that was added to the master schedule when the group met to assign deadlines. As you can see in the Gantt chart in figure 21, the group decided that rewriting the Meeting Room Use policy statement and regulations should begin in early January and that both elements could be completed and reviewed by the end of February. The Anytown Public Library Board meets on the final Thursday of each month, so the board members would be asked to review and approve the Meeting Room Use policy statement and regulations during their February meeting. The group making the assignments assumed that the policy statement and regulations would be approved during that meeting and scheduled the development of procedures to begin in early March and be completed in mid-April. The implementation date was set for late May to allow plenty of time to inform staff about the new policy, to provide any needed training, and to print any needed new forms or signs.

The group then looked at the other policies that needed to be scheduled. They decided that the Bulletin Board policy and the Parking policy might be affected by the decisions made concerning the Meeting Room Use policy, so they scheduled the development of those policy statements and regulations concurrently with the Meeting Room Use policy and decided to ask the same group of managers to deal with all three policies. They planned on presenting the draft policy statements and regulations for all three policies to the board during the February meeting.

The procedures for the Bulletin Board policy and the Parking policy were scheduled to be completed at the same time as the procedures for the Meeting Room Use policy, although the group decided that the procedures should be developed by three different subcommittees. The group felt that although the Bulletin Board policy might change, four to five weeks was sufficient time to inform and train staff and print new forms. However, if any changes were going to be made in the policies and procedures governing public parking, the group agreed that they should spend at least two to three months on informing the public about the proposed changes before the changes were implemented. Therefore the implementation date for the Parking policy was set for the first week in July.

When the group completed scheduling the three interconnected policies, they referred to their copy of Workform 8 to see what the next policy in the high-priority group was. They discovered that it was Loan Periods and Loan Limits and so they scheduled the development of the policy statement and regulations for that policy to begin in June, after the all of the work had been completed on the first three policies to be developed. The members of the management team agreed that the library had too few staff members to schedule work on more than three policies at a time. When the team finished scheduling all of the policies in the high-priority group, they moved on to the policies in the second-priority group and then to those in the third-priority group. When they completed their work they had several Gantt charts showing approximately how long it would take to develop all of the policies in the categories under review.

FIGURE 21

Completed Example of Workform 9, Master Schedule

Policy/Activity	Jan.	Feb.	Mar.	Apr.	May	June	July	Aug.	Sept.	Oct.	Nov.	Dec.
1. MNG-8 Meeting Room Use												
a. Policy Statement and Regulations	x—	—x										
b. Procedures			x—	—x								
c. ~~Guidelines~~ NA												
d. Implementation					*							
2. MNG-10 Bulletin Boards												
a. Policy Statement and Regulations	x—	—x										
b. Procedures			x—	—x								
c. ~~Guidelines~~ NA												
d. Implementation					*							
3. MNG-14 Parking												
a. Policy Statement and Regulations	x—	—x										
b. Procedures			x—	—x								
c. ~~Guidelines~~ NA												
d. Implementation					*							
4. CIR-3 Loan Periods and Loan Limits												
a. Policy Statement and Regulations						x—	—x					
b. Procedures								x—x				
c. ~~Guidelines~~ NA												
d. Implementation										*		

TASK 2: WRITE THE POLICY STATEMENT AND REGULATIONS

Step 2.1: Identify who needs to be involved.

Step 2.2: Identify and evaluate current practice in your library and best practice in other libraries.

Step 2.3: Write.

Step 2.4: Review and revise.

Step 2.5: Obtain approval.

Step 2.1: Identify Who Needs to Be Involved

Every library has some sort of governing authority. Some libraries have authority boards and others are a part of a city or county. In either case, the members of a library's governing authority are responsible for approving the library's policies and regulations. In rare instances, most commonly with library boards, one or more members of the board assume the responsibility for drafting library policy statements and regulations. This usually occurs with the assistance of staff, but the board members in question are clearly responsible for developing the policy statements and regulations. More often, members of the library board or other governing authority prefer to review and approve policy statements and regulations that have been drafted by staff rather than get involved in the actual writing of documents. The members of the governing authority of each library make the decisions about their part in the policy development process. The library director is responsible for ensuring the board's decisions are implemented. If you work in a library in which members of the library board assume responsibility for the development of policy statements and regulations, it is probable that the board chairperson will appoint members to a committee with that charge.

More often, however, it is the members of the library's management team who will select the people to be responsible for writing draft policy statements and regulations. There is no one set configuration of people who automatically can be identified as the best and only people to write or rewrite policy statements and regulations for your library. In fact, there are a number of options to consider, including senior managers, library board members, elected officials, members of the community, system or regional staff members, or some combination of these options. The choice of who to involve depends on a variety of factors.

If the policy in question is fairly straightforward and unlikely to be controversial, then one or two members of the management team should be able to develop draft policy statements and regulations with little trouble. However, if the policy is complex, you may want to include one or more experts on the subject of the policy along with the managers. The experts may or may not be staff members. For instance, it would probably be very helpful to have a day-care manager involved in discussions about the library's policy on services to day-care centers. You might want to involve a group of teenagers in the development of youth services policy statements and regulations.

The most challenging policies to address are those that are likely to be controversial with the staff or with the public—or, in particularly sticky situations, with both. A number of years ago there was a NAPA auto parts commercial with the tag line "you can pay me now or you can pay me later." The commercial suggested that it would be less expensive to do regular maintenance on your car (pay me now) than to wait until the car needed repairs (pay me later). In the same way, it is probably less trouble to involve a wide variety of people with differing points of view in the development of potentially controversial policies from the beginning rather than deal with their opposition and anger after the policy statement and regulations have been presented to your governing authority. That means that the group selected to draft policy statements and regulations for potentially controversial policies will be larger than the one or two managers who typically draft these elements. It also means that the most crucial appointment you make to this group will be the chairperson. The chairperson will need to have strong facilitation skills to ensure that all points of view are presented and to help the group reach consensus on the policy statements and regulations to recommend. There is more information on helping groups reach agreement in the Tool Kit in *The New Planning for Results.*[1]

If your library is a member of a library system or region, you may want to ask someone from the system to participate in the development of policy statements and regulations for policies in areas that are new to the library. For instance, a library that is adding a teen department for the first time may not know a lot about the issues to consider when developing policies for services to teens. An experienced system staff member will probably be familiar with a variety of library programs for teens and be able to provide needed expertise.

Ultimately, whoever is making the decision about whom to involve in the development of policy statements will have to identify both a chairperson and a list of participants. When that decision is made the name of the chairperson should be written in column E on Workform 8, on the line labeled "Policy/Regulations." The deadline for completion of the policy statement and regulations should be entered on the appropriate line in column F on Workform 8. Be sure that the deadline on Workform 8 is compatible with the master schedule you developed earlier.

You now have all of the information you need to make the final appointments to the group that will be responsible for developing policy statements and regulations. When they are notified of their appointments, they should receive the following information:

1. the name of the chairperson of the group
2. the names of the other members of the group
3. a description of the group's responsibility
4. the time frame for the group's work, including a final deadline
5. the date and time of the first meeting of the group
6. the copy of Workform 7, Policy Element Review Summary, that pertains to the policy they will be developing
7. a copy of the evaluation criteria for policy statements and regulations
8. a copy of the applicable policy development template from appendix A, if there is such a template

Step 2.2: Identify and Evaluate Current Practice in Your Library and Best Practice in Other Libraries

The members of the group responsible for developing policy statements and regulations will begin by reviewing the evaluation criteria for policy statements and regulations and the copy of Workform 7 for the policy under review. Remember that a member of the Policy Audit Advisory Committee has already identified the ways in which the policy statement and regulations do not meet the evaluation criteria for those elements and indicated the extent of revision required for each element. If all that is needed is minor revision in either element, the group should discuss the needed revisions briefly and decide on their recommended revision. However, if moderate or significant revisions are needed, or if one or both elements are missing entirely, then the members of the group may need to gather additional information before they can act.

There are two types of information that will prove useful. The first is information about current practice in your library. In chapter 1 *practice* was defined as "the way things are usually done in your library." There is often a gap between policy and practice, particularly if the policy is old or incomplete. Obviously, if you have no policy on a given subject, practice is all there is to guide staff. The only way to be sure that you have correctly identified current practice is to work with the staff who perform the activities being addressed by the policy. You could talk to them about what they do, you could spend some time working with them to learn firsthand about current practice, or you could ask the people who manage the staff who perform the activities to provide you with a written description of current practice. It is not a good idea to just assume that you know how things are handled on the front lines, particularly if it has been a while since you actually performed the activities being considered.

Other libraries can also provide you with information to consider as you develop policy statements and regulations. There are no real best practices in policies and regulations; each library operates in such a unique environment that it is impossible to say that a given policy is the industry standard. However, learning how other libraries have addressed the issues you are considering may suggest options that you had not considered. The information you gather on current practice in your own library and on policies from other libraries will provide a starting point for your deliberations in Step 2.3.

Step 2.3: Write

The step of writing any of the policy elements begins by understanding that committees do not write, individuals write. Most of us have had to sit through at least one meeting in which a group of people were trying to create a statement or document and everyone was so involved in wordsmithing each sentence that no progress was made. This is not the way to write effectively or efficiently. The process of writing, then, begins by deciding who is going to be responsible for actually writing the draft policy statements and regulations. The writer should be someone with the ability to write clear, simple, and easily understood prose. The writer will be producing policies, not novels or scholarly treatises, and the writing style should reflect that difference. The writer should also understand that his or her responsibility is to incorporate the group's ideas into a document and not try to use the control of the pen as a way to control the content of the final document.

When the writer has been appointed, you are ready to begin the actual process of determining the content of the new policy statement and regulations. Start by identifying the audience for the policy statement and regulations. Most policy statements and regulations are written for both internal and external uses. In other words, the policy statements and regulations must be understandable and appear to be reasonable to staff, your governing authority, elected officials, and the public. This has some important implications. The language used in the policy statement and regulations will have to be free from library jargon, which is surprisingly difficult to do. The regulations will have to be sufficiently clear and comprehensive to be understandable to people who know little or nothing about the inner workings of libraries. Everyone involved in the development of policy statements and regulations will need to keep the multiple audiences in mind during discussions about content and while reviewing draft documents.

Before the writer can write, he or she has to have something to say. In chapter 1 a *policy statement* was defined as "a brief, written statement that describes *why* the library does something." A *regulation,* on the other hand, was defined as "a specific, written rule that further defines the policy, describing *what* must be done to support the policy." The actual content of both the policy statement and the regulations will be developed through a consensus-building process. There is a great deal of information available to you about the policy under review. The evaluation criteria for policy statements and regulations define the qualities that need to be included in the final products. Workform 7, Policy Element Review Summary, includes very specific descriptions of how the current policy statement and regulations fail to meet the evaluation criteria. The information gathered during Step 2.2 details current practice in your library and in other libraries. What you must now do is find a way to use all of that information to create a new policy statement and regulations.

The most effective way to work toward consensus is to structure the discussion of the content of the policy statement and the regulations around a series of questions. That is the approach that was taken in the 36 templates that are included in appendix A. If appendix A includes a template for policy that you are discussing, you can use those questions as the framework for your deliberations. If not, then you will need to begin your work by identifying the questions to be considered. You can use the examples in appendix A to give you an idea of the types of questions to ask. As you work through the questions you develop, you may find that one question leads to another, which is a good thing. That means that you and your colleagues are truly thinking about the issues raised by the questions.

When you have considered all of the information about each element and answered all of the questions that you have, you are ready to see if the group can agree on the content that the writer should include in the element. In many instances, the content decisions will become self-evident at some point during your discussions. It is important that the writer keep track of the decisions made by the group as they are made. At the end of each meeting, the writer should read the notes he or she has taken and ask the group to verify that they are correct.

When the group has reached agreement on the content to include in the policy statement, the writer should create a draft policy statement for the group to review, discuss, and revise. The same process should be followed with the regulations. When writing the regulations you should be very careful not mix in directions on *how* to do something with the statements of *what* to do. How-to instructions are included in the procedures and not the regulations. In the case study below, staff from Tree County Public Library consider the policy statement for their new policy on Priorities for Assistance with Electronic Services.

CASE STUDY

TREE COUNTY PUBLIC LIBRARY POLICIES

Part 3
Writing a Policy Statement

In part 2 of the Tree County Public Library case study, the members of the Policy Audit Advisory Committee recommended that a new policy on Priorities for Assistance with Electronic Services be developed. A committee was appointed to create the policy statement and regulations for the new policy. During previous meetings of the committee, members had reviewed the committee charge and the evaluation criteria for policy statements and regulations. They had gathered data about current practice in the library and about the practices in other libraries around the country. They were now ready to write the policy statement.

The chairperson had checked appendix A, hoping to find a template with questions for a policy on Priorities for Assistance with Electronic Services. He was disappointed to discover that there wasn't such a template. However, he noticed that there was a template for the policy Priorities for Reference Service. Upon review, he decided that many of the questions in that template could be adapted for a discussion on providing electronic services. He made copies of the template for all of the members of the committee and they began the meeting by reviewing the questions for the policy statement in the reference service template:

1. What is the purpose of identifying priorities for reference service?
2. How does the establishment of priorities for reference service support the library's goals and objectives?

The members of the group started their discussion by changing the term *reference service* to *electronic services* in the two policy statement questions. This immediately resulted in a general discussion of what should be included in electronic services. There were a number of issues to address, the most contentious being whether helping someone with a basic software issue, such as a word processing problem, should be included as an electronic service. The committee had discovered that current practice varied throughout the library system and that there was no consensus on an approach in other libraries. Some staff would help people to use the online catalog but would not help them use the résumé program on the computer in the job center. Others would help with the résumé program but not with e-mail. During the discussion, it became clear various members of the committee held strong, and conflicting, opinions on the subject.

The chairperson suggested that a discussion of the second question might help resolve the disagreement among the members of the committee. He distributed the community needs assessment completed as a part of the library's recent strategic planning process and a copy of the Information Literacy service response, which had been selected as a high priority for the library by the planning committee and the library board. The planning information helped the members of the committee put the issues surrounding the definition of *electronic services* into a context and provided a framework for reaching agreement. The members of the committee finally agreed that *electronic services* included any service being provided electronically on library computers using library-supplied software or the Internet. The final draft of the policy statement they wrote said, "To ensure that residents of Tree County have the skills they need to find, evaluate, and use electronic information effectively, the staff of the Tree County Public Library will provide library users with assistance in using library computer terminals, library-provided software, the library's online catalog, electronic information databases, and the Internet."

The committee agreed to address the specific issues of assistance with Internet e-mail, listservs, and chat rooms in the regulations.

Step 2.4: Review and Revise

The review process that you use for policy statements and regulations will depend on the level of effort assigned to the policy. Policies requiring minimal effort (levels 0, 1, 2, or 3) will go through a much simpler review process than those needing significant or extensive effort (levels 4 and 5).

Library staff should have an opportunity to review and comment on all draft policy statements and regulations before those elements are sent to the board for action. Draft policy statements and regulations that required minimal effort (policies that reflect few changes, describe current practice, or address areas of little interest to the general staff) may be posted on an in-house Intranet or sent to the various units to be shared with staff. Staff can be encouraged to make comments or suggestions via e-mail or to their supervisors. There is no need for meetings or formal action on the part of library managers.

However, draft policy statements and regulations that require significant or extensive effort (policies that are intended to change current practice or that are likely to be controversial) should be made available for more comprehensive review and discussion. Those draft policy statements and regulations should be shared first with supervisors to get their opinions and answer their questions. It may be appropriate to make changes in the drafts before they are sent to the full staff for review. Depending on the extent of the changes, there may be a need for a second meeting with supervisors to review the new drafts and make sure that everyone understands the changes.

When the supervisors are in a position to answer staff questions, the draft policy statements and regulations should be distributed to all staff via the Intranet or in paper form. Supervisors should hold meetings with their staff members to discuss the policy statements and regulations and get comments and suggestions from the staff. Information from those meetings should be reported back to the committee that developed the policy statement and regulations, and changes or clarifications should be made if needed.

Some policy statements and regulations will have a significant effect on the public. If there is a chance that a policy statement and regulations may be controversial, the library's governing authority may want to hold public hearings on the topic. Occasionally such hearings are held very early in the process to provide the people developing the policy statement and regulations with an understanding of community concerns and preferences. More often public hearings are held after a draft policy statement and regulations have been developed but before official action is taken. In either case, library staff will follow the appropriate city or county rules for scheduling and publicizing such hearings.

There are some policy statements and regulations that may have legal implications that the library staff or members of the library's governing authority are not qualified to address. If there is any suggestion that a policy statement or regulation should be reviewed by legal counsel, that review should take place. This is an area in which it is better to be safe than sorry, and the relatively minor cost in time and money to get a legal opinion is an excellent investment.

Step 2.5: Obtain Approval

Final approval for policy statements and regulations will come from the library's governing authority. If you followed the advice earlier in this book, the members of the governing authority will have been kept informed about the policy review process and will be expecting to receive policy statements and regulations to review. If possible, you will want to present interrelated policy statements and regulations at the same time. That provides members with a more comprehensive picture of the issues and makes it less likely that they will approve conflicting policies.

Members of the governing authority should receive copies of all draft policy statements and regulations at least one week before the meeting during which the drafts will be discussed. Staff should come to the meeting prepared to answer questions. They may want to present some background information on the process used to develop and review the draft policy statement and regulations and on the library's current practice in the area covered by the policy, particularly if current practice is being substantially changed.

If the members of the governing authority approve the policy statement and regulations, you are ready to begin writing procedures. If the members recommend changes, then new drafts of the elements will have to be created. Depending on the extent of the changes the members of the governing authority want made, you may have to go back through the staff review process again before presenting the revised policy statement and regulations to the board. That will be time-consuming and may cause some staff frustration, but it is better to keep staff informed throughout the process than to end up with policy statements and regulations that look nothing like those reviewed by staff. Fortunately, members of the governing authority reject staff recommendations very rarely.

TASK 3: WRITE PROCEDURES

Step 3.1: Identify who needs to be involved.

Step 3.2: Identify and evaluate current practice in your library and best practice in other libraries.

Step 3.3: Write.

Step 3.4: Review and revise.

Step 3.5: Obtain approval.

Step 3.1: Identify Who Needs to Be Involved

When the policy statement and regulations have been approved, members of the library management team will be responsible for selecting the staff who will develop procedures. There were a variety of factors to consider when selecting the people to develop policy statements and regulations. That is not the case with procedures, which are almost always developed by the people who do the activities being described in the procedures. Circulation attendants are involved in the development of circulation procedures, accounting clerks participate in discussions about petty cash, and children's staff identify the procedures required to set up a school visit.

There are some choices to be made in terms of the number of people to ask to participate in the development of procedures. In libraries in which the circulation attendants meet regularly, it is common to ask that group to spend some time during each of their meetings developing procedures. The same request can be made of similar groups that meet regularly—youth services, reference, and so forth. Libraries that do not have such regular meetings of peers may want to consider establishing them. Such groups encourage peers to share ideas and concerns and can improve both service and morale in your library. If you decide not to form a permanent group of peers, you will want to be sure to select a representative group of staff to develop procedures. The group should include new staff and experienced staff and should have representatives from all library sites if the library has branches.

There is one exception to the general rule that people who do the activities are responsible for developing draft procedures. The person who actually writes the procedures will be selected based on the ability to write and not on content knowledge. In other words, the content of the procedures comes from the people who know the job best, but the writing is done by someone who can translate that content expertise into written procedures that are clear and easy to follow.

When the writer and the participants in the group have been selected and the chairperson has been identified, write the name of the chairperson in column E on Workform 8, Policy Revision and Development Summary, on the line labeled "Procedures." The deadline for completion of the procedures should be entered on the appropriate line in column F on Workform 8. Be sure that the deadline on Workform 8 is compatible with the master schedule you developed earlier.

You now have all of the information you need to notify the people you intend to involve in the development of the procedures for a given policy. When people are notified of their appointments they should receive the following information:

- The name of the chairperson of the group
- The names of the other members of the group
- A description of the group's responsibility
- The time frame for the group's work, including a final deadline
- The date and time of the first meeting of the group (If the group already meets regularly, indicate the date of the first meeting in which they begin to discuss procedures.)

- A copy of the approved policy statement and regulations for which they are developing procedures
- The copy of Workform 7, Policy Element Review Summary, that pertains to the policy they will be working on
- A copy of the evaluation criteria for procedures

Step 3.2: Identify and Evaluate Current Practice in Your Library and Best Practice in Other Libraries

In chapter 1, a *procedure* was defined as "a written, step-by-step description of *how* the staff will carry out a policy and regulations." The place to start any discussion of new procedures is by looking at how activities are completed now. This is relatively easy if the library has a single building or if the activities are completed by a single team. It is much more complicated if the same activity is completed by different groups of people in different facilities or departments. Even though the group that is charged with developing procedures consists of people who perform the activities, there is no guarantee that they perform the activities or the tasks within those activities in the same ways. The larger the library system, the more likely it is that the activities and tasks are completed in a variety of ways. In order to get a clear understanding of current practice, the group is probably going to have to complete a formal task analysis.

The book *Staffing for Results: A Guide to Working Smarter*[2] includes a complete description of the methodology to use to analyze a task. Basically, this involves identifying the task you want to study and the level of detail you want to include. Tasks can be defined as either metaprocesses or microprocesses. *A metaprocess, the big picture of an organization's functions, is made up of hundreds of microprocesses, the employee-level view of the work.*[3] Procedures describe microprocesses. Once you have identified the microprocess to study you will have defined the starting and ending points of the process. For example, does the task of shelving books in your library begin when the book is checked in, when it is placed on a book truck, when the book truck is organized, or when the book truck is rolled to the shelves to actually begin reshelving? After you have decided when the task starts and when it ends, you have to agree on a common vocabulary to describe the steps in each task. When you are sure that everyone is using the same term to describe a specific action, you are ready to begin collecting data about how the task is completed in different departments or units of the library.

It would very helpful for all concerned if the members of the groups charged with developing procedures were trained to analyze tasks using the process described in *Staffing for Results* before they begin to try to identify current practice. The process is not all that complex and the training could be provided in a half-day session for all of the staff who are likely to be involved in the development of any new or revised procedures for the library. The benefits of such training would be considerable. All staff would have a common understanding of how to determine current practice and a common vocabulary to use when discussing the process. Library managers could be sure that data gathered on current practice would be comparable even if it was gathered by different groups working on different procedures.

Current practice provides one part of the picture for people developing procedures. The remainder of the picture is filled in by determining the best practice in the area under consideration. Many library employees have worked in their current library for many years—sometimes for their whole careers. They rarely think about the actual process of what they do. They were trained to do a job in a certain way when they started work and they have done the job that way ever since. Learning about best practice in their area of work can be an eye-opening experience. Just discovering that there is more than one way to complete the task may change the way they look at their jobs.

There are a variety of ways to learn about the best practice in a given area. One of the most interesting ways is to visit other libraries and talk to the staff about how they do things. While visits to libraries that are similar to your library in size are normally most helpful, you can learn things from visiting any library. Another way to learn about best practice is to attend programs at state or national conferences. Many conference programs fall into the "how we do good things in our library" category and they can be very informative. Library journals often include articles with the same types of information. Staff from the system or regional library or from the state library agency may be able to provide information about the best practice that they have observed as they visit libraries. State and national listservs on library services provide an opportunity for staff to talk to their peers about a wide variety of issues.

Step 3.3: Write

In some ways procedures are easier to write than policy statements or regulations. The audience for the procedures is the staff who do the work, which means that the writer does not have to be as careful about library jargon as the person writing policy statements and regulations has to be. The writer can also assume that the staff have some general understanding of libraries, although the procedures will have to be clear and easily understood because they will be used by both new and experienced staff.

There are templates for the questions to ask when developing policy statements and regulations for 36 policy subjects in appendix A. You may have noted that there are no comparable templates for procedures. Practices in libraries vary far too widely to make it possible to develop an individual set of questions to guide the development of procedures for each policy. The process for analyzing a task, described in Step 3.2, is the most effective way to determine the procedures for each policy under review.

The easiest way to present procedures is in an outline format. That allows you to break the activity being described into a series of tasks and then to provide the level of detail needed under each task by identifying the steps required to accomplish the task. You will find that procedures often end up with a series of conditional possibilities that have to be addressed, as illustrated in the outline below.

I. What action starts the step?
   A. What are the possible responses to the action?
      1. Response 1.
         a. What to do—detail.
         b. What to do—detail.
         c. What to do—detail.
      2. Response 2.
         a. What to do—detail.
         b. What to do—detail.
         c. What to do—detail.

II. What is the next action in the step?
   A. What are the possible responses to the action?
      1. Response 1.
         a. What to do—detail.

If you apply the questions in the outline to the process of checking out materials, you can see how the conditional possibilities affect the development of the procedures.

I. Scan the user's borrower's card.
   A. User has fines below the fine threshold (see Policy XXX on Fines and Fees for more information).
      1. Tell user about the fines and ask if the user wants to pay them.
         a. If yes, take the money and enter the transaction in the user's record (see Policy XXX). Then proceed with checkout.
         b. If no, proceed with checkout.
   B. User has fines above the fine threshold.
      1. Tell the user about the fines and that he or she cannot check out materials until fines are paid to below the fine threshold of $XX. Ask what the user intends to do.
         a. It the user wants to pay enough to reduce the fine to below the fine threshold, take the money and enter

the transaction in the user's record. Then proceed with checkout.

b. If the user wants to pay the entire fine, take the money, enter the transaction in the user's record, and proceed with checkout.

c. If the user decides not to pay the fine, place the items the user was intending to check out with the other items to be reshelved.

d. If the user has questions or becomes angry, refer the user to your supervisor.

II. Scan items to be checked out to user.

A. First item is checked out to user.

1. Desensitize theft strip.

2. Stamp date due on slip inside back cover of book or on back of media case. [The example stops here, but the procedures go on to describe the remainder of the steps involved in checkout.]

As the committee responsible for developing the procedures considers each task and step of the procedure, it would be very helpful to continue to ask why that task or step is needed. This is where information on best practice in other libraries can prove to be valuable. For instance, in the example above, when a book is checked out, the circulation clerk has to open the back cover of the book and stamp the date due on a slip that was glued to the book by someone in processing. There are a variety of less time-consuming options being used by libraries, including using a grocery store labeler to stick the date due on the back cover of each book, using preprinted slips to insert into one of the books, and printing a receipt listing all of the items checked out and the due dates for each. The real value of developing or revising procedures comes from a careful review and questioning of every facet of every task and step involved in the activities under review.

As you can see, the development of procedures is an exercise in detail—some would even say in minutia. However, if the procedures are going to be of any value, they have to provide enough detail about the activity to ensure that the staff in every unit of the library know what is expected. Earlier there was a discussion of the role that policies play in ensuring that library users receive equitable library services. It is at the procedures level that the real issues of equity are defined. In the example above allowing users with fines over the threshold to check out materials has clear equity implications. Obviously if all staff members in every library unit do not follow the same procedures, then some users will be receiving preferential treatment and others will be receiving discriminatory treatment. There is a potential for serious legal problems if agencies funded with public monies discriminate in the application of policies and procedures.

Step 3.4: Review and Revise

It is probable that procedures will go through several drafts before they are ready to be approved by the library director. When the first draft has been completed, it should be distributed to everyone who is responsible for the activities described in the procedure. Each person should carefully review the procedures to be sure that every eventuality is covered and that the responses to each possibility are clear. If there are significant changes in current practice, then it would be helpful to include a description of those changes and the reasons for them in the cover memo that is sent with the draft procedures.

When the frontline staff have reviewed the procedures and agreed that they are accurate and complete, it is time to distribute the draft to the management team. Each library director will have his or her own methods for ensuring that managers have a chance to see and discuss policies. The chairperson of the committee developing procedures should follow the methodology used in his or her library.

Step 3.5: Obtain Approval

When the managers have completed their review and the committee members have made any needed changes, the procedures are probably ready to be submitted to the library director for approval. The only exception to this would be if the managers recommended extensive changes. In that case, it would be wise to send the revised procedures to the frontline staff with an explanation of the changes for review and comment before asking for final approval. It is always a good idea to avoid surprising anyone with procedures, and staff have a right to expect to see procedures before they are approved.

TASK 4: WRITE GUIDELINES (IF NEEDED)

Step 4.1: Identify who needs to be involved.

Step 4.2: Identify and evaluate current practice in your library and best practice in other libraries.

Step 4.3: Write.

Step 4.4: Review and revise.

Step 4.5: Obtain approval.

Step 4.1: Identify Who Needs to Be Involved

Before any decision is made about who to involve in the development of guidelines, the members of the management team may want to consider again whether or not guidelines are needed for the policy under review. If they decide that guidelines are needed, the members of the group should decide whether to develop them now or wait until after the rest of the policy manual is complete.

At the time that the members of the library management team decide it is appropriate to develop guidelines they will begin by identifying who to involve in that process. Guidelines have more in common with procedures than they do with policy statements or regulations and like procedures they are normally developed by a group of the people who perform the activities being described in the guidelines. In the case of procedures, the group was defined as people who have the same positions. Guidelines, on the other hand, are often written by all of the staff from a specific department to describe the services provided by that department. Reference guidelines are developed by reference staff of all levels. Guidelines for serving genealogists are developed by staff in the local history section.

The same exception to the general rule that the people who do the activities are responsible for developing draft procedures applies to guidelines. The person who actually writes the guidelines should be selected on the basis of his or her ability to write and not on content knowledge. The content of the guidelines comes from the people who know the job best, but the writing is done by someone who can translate that content expertise into clearly written and understood guidelines.

If your library has multiple units, you will have to decide if the guidelines that need to be developed will be systemwide or if they will pertain only to the services provided at one site. If the guidelines are systemwide, appropriate people from each site that will be affected by the guidelines should be included in the development process.

When you notify people of their appointments to the group that will be responsible for developing guidelines for a policy, send them the same types of information you sent the people who were selected to develop policies. See Step 3.1 for details.

Step 4.2: Identify and Evaluate Current Practice in Your Library and Best Practice in Other Libraries

Procedures and guidelines both present information on how to do something. Procedures are task and step descriptions of activities. Guidelines present more general information intended to provide an understanding of the purpose of the activities and a framework to ensure that the quality of the service provided is high. Although the two policy elements have very different purposes, the processes used to gather data about current practice and best practice are the same as those described previously in Step 3.2.

Step 4.3: Write

Guidelines are written for internal use. They are intended to provide staff with a framework and context for the policy statement, regulations, and procedures in a policy to ensure that staff provide consistently high quality services. Actually, it is the emphasis on quality that differentiates guidelines from procedures. Procedures are focused on uniformity of action and rarely address the more abstract issues that come up in any discussion of quality. This difference can be seen in the formats of the two elements. Procedures are tightly structured and written in an outline format. Guidelines are normally narrative documents with no set structure.

Just as there were no questions to guide the development of procedures included in appendix A, there are no questions pertaining to guidelines. The reason is the same: library practices vary far too widely to make questions specific to each policy useful. However, it is possible to identify some general questions that may be helpful to the people responsible for developing guidelines.

- What are the individual philosophical issues that affect the way the service is provided?
- What are the resource restrictions that affect the way the service is provided?
- What other factors affect the quality of the services provided?
- What specific activities need to be completed to ensure that the quality of the services provided is always high?

Although each library's guidelines reflect unique local conditions, it would be helpful for the committee to review a sampling of guidelines from other libraries as well as copies of previous guidelines from their own library. That would give the members of the committee a feel for the types of information that are typically included in guidelines and for the approaches that might be used. Staff from a system library or the state library agency can probably provide you with copies of guidelines from other libraries.

Step 4.4: Review and Revise

The review process for guidelines parallels the process for procedures described in Step 3.4, with one big difference. The outline format of the procedures encouraged people to focus on the actual steps being described. The narrative format normally used for guidelines can lead to discussions of style and the use of specific words—the very wordsmithing you were trying to avoid by making a single person responsible for writing each element of a policy. There is probably no way to avoid this during the guideline review process, and as long as the chairperson of the guidelines committee keeps substantive concerns separate from editorial concerns there should be no real problem. The committee will want to spend the time needed to resolve the substantive issues. The writer should be allowed to resolve the editorial comments.

Step 4.5: Obtain Approval

The review process for guidelines is the same as the process described in Step 3.5 for procedures.

Challenges

The challenges that you and your staff will face when writing policies are somewhat different from the challenges that occurred earlier in this process. For the first time you will actually be creating something new rather than reviewing and discussing existing documents. You will be moving from being reactive to being proactive and facing all of the potential pitfalls that can hamper any new endeavor.

The primary challenges include helping staff understand that it really is as hard or harder to fix an old policy as it is to write a new policy, keeping the distinctions among the four elements of a policy clear at every step of the process, and identifying staff members who can write effectively.

Writing versus Revising

Many staff members are going to find it hard to understand why you are not making a greater distinction between revising existing policies and writing new policies. Unless a person really understands the process required to do each, they seem like very different activities. It is going to take months and perhaps years to complete the revision of the library's policy manual. Inevitably, some staff are going to get sick of the whole thing and start second-guessing the process—and the distinction between creating a new policy and fixing an old one can provide them with a great starting point for their questions and complaints.

If most of the staff don't know that there is a master schedule or don't understand how it was developed, the complaints of a few malcontents may fall on fertile ground. If, on the other hand, all staff have been kept informed about the overall process as well as the progress being made on individual policies, most staff members will continue to support the process. The easiest way to be sure that all staff have the information they need to understand the big picture is to distribute the master schedule, along with a brief explanation of why you are scheduling new and revised policies together, before you make the first assignments to the committees that will be developing each element of the policies. Then distribute a revised master schedule every three or four months to show the progress that has made, any revisions to the schedule that have been needed, and the work left to be done. It is always easier to deal with anticipated problems than it is to manage actual problems.

Keeping Policy Elements Clear

There is no question that the most challenging aspect of this part of the process will be helping all staff to keep the distinctions among the four policy elements clear. This will be particularly true in libraries in which current policies are a jumble of all four elements in a narrative format. Everyone who is involved in developing any of the elements of the policy should be trained to understand what is included in each element of a policy and to learn how to recognize the various elements. Workform 5, Defining Policy Elements, can be used as a part of that training.

It is likely that no matter how much training you provide, some staff will continue to be a little fuzzy on the differences between regulations and procedures. For some reason, those are the two elements that staff seem to find hardest to keep separate in their minds. The issue is not critical as long as the person writing each element and the chairperson of the committee who is directing the work understand clearly what should—and should not—be included in the element.

Identifying Writers

Not every member of your staff has the skills to write regulations, procedures, or guidelines. Even the fairly straightforward policy statement can be difficult for some people to draft. It is going to be important to identify at least two or three people who have the writing skills necessary to create policy elements. As noted earlier, those people do not need subject expertise. That comes from the various people involved on the committees developing the elements.

In many libraries, senior managers are asked to do the actual writing of the policy elements. They normally have more experience writing than other staff members and a clearer understanding of the distinctions among the elements of a policy. The library director will have to make the final decision about who will be asked to do the writing. The director will have read dozens and dozens of memos and reports written by members of the senior management team and can use that knowledge to select the writers. The director will be looking for people who write clear prose. That excludes people who love complex sentences with lots of subordinate clauses, people who never met a noun they didn't want to modify, and people who always use a thousand words to say something that could be said in a hundred words—or in ten. Instead, the director is looking for people who are concise, who can organize information logically, and who use language precisely. As every director knows, most libraries do not have a surplus of managers with such skills. The limited number of choices should make the selection of the writers fairly easy. If two or three people are going to be responsible for all of the writing needed to create the library's new policy manual, the director should make some modifications in their other job duties. Otherwise, the policy elements may never get written, which would be too bad, given all of the work that has gone into the process.

Key Points to Remember

1. There is a very real difference between extent of revision required and level of effort.
2. You can base the priority of policies on urgency, importance, or momentum. The choice depends on conditions in your library.
3. Most of your staff are already fully occupied with their daily jobs. Be careful to spread the work of writing policy statements, regulations, procedures, and guidelines equitably among staff members.
4. It is going to take at least six months to complete the policies you need to develop and may well take more than a year.
5. Groups don't write—individuals do.
6. You need a controlled vocabulary to write effective policies. Everyone involved should understand the differences between policy statements and regulations, between regulations and procedures, and between procedures and guidelines.
7. The time spent during the review of draft policy elements is a sound investment. All interested parties should be given an opportunity to comment on the drafts before they are submitted for approval.
8. Get professional legal advice anytime there is a legal question that cannot be answered by staff or members of the governing authority.
9. No part of the final policy should be a surprise to staff. They should have had a chance to review and comment on every element before the element was approved.

NOTES

1. Sandra Nelson, *The New Planning for Results: A Streamlined Approach* (Chicago: American Library Association, 2001), 235–245.
2. Diane Mayo and Jeanne Goodrich, *Staffing for Results: A Guide to Working Smarter* (Chicago: American Library Association, 2002), 62–66.
3. Ibid., 64.

Chapter 5

Implementation

MILESTONES

By the time you finish this chapter you will know how to

- organize your policy manual effectively
- disseminate policies to library staff and members of the public
- design and deliver the training that staff need to implement policies
- monitor the implementation of new and revised policies
- establish a process to continually update and maintain your library policies
- deal with the challenges that you will face while implementing your policies

The whole point of writing policy statements, regulations, procedures, and guidelines is to ensure that all library staff members understand the library's priorities, the rules that govern the provision of services, and the actual processes that are to be used when delivering those services. Such things do not happen automatically just because the board approves new policy statements and regulations and the director approves new procedures or guidelines. They happen only when library managers put as much thought into implementing the library's policies as they did into developing those policies.

Although a number of issues affect the implementation of the library's policies, by far the most critical issue is communication. Every library has a different process for managing internal communications, and most of those processes are driven by the management philosophy of the library director. At one end of the spectrum are directors who want to control every piece of information that is disseminated to the staff as though each nugget of information was in fact made of gold. At the opposite end of the spectrum are library directors who inundate staff with e-mails and written memorandums, providing so much data that staff can't separate the important from the trivial and the relevant from the extraneous. Needless to say, a happy medium between these two extremes is desirable.

However, just saying that it is important to provide enough information but not too much does not give a great deal of help to the managers responsible for communicating policies to their staff members. Managers need to be familiar with both the theory and the practice of formal communication in organizations and with the specific issues pertaining to communicating in libraries. There is an overview of these issues in the "Library Communication" Tool Kit in *The New Planning for Results*.[1] The most important thing to remember when developing a communication strategy for your organization is that communication does not occur when you *send* the message. It occurs only when the message has been *received* and *understood* and when the person or people who receive the message have been *affected* by it. Figure 22 presents a model of effective communication.

The fact that people have been affected by a message does not mean that they agree with the message or are happy about the contents of the message. It simply means that they react to the message and, as every manager knows, there are messages that elicit positive reactions and messages that elicit negative reactions. The key is to be sure that the messages you send elicit the reaction you expected. There is nothing more frustrating than sending a message that you expected to be received with enthusiasm only to find that through some misunderstanding, the effect was quite different.

While internal communications may be challenging, at least library managers control the communication process. That is not the case when library managers try to communicate library policies to most external

FIGURE 22
Model of Effective Communication

EFFECTIVE COMMUNICATION OCCURS WHEN

a message

↓

is **understood by** its sender

↓

and **transmitted** through a medium

↓

to one or more **receivers**

↓

who **understand** it

↓

and **are affected** by it

Source: Sandra Nelson, *The New Planning for Results: A Streamlined Approach* (Chicago: American Library Association, 2001), 247.

audiences. The effective communication model from figure 22 is just as valid for communication with external audiences as it is with internal audiences—people have to receive information and be affected by it before communication can be said to have occurred. However, the mechanisms open to library staff members to deliver messages to external audiences are less direct than the mechanisms used to deliver internal communications.

It is even difficult to communicate effectively with the members of library support groups. While these people are included as a part of our external audiences, they clearly belong in a special category. Unlike the general public, members of our support groups are people who have expressed an interest in the library and who can be reached directly through library mailing lists and member newsletters. As a result, library managers often assume that it is relatively easy to communicate with them, even though repeated experience may have shown otherwise.

The remainder of this chapter will provide detailed information to help you communicate with both internal and external audiences. There also will be suggestions for ways to monitor the implementation of your policies and to make any changes that are required. The chapter will conclude by providing a framework for the ongoing review and development of your policy manual.

Definitions

The chapter includes a great deal of information about communication. Throughout the discussion, distinctions are made between the methodologies used to communicate with internal audiences, external audiences, and library support groups. To ensure that everyone has the same understanding of those three groups, they are defined below:

External Audience Residents of the library service area, elected officials, members of the media, and others who are not library employees or members of support groups.

Internal Audience Library staff members and volunteers.

Library Support Groups Members of library boards, friends groups, and foundations.

Policy Implementation

There are four tasks you will complete to implement your policies. The first two tasks involve making sure that the staff and the public are aware of the library's policies. The third task is to monitor the implementation of new and revised policies, and the fourth task addresses the need to update and maintain the library's policy manual. The four tasks are

Task 1: *Communicate with internal audiences.*

Task 2: *Communicate with library support groups and external audiences.*

Task 3: *Monitor* implementation.

Task 4: *Update and maintain* the policy manual.

These four tasks are each divided into a series of steps, which are listed at the beginning of the discussion of each task below. Figure 23 shows all of the tasks and steps associated with implementing your policies.

TASK 1: COMMUNICATE WITH INTERNAL AUDIENCES

Step 1.1: Organize policy manual.

Step 1.2: Publish and distribute policies internally.

Step 1.3: Train staff.

Step 1.4: Obtain needed supplies, forms, and so forth.

It should go without saying that if staff are going to be expected to observe library policies, it is essential that they understand the policies and have the tools they need to implement them. Sadly, it isn't necessarily so. There are far too many examples of libraries in which staff first saw new policies the day before they were expected to implement them. In at least one library, staff were instructed to implement new policies for

FIGURE 23
Tasks and Steps in Policy Implementation

Task 1: Communicate with internal audiences
- Step 1.1: Organize policy manual
- Step 1.2: Publish and distribute policies internally
- Step 1.3: Train staff
- Step 1.4: Obtain needed supplies, forms, and so forth

Task 2: Communicate with library support groups and external audiences
- Step 2.1: Inform library support groups
- Step 2.2: Inform other external audiences

Task 3: Monitor implementation
- Step 3.1: Observe implementation
- Step 3.2: Modify policies as needed

Task 4: Update and maintain the policy manual
- Step 4.1: Initiate development of next category or type of policy
- Step 4.2: Schedule regular review cycle for existing policies
- Step 4.3: Schedule annual review of master category list

managing cash six months before the cash registers—required in the policy—were received in the branches. In another library, circulation staff were expected to follow revised regulations and procedures when using a new automated circulation system but received no training in the revisions or the new system. They were told the new system was "very similar to our old system" and that they could "figure out the changes in procedures as they needed them." Well, they ultimately figured everything out, but not until they were all frustrated and angry because they felt that they had been made to "look stupid" in front of the library users. Things do not have to be this way if library managers spend the time needed to organize the library policy manual, disseminate it to staff in a timely manner and easily accessible format, provide training when needed, and ensure that staff have all of the tools they need to implement the new or revised policies.

Step 1.1: Organize Policy Manual

Before you can do anything with a policy, you have to make it available in some format. If you plan to make more than one policy available, you will need to decide how to organize the policies before you can publish them. As noted earlier, policy manuals are easiest to use and revise if each policy is published as a separate document. The most logical structure for the library policy manual is the master category list created by the Policy Audit Advisory Committee and submitted to the library director as a part of the committee's final report. The master category list includes the names of the policies in each policy category and the unique number assigned to each policy. All that remains to be added is the date each policy was issued or revised.

Some libraries choose to list all of the subjects for which policies will be developed in each category in the table of contents even if the policies are not yet available. Other libraries choose to include only those policies that actually exist in a given category, especially if managers believe it is going to take a long time to write and obtain approval for some of the policies included in the master category list. Either approach is acceptable. Consider the advantages and disadvantages of the two approaches and select the one that makes the most sense for your library.

The sample table of contents in figure 24 includes all of the policies that will be included in the categories of circulation services and information services, whether they were issued in the past, are newly issued or revised, or are not yet available. As policies are completed or revised, they are issued along with an updated table of contents. This ensures that staff have access to new policies as soon as possible. By continuously updating the table of contents, managers will ensure that staff have a way to determine if they have all of the policies that have been issued and if their copies of the policies reflect the latest revisions. In figure 24, note that the revision date of the table of contents is included at the bottom of the page.

Step 1.2: Publish and Distribute Policies Internally

At some point in time virtually every library has had a written policy manual. Older manuals were often narrative in form and focused heavily on policy statements and guidelines. Staff in most libraries could probably locate a copy of one or more of their old policy manuals in their files or on a bookshelf somewhere, and it might be worth the time to find a copy and look at it for a few minutes, if only to remind yourself of how hard the old manuals were to use and maintain.

You have already made decisions that guarantee your new policy manual will be easier to use and update than those older versions were. The choice to publish each policy as a separate document, the decision to use the master category list to organize the manual, and the decision to publish policies as they are completed instead of waiting until the entire manual has been finished all result in a more user-friendly and manageable policy manual.

The decisions you make about the format or formats in which you publish the policy manual will also affect the accessibility of the policies you have developed. The question of format for the policy manual is relatively recent. For over a hundred years the only option was to print the policy manual, bind it in some fashion, and distribute copies to the various library units. The widespread availability of library Intranets in the past decade opened a new and better option. Now policies do not

FIGURE 24

Sample Policy Manual Table of Contents

Circulation Services		Date Issued/Revised
CIR-1.	Library Cards for Residents	5/17/20xx
CIR-2.	Library Cards for Nonresidents	5/17/20xx
CIR-3.	Loan Periods and Loan Limits	2/9/20xx (rev.)
CIR-4.	Renewals	7/25/20xx (rev.)
CIR-5.	Reserves	7/25/20xx
CIR-6.	Claims Returned or Claims Never Had	Not Available Yet
CIR-7.	Lost or Damaged Materials	Not Available Yet
CIR-8.	Fines and Fees	7/25/20xx
CIR-9.	Borrowing Materials by Staff	2/17/20xx

Information Services		Date Issued/Revised
INF-1.	Priorities for Reference Service	6/16/20xx
INF-2.	Interlibrary Loan	Not Available Yet
INF-3.	Internet Use	11/21/20xx (rev.)
INF-4.	Use of Library-Provided Personal Computers	11/21/20xx (rev.)

TABLE OF CONTENTS REVISED ON 11/21/20xx

have to be printed on paper and placed in a binder in each library branch or department for the library to have a written policy manual; the manual can be written and maintained on the library's Intranet.

There are a number of advantages to maintaining the policy manual on the Intranet rather than relying on a printed version. The Intranet version can be available at any time to any staff member who has access to the library network. On the other hand, a printed version is often located in the manager's office and is not always available. The Intranet version can be changed quickly and easily, and everyone has access to the revised version at the same time. A printed version requires the copying and distributing of revisions with all the associated labor and supply costs, and even then, there is no guarantee that a new policy will actually be placed in the proper place in the policy manual in a timely manner.

Adding the library policies to the Intranet should not be a major undertaking. The library web master can use the table of contents as the home page and then post each of the new policies or revised policies as it is issued. Each entry in the table of contents should be linked to the appropriate policy to make it easy to navigate through the policy manual. The staff responsible for maintaining the Intranet will need to receive the new policy in ample time to get it posted to the Intranet. What constitutes ample time will of course vary from library to library based on workload. However, it is essential that the policy be available online by the date it goes into effect. It also will be important for the web master to remember to remove old policies when the revisions are posted.

To facilitate the staff's use of the policies, it would be very helpful if each of the policies was indexed and searchable by keyword. Even if the table of contents is organized by category and each entry is linked to a policy, all that does is help a staff member find the specific policy needed. It will still be time-consuming to scan through a lengthy policy looking for the one section that deals with exactly the issue that the staff member needs to locate. Most word processing applications include utilities that can index a document or documents, so indexing is no longer a time-consuming manual activity. Another advantage to indexing all of the policies is that it will facilitate the location of information on a topic that might be included in a variety of policies. For example, a search of the keyword index under *teacher* might indicate that the procedures to issue a library card to a teacher are covered in section III C 1 of the policy on Library Cards, that borrower limits for teachers are covered in section II F of the policy on Borrower Limits, and that information on scheduling a class visit is found in section II B 2 of the policy on Programs in the Library.

Managers in some libraries might not be comfortable with the idea of abandoning print versions of their policy manuals, and managers in other libraries may not have the resources at the present time to create Intranet versions of their manuals. Those managers will have to be very careful to ensure that each staff member has access to a complete and up-to-date manual, which is not easy. If the policy manual is being maintained in printed form, then copies of each policy published along with a revised table of contents need to be produced and distributed to every individual or unit that has a copy of the policy manual. To make certain that this occurs it is essential that an up-to-date distribution list be maintained by the staff member who is responsible for copying and distributing the policies. Ideally, moving toward an Intranet version of the library's policy manual should be the ultimate goal of every library.

Neither the posting of a policy to the Intranet nor the distribution of a print version of the policy to various library units is synonymous with communicating the policy. Supervisors need to be informed that a new policy is being issued. In virtually every case, the supervisors and staff should have had an opportunity to review draft versions of the elements of the policy and to recommend changes (see Steps 2.4, 3.4, and 4.4 in chapter 4). However, there is often delay between the last staff review of a policy and the actual publication of the policy. It is important that supervisors have a chance to read and discuss the final policy before it is distributed to all staff.

Many libraries have found that the best method to accomplish this is to include new policies as a regular item on the agenda of each supervisors' meeting. Once the supervisors have been informed about the publication of a new or revised policy and had an opportunity to discuss it, they are responsible for informing their staff and discussing the policy with them in a timely manner. Remember to share information about new policies also with volunteers and any contract employees, such as security guards or maintenance staff, if the policies in any way affect the work they are expected to perform.

Step 1.3: Train Staff

Staff training is one of the most critical issues in public libraries today. Library audiences and service priorities are changing, and the tools that are available to serve those audiences are evolving more rapidly than most staff can handle comfortably. Many staff members feel like new things are expected of them so often that they never have a chance to feel comfortable and in control of their jobs. It is important to acknowledge and address the frustration that many staff members feel when their jobs change.

This obviously has implications for managers who are issuing new or revised policies, particularly when those policies include significant changes in regulations, procedures, or guidelines. If the new or revised policy has only minor revisions to current practice, then training may not be needed. However, if the new policy is a departure from past practice, requires the use of new equipment, or includes new forms to be completed, then it is probable that training is necessary. Training will also be necessary if the new or revised policy affects the classification of staff who will be performing certain activities. Anytime staff members are given new duties, they must receive the training needed to accomplish those duties effectively. It is patently unfair to expect people to be able to do new activities with no prior training or instruction, and it is particularly unfair if the new activities involve serving the public. No one likes to look incompetent under any circumstances, and that is especially true of staff trying to serve library users.

Training involves identifying what the people to be trained currently know and what they need to know and then developing a program to provide the needed information. In other words, training in the context of this discussion is a formal activity. You cannot assume that asking the library's supervisors to review the final copy of a policy with staff constitutes training. It almost never does.

You will need to allow ample time to develop a training agenda, to design training materials, to schedule staff to attend the training, and to schedule time for staff to practice what they have learned before you actually implement a new or revised policy that includes significant changes. The amount of time required will vary depending on the number of staff to be trained, the complexity of the training, and how quickly the staff can be scheduled to attend.

Step 1.4: Obtain Needed Supplies, Forms, and So Forth

It should be self-evident that staff cannot implement a new policy that requires them to use equipment, supplies, or new forms if what they need has not yet been provided. Ordering new equipment takes time. It also takes time to purchase supplies and print forms. Be certain that the items that the staff needs have been purchased, produced, and distributed in adequate quantities prior to the implementation date of the new policy.

Managers and supervisors will also want to discuss whether signs or other printed materials need to be produced. If changes are being made to policies that are outlined in existing library publications, then those publications will need to be revised prior to the implementation of the new policy. Changes to library policies are hard enough to implement without the added burden of expecting staff to enforce regulations that are not supported by printed materials available for distribution to the public. Allow time for the printing and distribution of all needed materials. Remember to instruct staff to remove old signs and discard—or better yet, recycle—out-of-date printed materials.

CASE STUDY

TREE COUNTY PUBLIC LIBRARY POLICIES

Part 4
Preparing the Staff

In the earlier parts of this case study we learned that the new Tree County Public Library strategic plan included Information Literacy as a service priority and that this was a new emphasis for the library. In fact, general practice in the various library units limited staff assistance with computers and the Internet. Part 1 of the case study provided details about staff concerns regarding the new priority. In part 2 of the case study, the members of the Policy Audit Advisory Committee identified the policies that needed to be revised to reflect the new priority and the new policies that needed to be developed. In part 3 of the case study, a group of library managers wrote the policy statement for the new policy called Priorities for Assistance with Electronic Services. Between the end of part 3 and the beginning of this part of the case study, regulations and procedures have been drafted, reviewed, and revised, and the entire policy has been approved by the library's governing authority. The library director has reallocated some existing funds to purchase more terminals to balance the distribution of PCs throughout the system in response to the recommendation made by the Policy Audit Advisory Committee. The managers now have to decide how and when to implement the new policy.

The library director scheduled a discussion of the issues to be addressed before the new policy could be implemented as a part of her regular meeting with the senior managers. The director identified two issues as critical: training and forms.

The managers all agreed that there was a clear need for training in a number of areas before the library staff could be expected to provide library users with the levels of electronic assistance included in the new policy. There was less agreement on what types of training should be provided. Some managers believed that every staff member had a personal responsibility to learn to use the Windows operating system, just as every staff member had to know how to read to work in the library. Others thought that the library should provide training in even such basic computer skills for older, long-term employees. The group finally agreed that training would be developed based on the assumption that staff were comfortable with Windows but needed to know more about searching the Internet and the library's information databases. The few individuals who had trouble with Windows would be given special assistance.

There was also disagreement on what specific staff members needed to know. For example, everyone agreed that all of the staff working in the Business and Sciences unit needed to know how to use the résumé software on the computers in the job center. The problem was that occasionally, staff from Arts and Humanities filled in for staff in the Business and Sciences unit if there were an unusual number of absences. Did that mean that everyone in Arts and Humanities also had to understand the résumé software? After discussion the managers agreed that only the staff in Business and Sciences needed to be able to use the résumé software. Staff from other units working temporarily in the Business and Science Unit would be instructed to refer any questions about résumé software to a staff member who knew how to use the program. The same principle was used to decide about the audiences to be trained in other unit-specific software (children's games, literacy programs, and so forth).

When the managers had reached agreement on the audiences to be trained and the skills to be included in the training, they selected one person to be responsible for coordinating the training and asked that he prepare a detailed training plan for their review. The training plan was to include a timeline so that the managers could determine when the new policy could be implemented. The library director encouraged the training coordinator to schedule the training as expeditiously as possible.

The managers then moved on to the issue of new forms. The procedures for the new policy included three new forms to be completed by staff. The forms needed to be printed and available to all staff before the policy could be implemented. The person responsible for coordinating training requested that the forms be available for use during training and the group agreed. One manager was assigned to coordinate the printing process.

The library director concluded the meeting by asking the managers responsible for training and printing to be ready to provide the group with a preliminary timeline by their next meeting.

TASK 2: COMMUNICATE WITH LIBRARY SUPPORT GROUPS AND EXTERNAL AUDIENCES

Step 2.1: Inform library support groups.

Step 2.2: Inform other external audiences.

Step 2.1: Inform Library Support Groups

Library support groups include members of the library's governing authority, members of advisory boards, members of the library friends group, and members of the library foundation board. The members of the library's governing authority, of course, will know about all changes in policy statements and regulations because they must approve those policy elements. However, there will be a delay between the time that the governing authority approves the policy statements and regulations and the actual implementation of the final policy. That delay can be considerable, depending on the time it takes to develop procedures and guidelines (if any). It is good politics to inform the members of the governing authority before new or revised policies go into effect and to remind them that they approved the policy statements and regulations during a previous meeting.

It is probable that members of the advisory boards and the boards of the friends group and the foundation would also like to be kept informed about significant changes in library policy statements or regulations. One of the side benefits of serving on such boards is the opportunity to be in the know. If a board member first hears about changes at the library from colleagues rather than from staff, the member may feel slighted or neglected. It is easy enough to include a brief review of any new or revised policies that are scheduled to be implemented between one meeting and the next as a regular part of each board meeting.

Step 2.2: Inform Other External Audiences

External audiences include, but are not limited to, library users, community residents, appointed and elected officials, and members of the media. Obviously, there is some overlap in these groups. Some but not all library users are community residents. Some community residents are library users while others are not. Appointed or elected officials are probably community residents but they may or may not be library users. Members of each of these groups start with different information and want to know different things.

There are eight questions to ask when determining how to inform an external audience about new or revised policies. These questions underscore the importance of identifying your target audience before you develop a communication plan.

1. Who is your target audience?
2. What do you want the members of the target audience to do as a result of your communication?
3. What do the members of the target audience know now?
4. What facts do they need to know if they are going to do what you want them to do?
5. How do the members of the target audience feel about the topic of your communication?
6. How do you want them to feel?
7. What information is likely to persuade the members of the target audience to do what you want them to do?
8. What is the most effective way to deliver the information the target audience needs to act and feel the way you want them to act and feel?

As you can see in these questions, the assumption is that you are telling external audiences about the new or revised library policies because you want them to do something or feel something or both. For instance, you may want residents to come to the library when they want to read a best seller because they feel that the library often has the materials they want when they want them. Or perhaps you want parents of young children to believe that the library can help create a love of reading in their children, so that they will bring the children to the library.

There is absolutely no point in trying to inform external audiences about new or revised policies if you can't identify the audience for your message or if you do not have a specific outcome you expect to result from the communication. Everyone is inundated with information every day. Messages that are not specifically targeted and clearly stated are buried and ignored.

Although all eight of the questions to ask when developing a message for external audiences are important, questions 4 and 7 are the most critical. Those two questions ask you to identify the information that will encourage people to do what you want them to do or to feel what you want them to feel. Accurate answers to those two questions almost always include less information than you and your colleagues want to provide. It is highly unlikely that any of your external audiences will need or want to see the detailed procedures for any policy. In most cases it will be sufficient to post the policy statement and the regulations for each of the policies. Occasionally, it may be appropriate to post additional specific information, such as a fee schedule or a meeting room application form.

There are various means the library may choose to inform external audiences about new or revised policies, including posting on the library's web page, posting in the library, printing a flyer or brochure, issuing press releases, or developing public service announcements.

LIBRARY WEB PAGE

The library's web page is one of the most effective means that the library has to communicate with its customers, potential customers, and other community residents. Information on the library's web page is available twenty-four hours a day and it is easy to keep a web page current and up-to-date, especially when you compare it with other methods of communication. Make sure that it is easy for users to find the link to the policy section from the home page. Give some thought to how people will access that information. It might make sense to list the policies alphabetically by keyword instead of arranging them in the same order that they appear in the library policy manual.

Apply the same security considerations to the library policy portion of your web page that you use for other sections that contain important and sensitive information. Do not make it easy for hackers to get into your policy files or you may find that someone has changed your policies to eliminate fines and provide free delivery of materials to every home in the city or county.

If the library serves customers who speak languages other than English, it is important to provide access to library policies in those languages. Posting translations of library policies on the library web site is one of the most effective and efficient ways to provide access to this important information to customers in their native language.

POSTING IN THE LIBRARY

Every library staff member knows that the typical library user does not read signs. However, there may be some policies that merit posting in specific areas of the library, especially if you want staff to be able to easily and quickly refer the public to the policy. For example, if the library has a policy statement and regulations governing access to the Internet, it might be useful to post them in the area near the computers. It is also often useful to post a copy of the meeting room policy statement and regulations in the meeting room.

If the new or revised policies are going to lead to changes in current library practice, you might wish to post the policy statement and regulations for those policies for a designated period of time before and after the changes take place. For example, if a new fines and fee structure is going to take effect on July 1, you might wish to post the new policy as soon as it has been approved and indicate that the changes will take place on July 1. Once the new fee structure has been in place for a month or two, you can remove the posted copy and rely on other methods of communication, such as a flyer or the library's web page, to document the fee structure.

If you decide to post policy statements and regulations for one or more policies, it would be advisable to print them in a large and easily readable font. Consider laminating the policies or using some other type of protective cover to minimize the opportunities for vandals to write their opinions about the policy or other matters for all to see. Remember that all of your customers may not speak English and items may have to be posted in other languages.

PRINTING FLYERS, BOOKMARKS, AND BROCHURES

Most libraries print flyers, bookmarks, or brochures that summarize the library's loan periods, borrowing limits, reserves, renewals, fines and fees, and so forth. The information in such publications is usually derived from library policies, even if a specific policy is not actually cited as part of the publication. There are some policies that may merit printing in large quantities as well. This can be an effective method to use when you want to encourage or enable library users to take copies of a policy home.

There is no right or wrong answer on whether a specific policy should be made available in this format. Ask the staff who work at the circulation desk and the reference desk. They will have a good idea of what is needed. You can always do a modest first printing and then print more if there is a need. It is not necessary for an entire policy statement and every related regulation to be listed verbatim in a flyer, bookmark, or brochure. Of course, the publication needs to be an accurate reflection of the policy statement and regulations, but in most cases, it is more appropriate to create an attractive user-friendly publication than to distribute an 8½-by-11-inch copy of a bureaucratic policy from the library's policy manual. Remember that if a policy is important enough to distribute in English, it is also important enough to be made available in the other languages spoken by community residents.

Although printed flyers, bookmarks, and brochures are among the most effective ways to distribute information to a large number of library users, there are some disadvantages to using them. The most obvious is cost. Printing large numbers of flyers, bookmarks, or brochures is almost always more expensive than any of the other means of communicating with external audiences. A less obvious but potentially more damaging disadvantage is that it seems to be almost impossible to discard all of the older versions of a publication when a new version is issued. One way to address this challenge is to change the color of the paper or the ink that is used on the new publication to make it easier to distinguish any older version from the new version. Of course, it is also important to prominently display a date on the publication so that staff and library customers will know when it was issued.

PRESS RELEASES

It is not common to issue a press release to announce a new or revised library policy, but there are occasions when it is both appropriate and effective. Press releases are normally used to announce the beginning of a new or expanded service or to let people know about a significant change in policy that will affect most users. For example, if a library were going to begin to display works produced by local artists, a press release could be prepared that included a brief description of the new service, an invitation to artists to participate in the program, and the key regulations that artists would need to know and observe if they wanted to participate. On the other hand, if the library fee structure had been revised to increase overdue fees, it would be advisable to issue a press release as one of the many ways that staff endeavored to promptly communicate this change to as many library users as possible.

When writing a press release, remember that the audience will be far wider than just library users. Avoid the use of jargon and be sure that the press release can be easily understood by nonusers as well as users. The press release format provides a good opportunity to change the way people feel about the library as well as to provide specific information. Therefore, you will want to include the reasons for the new policy as well as the main points of the policy itself.

PUBLIC SERVICE ANNOUNCEMENTS

With so many worthy organizations and causes competing for the limited amount of time available for public service announcements on local radio and television, it will probably be difficult to get air time to publicize a new or revised library policy unless it is truly newsworthy. However, if the policy pertains to a new program, such as computer classes for seniors or tours of the library conducted in sign language, it might be possible to promote the service and its corresponding regulations by using public service announcements. If the library is located in a community that has a local cable television station that devotes some or all of its programming time to local government, then it might be easier to use that method to communicate new or revised policies.

As with press releases, the audience that can be reached by a public service announcement is much broader than just library users. Remember, the typical community resident does not care about the library's rules. At best, he or she might want to know about the services that are available, but the restrictions on those services are of little interest. Communicate the policy statement and regulations in a positive manner rather than a negative one, and focus on the big picture of what and why instead of the minutia of how many or who is eligible.

In most cases, one or two of the preceding methods will be sufficient, but in some cases it might be necessary to employ all of them. The choices you make will depend on your answers to the eight key questions, as you can see in the case study below.

CASE STUDY

ANYTOWN PUBLIC LIBRARY POLICIES

Part 5
Informing the Public

In earlier parts of this case study we learned that the new Anytown Public Library strategic plan included Commons as a service priority, which meant that the library staff had to revise the existing Meeting Room policy. This part of the case study begins after all elements of the policy have been approved and the staff have been trained to use the required new procedures and forms, but before the policy has been initiated.

The new Meeting Room policy allows organizations and groups to use the library's four meeting rooms, which is a change from the previous practice of allowing only staff to use the rooms. The new policy is in support of an objective in the new strategic plan that states, "Each year, community organizations and groups will hold at least one hundred meetings in one of the library's meeting rooms." If the library is going to meet the target set in the objective, it seems clear that library staff members are going to have to develop an aggressive plan to publicize the availability of the meeting rooms.

The library director called a meeting of staff members who have had some experience with marketing the library's services in the past. The purpose of the meeting was to develop a plan to publicize the new Meeting Room policy. The director developed her agenda around the eight questions to answer when creating a communication plan (presented earlier in this chapter), and the group discussed each in turn. Their decisions are summarized below.

1. Who is our target audience?

   Elected officers of community organizations and groups.

2. What do we want the members of the target audience to do as a result of our communication?

   We want them to schedule one or more of their meetings in the library each year.

3. What facts do the members of the target audience know now?

   They may know that library meeting rooms have never been available to outside groups or organizations.

4. What do they need to know if they are going to do what we want them to do?

   They need to know that the library meeting rooms are available, convenient, and free.

5. How do the members of the target audience feel about the topic of our communication?

   It can be difficult to find places to meet in our community. In the past the library has refused requests from a number of groups to use the meeting rooms. People in those groups probably have negative feelings about the library and the possibility of using our meeting rooms.

6. How do we want them to feel?

   We want them to feel like welcome and valued guests.

7. What information is likely to persuade the members of the target audience to do what we want them to do?

   The communication to the elected officials is going to have to be personal and positive. We can't just inform them that the meeting rooms are available. We will have to invite them to use the rooms and make them believe that we want to serve them.

8. What is the most effective way to deliver the information the target audience needs to act and feel the way we want them to act and feel?

   We will use a variety of communication methods, including

   a. Send a personal letter to the chairperson of each group explaining the change in policy and inviting the group to use the room. The letter will stress the benefits of using our meeting rooms and make it clear that we would welcome each group to the library.

   b. Issue a press release and include pictures of the nicest meeting room.

   c. Include information about the availability of the meeting rooms in all presentations staff give to the public groups.

   d. Post the new policy prominently in the foyer of the library and in each of the meeting rooms.

   e. Highlight the new policy on the home page of the library web page.

The group agreed to review the effectiveness of these communication methods in six months and develop a follow-up plan, if necessary.

TASK 3: MONITOR IMPLEMENTATION

Step 3.1: Observe implementation.

Step 3.2: Modify policies as needed.

Step 3.1: Observe Implementation

Only the most naïve supervisor would assume that merely because a new policy has been distributed and all of the supporting services (training, supplies, printed forms, and the like) have been made available, all staff will promptly, willingly, and accurately implement the new policy. Even the best-intentioned staff member might make a mistake and forget one or more of the new regulations. If and when that occurs, a gentle reminder that a new policy has been adopted is usually sufficient to prevent the mistake from happening again.

However, many supervisors have had an experience with one or more staff members who disagree with a policy and express their disapproval in a variety of overt ways. There is the "I know best" staff member who substitutes his or her judgment for that of the library's governing authority and knowingly violates library policy on a regular basis for some or all library users, or perhaps for his or her own advantage. In some cases, this is not a new behavior for these staff members as they may have been selectively violating library policy for years without any negative consequences from their supervisors.

Then there is the "I know it's a dumb rule" approach taken by those staff members who do not like the new policy but aren't willing to break the rules. Instead they make it very clear to library users via verbal and nonverbal means that they think the policy is stupid and that they are being forced to implement it.

Behaviors such as these cannot be tolerated. Every staff member must observe all library policy statements, regulations, procedures, and guidelines. If they don't, there is no point in having policies at all. While policies should have provisions for exceptions, those exceptions should be made in accordance with the procedures outlined in the policy and not because one or more staff members disagree with the policy and some or all of its provisions.

When a supervisor observes or is informed that a staff member is deliberately circumventing or undercutting library policies, the supervisor should take prompt action to address the situation. After clearly explaining the rationale for the policy and making certain that the staff member understands what is expected, the supervisor should monitor the situation to make certain that the staff member is properly implementing the policy. If the staff member continues to violate the policy, then appropriate disciplinary action should be taken.

As unpleasant as it is to deal with the occasional staff member who chooses not to follow library policy, it is even more challenging to identify and deal with a rogue supervisor or a rogue branch. When this occurs, the entire unit is violating library policy by choosing to ignore the approved policy statements, regulations, or procedures and substituting instead their own preferred practice. This situation seldom comes to the attention of library administrators until a library user comments to a staff member at one branch that the staff at another branch do not require him to pay for reserves or that they do allow him to renew items as often he wants although doing so is a violation of library policy. When comments like that are made by users, they should be reported to someone in the library management team. Once the members of the library management team have been informed, they need to take immediate steps to find out if the library user was accurately describing staff actions in the branch in question. If it turns out that the user's report was accurate, then the branch manager's supervisor will have to deal with the branch manager. As in the earlier examples of blatant disregard for library policy, this is a time for appropriate disciplinary action.

Fortunately it is not common for staff or the public to blatantly disregard policies. More often what happens is that a policy that was carefully developed and sensitively implemented still leads to complaints from library users or library staff. When this occurs, do not be afraid to analyze the situation to determine whether the policy needs to be modified. However, you will want to be careful not to assume immediately that a new or revised policy should be changed merely because a few customers or a few staff express concerns about it.

Remember the old adage—change is hard. Library users and library staff were probably quite comfortable with the previous policy or practice and may be reacting negatively to the fact that any changes were made as opposed to the specifics of those changes. There is a real distinction between the causes of those two reactions. While you could resolve concerns about the specifics of a given change if you chose to, there is no way you could make people feel better about the fact that the change occurred. When you are evaluating public or staff reaction to a new or revised policy, keep in mind that you probably are hearing only from those who are displeased about the change. They may not be representative of the rest of the library users or library staff. In cases like this, taking the time to explain to the library user or the staff member why the change has been made may help resolve the situation even if the individual still does not like the fact that any change was made.

Step 3.2: Modify Policies as Needed

The law of unintended consequences states that any large-scale activity, no matter how well intentioned, is often accompanied by unforeseen circumstances that can overshadow the original purpose of the activity. Most library managers and administrators can attest to the applicability of that law, particularly in the case of new or revised policies. An amazing number of unanticipated things can come up when you begin to implement a new or revised policy. As you will see in the examples that follow, you have to be prepared to deal with the unexpected.

In Library A the community members responsible for identifying library priorities during the strategic planning process strongly recommended that the library shift emphasis from formal learning support to encouraging children to read for fun. The library had been providing extensive support to schools for several decades, including allowing teachers to check out large classroom collections. The members of the library board recognized the potential political challenges of reducing support to the schools and held meetings with the school board, the superintendent, and a group of principals to discuss the change and explain the reasons for it. The meetings went well, and the board adopted the new priority. Based on the change in priority the regulations for borrowers' cards were revised and teachers' cards were discontinued. The regulations pertaining to lending limits were also revised to remove all mention of classroom collections. The revised circulation policies were issued in the late spring. Everything seemed fine until mid-August, when the first teacher came in to get her classroom collection. She was told about the change in policy and became very angry. As luck (or lack of it) would have it, she was the incoming president of the local teachers' union and decided to make a political issue of the changes.

In Library B the group revising the policy statement and regulations for co-sponsorship of library programs decided to limit all such partnerships to non-profit agencies. The staff and the board reviewed the draft policy statement and regulations, and everyone thought it seemed reasonable. In fact, that policy elicited less discussion than any other during the revision of the policy manual. Six months after the policy had been adopted and put into the practice, the president of the foundation asked to make a presentation to the library board. He told the board that the new restriction on co-sponsorships was causing significant problems with fund-raising. He said the most recent issue was with local bank officials. They had agreed to donate $5,000 for children's materials, in return for which they wanted the library to put the bank logo on all bookmarks in the children's room. Library managers had refused to put the logo on the bookmarks and cited the policy as the reason.

Library C had never had a policy regarding the distribution of nonlibrary materials in the library. However, the proliferation of such materials had made it very difficult to keep the display area neat, so the library managers decided it was time to put some limits on the types of materials displayed. They reviewed the policies of other libraries in the area and found that most of them allowed only non-profit groups within the library's service area to distribute materials. Everyone agreed that restriction was a reasonable and equitable way to resolve the problem of overcrowding and the policy was approved and implemented. Nine months later a new white-supremacist group was established in a far corner of the county and its members wanted to include their publications in the display area. The publications were overtly racist and the members of board and the staff were opposed to making them available.

In each of these examples the policies that resulted in unintended consequences had been carefully thought out, reviewed by staff and board, and, in Library A, discussed with members of the external group affected. While the negative reactions could not be blamed on poor planning, in retrospect, managers in each library identified things they would have done differently had they been able to see into the future. Managers in Library A would have included the teacher's union in their discussions. Managers in Library B would have talked more to the members of the foundation board before approving the co-sponsorship policy. Managers in Library C would have looked beyond their own backyard when gathering data about how other libraries handle the distribution of nonlibrary materials. If they had, they would have found that a number of libraries had been faced with problems similar to the one they were now dealing with.

Although it is often easy to see what we should have done in the past, it can be more difficult to resolve current problems. Staff and board members in Libraries A, B, and C are going to have to decide how to address the unintended consequences of their policies. There are several things they need to consider during their deliberations. The first, and perhaps most important, is that the members of the library board approved the library policy and they can change it if they choose. No policy is carved in stone. That is not to say that policies should be automatically changed every time a negative issue arises. It is simply a reminder that there are always options available. The second thing to recognize is that some negative consequences are worth the short-term pain for the long-term gain. The challenge is to determine the balance between pain and gain. The third factor to consider is the legal position of the library and board. Occasionally the unexpected problems that arise have legal implications.

The members of the library boards of Libraries A, B, and C reviewed their options and reached three different solutions to their problems. The board members of Library A decided that the new library priority and policies reflected the needs of the community members and that they weren't willing to make any changes. The board met with the members of the executive board of the teachers' union to explain the reasons for change and to tell them that the changes had been discussed with the school board, the superintendent, and the school principals before they were implemented. The president of the library board wrote an op-ed piece describing the new priorities for children's services that was published in the local newspaper. Some teachers remained unhappy about the changes, but the political furor died down fairly quickly.

In contrast, the board members in Library B listened carefully to the concerns of the foundation president and decided to change the policy on co-sponsorship. It had never been the intent of the board members to close the door on public-private partnerships and they revised the policy to make that clear.

Board members in Library C had the biggest challenge. Their current policy clearly allowed any non-profit group in the county to distribute materials in the library. There was no legal way for staff or board members to discriminate against the publications of one group, no matter how great the provocation, because the First Amendment to the Constitution prohibits such discrimination. Furthermore, it is quite possible that attempts to change the policy to ban distribution of materials some find offensive would be challenged legally. The board members finally retained a lawyer who had First Amendment experience to help them resolve the issue. The lawyer told the board members they had two choices. They could leave the policy as it was and display all publications that were covered in the policy, or they could change the policy to bar the distribution of any nonlibrary materials in the library. The board members didn't like either choice, but finally, after several months of deliberation, they voted to ban the distribution of all nonlibrary materials.

TASK 4: UPDATE AND MAINTAIN THE POLICY MANUAL

Step 4.1: Initiate development of next category or type of policy.

Step 4.2: Schedule regular review cycle for existing policies.

Step 4.3: Schedule annual review of master category list.

Step 4.1: Initiate Development of Next Category or Type of Policy

Early in the process of revising and developing new library policies, you determined the scope of the policies to be included in the first phase of the process. If you decided to limit the development of policies to one category, you will want to initiate action on a second category shortly after you complete all of the policies in the first category. You will find the process is much easier to manage the second time around. The staff involved in the first phase of the process gained an understanding of the process, learned a new vocabulary, and became skilled at reviewing and writing policy elements. If you wait too long to begin to develop the policies in a new category, staff will lose those skills and you will be starting all over again.

Remember too that most libraries need several types of policies. This book focused on public service policies, but public libraries typically have at least four other types of policies: technical services, financial, personnel, and collection development. The processes used to develop policies in those areas are exactly the same as the processes used to develop public service policies. Only the content will be different.

Step 4.2: Schedule Regular Review Cycle for Existing Policies

In some ways library policies are like housework—never truly done. Each library should establish some sort of review process for existing policies to be sure that they remain current and relevant. The process used to review policy statements and regulations will probably be different from the process used to review procedures or guidelines. That makes sense when you remember that the elements were developed and approved by different groups.

There are a couple of methods you might use to organize the review of policy statements and regulations. The library director could assign one or two people to read through all of the policy statements and regulations each year to see if changes need to be made. Alternatively, the director could divide the review responsibilities among all of the senior managers and assign four or five policies to each. The reviewers would use the evaluation criteria developed during the policy audit review process and recorded on Workform 6, Evaluation Criteria, as the basis for their work. They would then bring any needed changes to a meeting of senior managers for discussion and resolution.

Perhaps the easiest way to set up an annual review of procedures and guidelines would be ask the groups that were responsible for writing the procedures or guidelines to review them. If the groups that developed most of the procedures meet regularly (circulation attendants, youth services, and the like) they could just schedule one meeting each year to review and discuss procedures. If a special committee was formed to develop one or more sets of procedures, the committee can be reconvened so that members can review their work. Guidelines are often developed by individual units of the library, and the responsibility for annual review of that element can be assigned to the appropriate units.

Any recommended changes in policy statements or regulations must go through the review and approval process described in Step 2.4 in chapter 4. Any recommended changes in procedures or guidelines should go through the review and approval process described in Steps 3.4 and 4.4 in chapter 4.

Step 4.3: Schedule Annual Review of Master Category List

By scheduling an annual review of existing public services policies you will ensure that your policy manual will never again include outdated or inappropriate policies. However, that annual review is no guarantee that there will not be gaps in your policies as conditions change in your library and in libraries in general. The only way to be sure that your policy manual is complete is to schedule an annual review and discussion of the master category list. Ideally this review will be completed in two phases. First the senior management team will meet to consider the master category list and make recommendations. Then both the master category list and the staff recommendations will be taken to the board for further discussion and action. Any new policies should be developed using the processes described in this book.

Challenges

As you come to the end of the initial phase of the policy development process, there are two final challenges you and your colleagues will face. The first challenge is similar to the first challenge in chapter 1, which was finding the time and energy to begin the process. In this instance the challenge is going to be finding ways to keep the staff involved and focused. The second challenge will be coping with the inevitable changes that will result from revising and developing new policies.

Keeping Staff Involved and Committed

It is clear by now that the processes described in this book do not have a neat beginning, middle, and end. Instead they are ongoing processes that will have to be integrated into the overall management of your library. To do that successfully you and your colleagues are going to have to find ways to keep yourselves and everyone else involved in and committed to the process.

One of the most important ways to ensure continued buy-in to the process is to acknowledge the contributions of staff members at every step. Ask the staff members who developed the drafts of a policy statement and regulations to attend the board meeting during which the drafts will be discussed. Introduce the staff members to the board and tell the board about their work on the drafts being reviewed. Go through the same steps when draft procedures or guidelines are being discussed by the senior management team. Invite the people who drafted the procedures or guidelines to be present during the discussion and publicly thank them for their efforts.

There are other things you can do to acknowledge staff participation in the process too. You could include the names of the staff members who were involved in developing a new policy in the memorandum that is prepared to announce the approval of the policy. Staff members could be thanked for work during all-staff meetings or meetings in the various units of the library. Staff members who serve on any committee involved in the policy development process could be given certificates or receive a personal thank you from the library director.

By making an ongoing effort to recognize the work being done by staff to develop policies, the library director and senior managers are sending the message that the work is important to the organization. On the other hand, if the efforts of staff are ignored, a very different message is sent. The message in that case is that the work is not even worthy of mention, which trivializes all of the efforts that staff have been making.

Another way to keep yourself and others from getting frustrated by the process is to celebrate benchmarks. It is easy to get so involved in the minutia of a project, particularly a long-term project like policy development, that you lose track of the big picture. While it may seem that you have been working on policies forever and not making any progress at all, the truth is that you have been moving forward all of the time. Charitable organizations often use giant thermometers to measure their movement toward their final goal. Every time the total amount of money received increases by a certain amount another segment of the thermometer is filled. You could use the same type of graphic to record the approval and implementation of new or revised policies. If that approach seems a bit more dramatic than necessary, you could periodically issue a general memo listing all of the policies that have been completed and reminding staff that real progress is being made.

All of these recommendations are based on the assumption that the library manager and senior managers remain committed to the policy development process. If the library management loses interest in the process, inevitably the rest of the staff will lose interest too. There is no way for managers to fake an interest. Either policies matter to them or they don't, and staff are very good at reading what managers really think as opposed to what they say they think. That means that involvement and commitment must start at the top and spread throughout the organization. This is not a grassroots process.

Managing Change

There is no question that the processes described in this book will lead to new and revised policies and that those policies will in turn result in changes in the way the library does business. Many people find change hard, and that is as true of administrators as it is of frontline staff. It helps if everyone involved in the process acknowledges that change can be difficult. Denial just makes the situation worse, and that is particularly true if library managers refuse to acknowledge the emotions that can result from change.

One way for library managers to deal with their own emotions about change and the emotions of others is to follow some basic change management guidelines. The recommended guidelines appeared in a slightly different form in *The New Planning for Results,*[2] and they have been incorporated in every task and step in this book. They will make it easier for you to help your colleagues, your staff, your governing authority, and the public to adapt to the changing environment in which we all find ourselves.

Involve staff at every step of the process. The more staff have to do with designing the changes, the more comfortable they will feel with them.

Don't get so involved in the process of change that you lose track of the reasons for the changes. Always know why you are making changes and always include the reasons when discussing changes with staff, the board, and the public.

Acknowledge the emotional reactions that we all have when faced with change. Some change experts suggest that people dealing with change go through much the same process as people dealing with grief: shock, denial, anger, guilt, depression, acceptance, and growth. These are strong emotions and they won't just go away if you ignore them.

Acknowledge the contributions made by the services and programs that are being phased out. A decision to change the priority of a service based on new community needs in no way diminishes the value of that service in the past. Celebrate your achievements and link your past successes at meeting community needs with your current efforts to continue to do so.

Don't expect change to be quick. It took a long time to establish your current organizational norms and it will take a long time to change them. Furthermore, the larger your library is, the longer it will take to change things. It is much like the difference between trying to turn an ocean liner (remember the *Titanic*?) and a canoe.

Stay focused on the end result. Your plan is intended to improve the library's service to the people of your community.

Don't automatically assume that all changes will be equally effective. Monitor changes carefully and make adjustments as needed. Be willing to publicly acknowledge that a change did not lead to expected results, if necessary.

Don't expect to control the change process. No single person can control organizational change. What you and other library managers can do is understand the change process and manage it.

Key Points to Remember

1. Communication is critical. Staff can't implement policies they haven't received or don't understand.

2. You need to allow enough time between the approval of a policy and the implementation of that policy to train staff, print any needed forms or signs, and inform the public of the change.
3. Library users and community residents should have access to information about library policies, and the library should use appropriate and effective means to make that information available.
4. If community residents speak and read languages other than English, it is essential that library policies be available in those languages.
5. Supervisors will have to monitor the implementation of policies to ensure that library users receive consistent and equitable service whenever and wherever they use the library.
6. Library employees who gratuitously violate library policies must be disciplined appropriately.
7. The review and maintenance of the library policy manual should be an ongoing part of managing the library.
8. Managers and members of the governing authority should be prepared to deal with the unintended consequences of new or revised policies.
9. Library managers should acknowledge the work of all staff members who participate in the policy development process.
10. Change is inevitable. It is better to manage change than to be managed by it.

NOTES

1. Sandra Nelson, *The New Planning for Results: A Streamlined Approach* (Chicago: American Library Association, 2001), 246–61.
2. Ibid., 133.

Appendix A

Policy Development Templates

GOVERNANCE AND ORGANIZATIONAL STRUCTURE

GOV-1 City/County Organization Chart (no template)
GOV-2 Locations and Hours of All Units (no template)
GOV-3 Library Board Bylaws (no template)
GOV-4 Library Board Standing Committees (no template)
GOV-5 Library Organization Chart (no template)
GOV-6 Staff Association Activities

Management Policies

MNG-1 Confidentiality of Library Records
MNG-2 Statistics
MNG-3 Petty Cash
MNG-4 Fund-Raising and Donations
MNG-5 Reconsideration of Library Materials
MNG-6 Building Maintenance
MNG-7 Emergencies and Disasters
MNG-8 Meeting Room Use
MNG-9 Exhibits and Displays
MNG-10 Bulletin Boards
MNG-11 Distribution of Nonlibrary Materials
MNG-12 Staff Committees and Staff Task Forces
MNG-13 Inclement Weather and Closing

Customer Services

CUS-1 Customer Service
CUS-2 Customer Behavior
CUS-2 Unattended Children

Circulation Services

CIR-1	Library Cards for Residents
CIR-2	Library Cards for Nonresidents
CIR-3	Loan Periods and Loan Limits
CIR-4	Renewals
CIR-5	Reserves
CIR-6	Claims Returned or Claims Never Had
CIR-7	Lost or Damaged Materials
CIR-8	Fines and Fees
CIR-9	Borrowing Materials by Staff

Information Services

INF-1	Priorities for Reference Services
INF-2	Interlibrary Loan
INF-3	Internet Use
INF-4	Use of Library-Provided Personal Computers

Group Services

GSV-1	Programs in the Library
GSV-2	Co-Sponsored Programs in the Library
GSV-3	Community Presentations
GSV-4	Special Events
GSV-5	Tours
GSV-6	Computer Training for the Public

STAFF ASSOCIATION ACTIVITIES

Policy Questions to Address

1. What is the purpose of the staff association according to their bylaws or other organizational document?
2. How does the presence of a staff association support the library's goals and objectives?

Regulations Questions to Address

1. May library staff attend staff association meetings on work time? If so, is there a limit on how much time may be spent per staff member in a given period of time?
2. May staff association officers or committee chairs perform staff association activities on work time? If so, is there a limit on how much time may be spent per staff member in a given period of time?
3. May staff association members use library facilities to hold staff association meetings or activities? If so, are they subject to the same regulations as other organizations or are some regulations waived?
4. May staff association members use library equipment or resources (such as e-mail or the library delivery system) to create or disseminate information about staff association activities? If so, are there any restrictions on this usage?
5. Are there restrictions on the types of activities that the staff association can undertake on library time, in library facilities, and/or with library equipment, and so forth? For example, may the staff association
   a. hold fund-raisers to support their activities?
   b. support political candidates?
   c. hold programs that are open to the public?

CONFIDENTIALITY OF LIBRARY RECORDS

Policy Questions to Address

1. Why does the library maintain the confidentiality of library records?
2. How does the implementation of confidentiality of library records support the library's goals and objectives?

Regulations Questions to Address

1. Are there any state laws or regulations that address the confidentiality of library records?
2. Has the library adopted the Library Bill of Rights, the Code of Professional Ethics, or other similar documents produced by the American Library Association or a state library association?
3. What information, if any, is considered confidential? For example, are the following considered confidential:
   a. existence of a library card?
   b. identification of materials currently on loan to a specific customer?
   c. identification of materials previously borrowed by a specific customer?
   d. attendance logs for library programs?
   e. participation in library programs such as the summer reading program?
   f. Internet sign-up sheets? (See Policy INF-3 for more information on Internet use.)
   g. other?
4. Under what circumstances, if any, will library staff provide borrower-related information concerning a minor child to his or her parent or legal guardian? May any member of the library staff provide this information, or may only supervisors or staff with a particular classification provide the information?
5. Which staff members have been designated to respond to court-approved requests and/or other requests for borrower-related information?
6. How is this policy implemented if the library issues borrower cards to institutions, schools, organizations, or businesses from which multiple individuals may have had access to the same library borrower card?

STATISTICS

Policy Questions to Address

1. Why does the library collect statistics?
2. How does the collection and use of statistics support the library's goals and objectives?

Regulations Questions to Address

1. Is the library required to report statistical information to the federal government? If so, what data elements need to be reported? Who is responsible for collecting and reporting the data in a timely manner? In what format is the report submitted?
2. Is the library required to report statistical information to the state library or other state agency? If so, what data elements need to be reported? Who is responsible for collecting and reporting the data in a timely manner? In what format is the report submitted?
3. Is the library required to report statistical information to local government? If so, what data elements need to be reported? Who is responsible for collecting and reporting the data in a timely manner? In what format is the report submitted?
4. Is the library required to report statistical information to the library board? If so, what data elements need to be reported? Who is responsible for collecting and reporting the data in a timely manner? In what format is the report submitted?
5. Is the library required to report statistical information to the Friends of the Library or the library foundation? If so, what data elements need to be reported? Who is responsible for collecting and reporting the data in a timely manner? In what format is the report submitted?
6. Is the library required to report statistical information to any other organization, funding source, and so forth? If so, what data elements need to be reported? Who is responsible for collecting and reporting the data in a timely manner? In what format is the report submitted?
7. Does the library produce an annual report for distribution to the public? If so, who is responsible for producing the report? What statistical information is reported?
8. What statistics are staff collecting and reporting to library administration? Who is responsible for collecting and consolidating the data? In what format are the consolidated data reported? To whom is the report distributed?
9. Has the library developed guidelines for the collection and reporting of all required statistics? Do these guidelines contain clear definitions for all data elements being collected? If so, please attach a copy to this policy.

(Cont.)

10. How does the library use the statistics it is collecting to manage and evaluate the services it is offering?
11. Does the library conduct a periodic review of the statistics being collected to make certain that all needed data are being collected and that data no longer needed have ceased being collected? If so, who is responsible for conducting this review and to whom are the results of the review reported?
12. Does the library conduct periodic training sessions on this topic? Is this topic addressed in new employee orientation?

PETTY CASH

Policy Questions to Address

1. Why is a petty cash fund necessary?
2. How does a petty cash fund support the library's goals and objectives?

Definition

What is a *petty cash fund?*

Regulations Questions to Address

1. Are there city, county, or other governmental regulations that govern the existence and use of petty cash funds?
2. Who has the authority to authorize the creation of a petty cash fund?
3. How many petty cash funds exist? Do different funds exist for different purposes?
4. What amount has been authorized for each fund?
5. Who is responsible for the proper administration, use, and safeguarding of each petty cash fund?
6. How are petty cash funds stored to maintain their security?
7. Who has access to the petty cash funds?
8. For what purposes may petty cash be used? For what purposes, if any, is the use of petty cash expressly prohibited?
9. Who has the authority to authorize the expending of petty cash?
10. Is there a maximum amount that can be spent with any one vendor at one time or within a period of time?
11. What types of receipts need to be kept to document expenditures from the fund?
12. How is the fund replenished when expenditures are made? How often can the fund be replenished? Who is responsible for requesting replenishment of the fund?
13. Under what circumstances, if any, are the petty cash funds audited?

FUND-RAISING AND DONATIONS

Policy Questions to Address

1. What is the purpose of fund-raising and accepting donations?
2. How do fund-raising and the acceptance of donations support the library's goals and objectives?

Definitions

1. What does the library mean by the term *fund-raising?*
2. What does the library mean by the term *donations?*

Regulations Questions to Address

1. Does the library accept donations of cash or checks? If so,
   a. may the donor request that the cash or checks be used for a particular purpose?
   b. is the donor given a receipt?
   c. how does the library indicate its appreciation to the donor?
   d. to whom is the cash or checks sent?
2. Does the library accept donations of
   a. equipment?
   b. furniture?
   c. books, DVDs, and/or other library materials?
   d. land?
   e. other?
3. If the library does accept donations, what criteria are applied for each type of donation that the library accepts?
4. Who is responsible for determining whether or not the library will accept a donation?
5. How is the decision about whether or not the library will accept a donation communicated to the potential donor?
6. If the donation is accepted, how does the library express its appreciation to the donor?
7. Under what circumstances, if any, is the donation publicly acknowledged? What form does that acknowledgment take?
8. Does the library actively solicit donations of
   a. equipment?
   b. furniture?
   c. books, DVDs, and/or other library materials?
   d. other?

   If so, how is this active solicitation accomplished?

(Cont.)

9. Does the library have an organized, ongoing fund-raising effort? If so, is this effort managed primarily by library staff or by another organization, such as a library foundation or the Friends of the Library?
10. If the organized fund-raising effort is managed primarily by library staff,
    a. who is responsible for determining the scope of the fund-raising effort and the intended use of the funds that will be raised?
    b. what is the role of the library board in the fund-raising efforts?
    c. may a prospective donor indicate how he or she wishes the funds to be expended?
    d. who is responsible for managing the fund-raising effort?
    e. where are the funds that have been collected deposited?
    f. are the funds invested? If so, who has approved the investment plan?
    g. how is the community informed about the library's fund-raising effort?
    h. how are donors recognized for their contributions? Does the form of recognition vary depending on the amount that was contributed?
    i. other?
11. If the organized fund-raising effort is primarily managed by another organization, such as the library foundation or the Friends of the Library,
    a. how are the library director and staff involved in the process?
    b. how is the library board involved in the process?
    c. who is responsible for determining the scope of the fund-raising effort and the intended use of the funds that will be raised?
    d. may a prospective donor indicate how he or she wishes the funds to be expended?
    e. who is responsible for managing the fund-raising effort?
    f. where are the funds that have been collected deposited? Are the funds under the control of the library or the other organization?
    g. are the funds invested? If so, who has approved the investment plan? How are the investments monitored?
    h. how and when are the funds disbursed to the library?
    i. is a portion of the funds retained by the organization to support the fund-raising efforts? Is there a maximum amount or percentage that can be withheld for that purpose? If funds are being withheld for that purpose, are potential donors aware that funds are being withheld?
    j. how is the community informed about the fund-raising efforts being conducted on behalf of the library?
    k. how are donors recognized for their contributions? Are donors recognized by the organization managing the fund-raising and/or the library? Does the form of recognition vary depending on the amount that was contributed?

MNG-5

RECONSIDERATION OF LIBRARY MATERIALS

Policy Questions to Address

1. Why does the library have a process for the reconsideration of library materials?
2. How does having a process to facilitate the reconsideration of library materials support the library's goals and objectives?

Regulations Questions to Address

1. Does the library have a collection management policy?
2. Has the library adopted or endorsed the American Library Association's Library Bill of Rights and/or its statements on Freedom to Read and Freedom to View?
3. If a customer, when in the library, expresses concern about the suitability or classification of a particular item to a staff member, what should the staff member do?
4. If a customer calls the library to express concern about the suitability or classification of a particular item, what should the staff member who takes the call do?
5. If a customer writes or e-mails the library to express concern about the suitability or classification of a particular item, what should the staff member do with the correspondence?
6. Is there a form that the customer will be asked to complete that requests information about the item and why the customer feels that it is unsuitable or improperly classified? If so,
   a. to whom are such forms sent for review and resolution?
   b. are the forms retained after a final decision is made? If so, how long are they kept and where are they kept? Who is responsible for maintaining the files?
7. What process will library staff follow to review the request for reconsideration and to respond to the customer? How is the customer made aware of the library's decision?
8. If the customer disagrees with the library's response, to whom can he or she address an appeal? What is the appeal process?
9. Who has the ultimate say on whether an item is suitable for the collection or whether it has been properly classified?

BUILDING MAINTENANCE

Policy Questions to Address

1. Why does the library maintain library buildings?
2. How does the library's policy on building maintenance support the library's goals and objectives?

Regulations Questions to Address

1. What types of building maintenance are performed by library custodial staff?
2. When should other library staff assist with or resolve building maintenance matters?
3. Are any types of building maintenance managed by another city or county department? If so, what services are provided by which departments?
4. Are any types of building maintenance managed by outside contractors? If so, what services are provided by which firms?
5. To whom do staff report facility-related problems that do not present an immediate danger to the public, the staff, or the facility?
6. Who is responsible for contacting service providers to inform them that a facility-related problem exists and needs attention? Where can staff obtain the contact information (such as name, phone number, or emergency pager number) for each of the departments or companies that provide service to the library?
7. What should a staff member do when there does not appear to be a designated service provider for the type of problem that exists?
8. Does the library maintain a log of facility-related problems, routine maintenance, and the like? If so,
   a. who is responsible for maintaining the log?
   b. how is the information used?
   c. how long is the log retained?
9. Under what circumstances is library administration informed that a building-related problem exists?
10. Under what circumstances, if any, are city or county staff informed that a building-related problem exists?
11. Under what circumstances, if any, is the library board informed that a building-related problem exists?
12. Under what circumstances, if any, are the local media informed that a building-related problem exists?

EMERGENCIES AND DISASTERS

Policy Questions to Address

1. What is the purpose of preparing to deal with emergencies and disasters?
2. How does the library's policy on emergencies and disasters support the library's goals and objectives?

Definitions

1. How does the library define the term *emergency?*
2. How does the library define the term *disaster?*

Regulations Questions to Address

1. Who is responsible for reporting that an emergency situation exists and requesting assistance from police, fire, paramedics, and others?
2. Where can staff obtain the phone numbers and other contact information to report an emergency?
3. Under what circumstances, if any, are staff authorized to provide emergency medical assistance?
4. Under what circumstances should staff evacuate the facility?
5. Who is responsible for informing library administration that an emergency exists?
6. Under what circumstances, if any, are city or county staff informed that an emergency exists or has happened at the library?
7. Under what circumstances, if any, is the library board informed that an emergency situation exists or has happened at the library?
8. Under what circumstances, if any, are the local media informed that an emergency exists or has happened at the library?
9. Who is responsible for handling inquiries if members of the media contact the library for information or a statement about an emergency?
10. Are emergencies or disasters handled differently if they occur when the library is closed? If so, how are they handled?
11. Are staff expected to submit a written report after the emergency or disaster is under control? If so,
    a. who is responsible for submitting the report?
    b. to whom is the report sent?
    c. how soon after the event is the report to be submitted?
    d. how will the report be used?

MEETING ROOM USE

Policy Questions to Address

1. Why does the library have a meeting room or meeting rooms?
2. What is the primary purpose of the meeting room(s)?
3. How does the use of the meeting room(s) support the library's goals and objectives?

Regulations Questions to Address

1. What events or programs may occur in the meeting room(s)?
2. What events or programs, if any, are prohibited in the meeting room(s)?
3. What is the occupancy code limit for the meeting room(s)?
4. Who may reserve the meeting room(s)? Adults only? Young adults? Children?
5. Is there a fee for the use of the meeting room(s)? If more than one room is available, does the amount of the fee depend on which room is reserved?
   a. If there is a fee, must it be paid at the time the meeting room is reserved?
   b. Under what circumstances, if any, are the fees waived? For example, are they waived if another city or county department is using the room for official business or if the library is co-sponsoring the program?
   c. If a meeting is canceled, will the fee be refunded? If so, under what circumstances? (See Policy CIR-8 for more information on fees.)
6. May the meeting room be used when the library is closed? If so, is there an additional fee to cover the cost of staff who must stay until the event is over?
7. May the individual or group that is using the meeting room charge a fee for people to attend a program they are offering in the meeting room? If so, may fees be collected on library premises?
8. Will the individual or group that is renting the meeting room be expected to sign an agreement that states the terms and conditions of the usage of the room?
9. How far in advance may meeting rooms be reserved? Does this vary depending on the user? For example, may the library staff reserve the meeting room with more lead time than community organizations are allowed?
10. Who is responsible for meeting room setup and cleanup?
11. May food and beverages be consumed in the meeting room? May alcohol be consumed in the meeting room?
12. May the individual or group using the meeting room borrow or rent the library's audiovisual equipment or supplies? If so, is there a fee? If equipment may be rented, must a library staff member operate it?

(Cont.)

13. May an individual or group that is using the meeting room on a regular basis store any of their literature or equipment at the library? If so, under what terms and conditions? (See Policy MNG-11 for more information on distributing nonlibrary material.)
14. May an individual or group using the meeting room offer items for sale to the attendees of an event or program being held in the meeting room?
15. May an individual or group using the meeting room post or distribute a flyer in the library about the upcoming event or program? Will the library advertise or announce the event in its calendar of events?
16. If the library has more than one meeting room, are the regulations the same for all of the rooms? If not, which regulations apply to which rooms?
17. If there is a Friends of the Library, library foundation, or other group of advocates and supporters, are they bound by the same regulations that apply to other community organizations? If not, which regulations apply and which do not?
18. Under what circumstances, if any, will the library co-sponsor an event or program? If the library does co-sponsor an event or program, which regulations apply and which do not? (See Policy GSV-2 for more information on co-sponsored programs.)
19. If there is a complaint about the meeting room policy or how it was implemented,
    a. to whom is that complaint submitted?
    b. what process will be followed to address the complaint?
20. If there is a complaint about the content of a program presented in the meeting room,
    a. to whom is that complaint submitted?
    b. what process will be followed to address the complaint?

EXHIBITS AND DISPLAYS

Policy Questions to Address

1. Why does the library create or authorize the creation of exhibits or displays?
2. What types of items may be included in an exhibit or display?
3. How do exhibits and displays support the library's goals and objectives?

Definitions

1. What is an *exhibit?*
2. What is a *display?*

Regulations Questions to Address

1. Are exhibits or displays created only by library staff, or are other organizations and individuals authorized to mount exhibits or displays in the library?
2. If other organizations and individuals are authorized to mount exhibits or displays,
   a. how do they indicate their interest in mounting an exhibit or display?
   b. what criteria are used to determine which exhibits or displays will be accepted, and who is responsible for enforcing the criteria?
   c. are there rules for signage, size, content, and the like that must be observed?
   d. must a release from liability form be signed that describes and limits the library's responsibility in the event that an exhibit or display is damaged or items become lost?
   e. may an exhibit or display contain items (such as artworks or crafts) that are for sale?
   f. may an exhibit or display contain the name, address, and phone number of the person or group that created it?
3. Who is responsible for the content and quality of exhibits or displays produced by library staff?
4. How are exhibits or displays scheduled and by whom?
5. Where does the library allow exhibits or displays to be mounted?
6. If there is more than one exhibit or display area, do the regulations vary from area to area? If so, which regulations apply to which area?
7. Is there a maximum, minimum, or fixed period of time for exhibits or displays?
8. Under what circumstances, if any, are library materials used in exhibits or displays?

(Cont.)

9. If library materials are used in exhibits or displays, are the materials available for circulation? If they are not available for circulation, may reserves be placed on them?
10. If there is a complaint about the Exhibits and Displays policy or how the policy was implemented,
    a. to whom is that complaint made?
    b. what process will be followed to address the complaint?
11. If there is a complaint about the content of an exhibit or display,
    a. to whom is that complaint made?
    b. what process will be followed to address the complaint?

MNG-10

BULLETIN BOARDS

Policy Questions to Address

1. Why does the library have a bulletin board or bulletin boards in the public service area of the library? What is the purpose of each?
2. How do the provision of a bulletin board or bulletin boards and their usage support the library's goals and objectives?

Regulations Questions to Address

1. Is the use of the bulletin board restricted to library-created or -sponsored announcements?
2. If individuals or organizations are authorized to post items on the bulletin board, which organizations are eligible:
   a. local, state, or federal governments?
   b. educational institutions? public schools? private schools?
   c. non-profit organizations?
   d. Friends of the Library? the library foundation?
   e. community organizations and clubs?
   f. for-profit companies?
   g. individuals offering services?
   h. other?
3. If individuals or organizations are authorized to post items on the bulletin board,
   a. how do they indicate their interest in having an item posted?
   b. what criteria are used to determine which items may be posted, and who is responsible for enforcing the criteria?
   c. may items advertising programs and events for which there is a fee be displayed?
   d. are there guidelines that govern the size of a posting, how long it may be posted, and so forth?
   e. is there a maximum, minimum, or fixed period of time that items may be posted on the bulletin board? If so, is each item marked with the date it was posted or is to be removed?
4. If individuals or organizations are authorized to post items on the bulletin board, must the individual or organization reside within the immediate service area of the library?
5. Who is responsible for the appearance and timeliness of items posted on the bulletin board?
6. What will be done with an unauthorized item posted on the bulletin board?

(Cont.)

7. If there is a complaint about the Bulletin Boards policy or how it was implemented,
   a. to whom is that complaint made?
   b. what process will be followed to address the complaint?
8. If there is a complaint about an item on the bulletin board,
   a. to whom is that complaint made?
   b. what process will be followed to address the complaint?
9. If there is more than one bulletin board, do the regulations vary from bulletin board to bulletin board? If so, which regulations apply to which bulletin board?

DISTRIBUTION OF NONLIBRARY MATERIALS

Policy Questions to Address

1. Will the library distribute nonlibrary materials to library users or allow its premises to be used for the distribution of nonlibrary materials?
2. Why was the decision to distribute or not to distribute nonlibrary materials made?
3. How does the decision pertaining to the distribution of nonlibrary materials support the library's goals and objectives?

Regulations Questions to Address

1. If the library is willing to distribute nonlibrary materials, which organizations are eligible to have their materials distributed:
   a. local, state, or federal governments?
   b. educational institutions? public schools? private schools?
   c. non-profit organizations?
   d. Friends of the Library? the library foundation?
   e. community organizations and clubs?
   f. for-profit companies?
   g. individuals offering services?
   h. other?
2. If the library is willing to distribute nonlibrary materials,
   a. how do individuals or organizations indicate their interest in having their items distributed?
   b. what criteria are used to determine which items may be distributed, and who is responsible for enforcing the criteria?
   c. who determines whether material meets the criteria for distribution?
   d. may items advertising programs and events for which there is a fee be distributed?
   e. are there rules that govern the size of the literature, how long it will be available for distribution, and so forth?
   f. is there a maximum, minimum, or fixed period of time that items may be made available for distribution?
   g. will surplus copies be returned to their owners? If so, under what circumstances?
3. If the library is willing to distribute nonlibrary materials, must the individuals or organizations that developed them reside within the immediate service area of the library?
4. If the material will be distributed inside the library, where may it be placed?
5. May individuals or organizations provide display racks for the material that is to be distributed?

(Cont.)

6. Who is responsible for the appearance of the area where the material is stored?
7. May storage containers (such as display racks) be placed outside the library to facilitate the distribution of nonlibrary materials? If so,
    a. are the distribution racks provided by the library, or are they provided by the individuals or organizations that wish to have material distributed?
    b. how do individuals and organizations indicate their interest in distributing their material outside the library?
    c. where may the racks be placed?
    d. are there limits on the size or type of distribution rack that may be used?
8. What will be done if materials that do not meet the library's criteria are left for distribution?
9. If there is a complaint about the Distribution of Nonlibrary Materials policy or how it was implemented,
    a. to whom is that complaint made?
    b. what process will be followed to address the complaint?
10. If there is a complaint about an item that is being distributed,
    a. to whom is that complaint made?
    b. what process will be followed to address the complaint?

STAFF COMMITTEES AND STAFF TASK FORCES

Policy Questions to Address

1. What is the purpose of staff committees?
2. What is the purpose of staff task forces?
3. How do the existence and use of staff committees and staff task forces support the library's goals and objectives?

Definitions

1. A *committee* is an ongoing work group with membership determined by position or responsibility (example: Youth Services Committee).
2. A *task force* is a working group appointed for a specific period of time to accomplish a clearly identified task with membership determined by specialized knowledge or based on specific groups or units to be represented (example: Automated Vendor Selection Task Force).

Regulations Questions to Address

1. What types of staff committees does the library have?
2. What types of staff task forces does the library have?
3. Who is responsible for determining that a staff committee or task force is needed for a particular purpose?
4. Who is responsible for determining the charges for the staff committees and task forces?
5. Who is responsible for selecting the staff member who will serve as chairperson of a committee or task force and the length of his or her term of office?
6. Who is responsible for selecting the members who will serve on each staff committee or staff task force and the lengths of their terms?
7. Are there guidelines that staff committee and task force chairpersons and members are expected to follow when performing their assignments? If so, please attach a copy to this policy.
8. How do staff committees and task forces report their progress to the group or person that appointed them?
9. How do staff committees and task forces report their progress to the library staff?
10. Are staff committee and task force chairpersons expected to evaluate the performance of the members of their committees or task forces? If so, how is the evaluation performed, and how is feedback given to the employee and his or her supervisor?

INCLEMENT WEATHER AND CLOSING

Policy Questions to Address

1. What is the purpose of having a policy related to inclement weather?
2. How does the existence of a policy related to inclement weather support the library's goals and objectives?

Definition

What does the library mean by the term *inclement weather?*

Regulations Questions to Address

1. When the library is open for service, who is responsible for determining that weather conditions warrant closing? If that person is not available, who is responsible for making the decision?
2. What criteria will be considered when determining if weather conditions warrant closing the library?
3. Will a minimum amount of advance notice be given before the library closes? If so, how much advance notice will be given?
4. How will customers who are currently in the library be informed that the library will be closing?
5. How will staff be informed that the library will be closing?
6. Will staff be paid for the hours they were scheduled to work or only for the hours they actually worked? Will full-time staff and part-time staff be treated the same? Will exempt staff and nonexempt staff be treated the same?
7. How should library staff respond to children or adults who do not have transportation available at the library?
8. Should city or county government officials be informed that the library is closing due to inclement weather? If so, who is responsible for notifying them?
9. Should the local radio or television stations be informed that the library is closing due to inclement weather? If so, who is responsible for notifying them?
10. Under what weather-related circumstances, if any, will the library remain open longer than its regularly scheduled hours? If this occurs, will staff be paid overtime or compensated for the additional hours they remain at the library?
11. Who is responsible for determining that weather conditions warrant not opening the library at its regularly scheduled time? If that person is not available, who is responsible for making the decision?

(Cont.)

12. What criteria will be considered when determining if weather conditions warrant not opening the library at its regularly scheduled time?
13. How will staff be informed that the library will not open at its regularly scheduled time due to weather conditions?
14. Will staff be paid for the hours they were scheduled to work? If not, may they use vacation time or some other form of paid leave to avoid receiving a smaller paycheck?
15. Should city or county government officials be informed that the library will not be opening at its regularly scheduled time due to weather conditions? If so, who is responsible for notifying them?
16. Should the local radio or television stations be informed that the library will not be opening at its regularly scheduled time due to weather conditions? If so, who is responsible for notifying them?
17. Will library borrowers be charged overdue fines for the period of time that the library was closed due to inclement weather?
18. If customers claim they could not get to the library because of inclement weather, will the library waive or reduce fines?
19. If the library serves a large geographic area and it is possible for inclement weather to strike a portion of the service area but not the entire area, do different regulations apply? If so, what regulations should staff observe?

CUSTOMER SERVICE

Policy Questions to Address

1. How does the library describe the type of customer service it expects the staff to provide to library customers?
2. Does the library offer the same quality of service to all customers regardless of age, race, nationality, educational background, physical condition, or other factors?
3. How does the library's approach to customer service support the library's goals and objectives?

Regulations Questions to Address

1. Does a staff member's classification determine the type of customer service that a staff member is expected to provide? If so, what types of customer service are provided by each classification?
2. Are staff expected to wear name tags or other forms of identification so that members of the public can recognize them as library employees?
3. What form of greeting are staff expected to use when they answer the telephone?
4. Is there a dress code that staff are expected to observe? If so, does it vary based on the classification or duties of the staff member?
5. May staff work on other tasks while they are scheduled on a public service desk? If so, are there any types of work they should not perform when they are scheduled on the desk?
6. May staff have food or drinks at the public service desk?
7. Under what circumstances, if any, may staff make or receive personal phone calls when they are scheduled on the public service desk?
8. Are staff expected to stay at the service desk if they are not assisting a customer, or are they expected to periodically walk around and offer service to customers?
9. Are staff assigned to the public service desk expected to provide assistance with or service for library equipment such as computers and photocopy machines?
10. Are there limits on how much assistance any customer should receive? Does this vary if other customers are waiting?
11. What should a staff member do if there are a number of customers waiting for service?
12. How should staff balance requests for service from customers who are in the library and those who are calling by phone?
13. What should staff do if they are unable to answer a customer's question?
14. What should staff do if the library does not own the material that a customer has requested?

(Cont.)

15. If the library has more than one service point, how should staff handle customer referrals from one point to another?
16. What other expectations does the library have for staff behavior?
17. How will staff members be informed of the library's Customer Service policy?
18. What should a staff member do if he or she observes that another staff member is not following the library's Customer Service policy?
19. To whom should customers be referred if they wish to lodge a complaint about the quality of service they have received? What process will the library follow to respond to such complaints?
20. Will a staff member's observance of the Customer Service policy be reflected on his or her performance evaluation?
21. Does the library have a program to recognize outstanding customer service?

CUSTOMER BEHAVIOR

Policy Questions to Address

1. What type of experience does the library wish its customers to have when they come to the library?
2. How do the library's expectations for customer behavior support the library's goals and objectives?

Regulations Questions to Address

1. Do any state laws or local regulations specifically address behavior in the library? If so, what aspects of behavior are addressed?
2. What expectations does the library have for each customer's behavior to ensure that every customer has a pleasant and successful visit to the library?
3. May a customer use a cell phone or pager in the library?
4. May a customer bring food or drink into the library?
5. May a customer bring any animal other than a service animal into the library?
6. May a customer carry a concealed weapon in the library?
7. What behaviors does the library consider unacceptable when they occur in the library or on library property?
8. How are customers made aware of the expectations the library has for their behavior?
9. What should a staff member do when he or she is aware that a customer is not observing the library's Customer Behavior policy?
10. What should a staff member do if a customer does not respond to the staff member request to cease unacceptable behavior?
11. If the library has security staff, how are they involved in enforcing the library's Customer Behavior policy?
12. Under what circumstances are the police notified when a customer's behavior is inappropriate?
13. To whom should a customer be referred if he or she feels wrongly accused of violating the library's Customer Behavior policy? What process will the library follow to respond to such complaints?
14. To whom should a customer be referred if he or she believes that the library's Customer Behavior policy is inappropriate? What process will the library follow to respond to requests for revision of the Customer Behavior policy?

UNATTENDED CHILDREN

Policy Questions to Address

1. Why does the library have a policy relating to unattended children?
2. How does having a policy for managing unattended children support the library's goals and objectives?

Definition

What does the library mean by the term *unattended children?*

Regulations Questions to Address

1. What should a staff member do when he or she sees an unattended child in the library? Should the staff member's actions vary based on the age of the child?
2. What should a staff member do when a child says he or she cannot find the parent or adult who brought him or her to the library?
3. What should a staff member do when an unattended child is in the library during school hours?
4. What should a staff member do when there is an unattended child in the library and it appears that the library will be closing early due to unexpected circumstances such as inclement weather or a power outage?
5. What should a staff member do when an unattended child is being disruptive?
6. What should a staff member do when an unattended child is engaging in behavior that could be harmful to himself or herself or to other children?
7. What should a staff member do when an unattended child is still at the library at closing time? Is a staff member authorized to drive the child home?
8. Under what circumstances, if any, should a staff member contact the police, social services, or another agency about an unattended child at the library?
9. What information has the library produced for parents and adult caregivers to explain its Unattended Children policy?

CIR-1

LIBRARY CARDS FOR RESIDENTS

Policy Questions to Address

1. Why does the library issue library cards?
2. How does providing library cards and requiring their use support the library's goals and objectives?

Regulations Questions to Address

1. Does the library require an individual to present verification of identity to obtain a library card? If so, what constitutes acceptable verification?
2. Does the library require an individual to present verification of current residence to obtain a library card? If so, what constitutes acceptable verification?
3. What source(s) should staff use to determine whether or not a specific address is within the service area of the library?
4. Does the library require a parent's or legal guardian's signature for a child or young adult under a certain age to obtain a library card?
5. Does the library issue a card to a child or young adult when a parent or legal guardian is not present? If so, what verification of identity or current residence must the child or young adult present?
6. Under what circumstances, if any, may an individual use a post office box as a mailing address?
7. May a teacher or other responsible adult present verification of address for a group of students he or she is bringing to the library?
8. Does the library allow a resident to register online for a library card? If so,
   a. how and when does the library verify the applicant's identity?
   b. how and when does the library verify the applicant's current residence?
   c. how and when does the applicant receive his or her library card?
   d. is there a delay between the time an applicant applies for a library card and when he or she can use library services that require the use of that card (such as borrowing materials or remote access to electronic databases)?
9. If the library has established different borrower types in order to govern circulation policies or gather statistics, what are those categories? What verification of identity, address, or authority to request a library card is required for each borrower type? For example, does the library issue cards to
   a. businesses within the service area of the library?
   b. institutions or organizations within the service area of the library?
   c. schools within the service area of the library?
   d. homebound users?

(Cont.)

10. If a user lives outside the service area of the library but owns a property or business within the service area, may he or she obtain a library card without paying a fee if other nonresidents are charged for a library card? If so, what verification of identity, property ownership, or payment of taxes must be shown?
11. If a teacher lives outside the service area of the library but teaches in a school within the service area, may he or she obtain a library card without paying a fee if other nonresidents are charged for a library card? If so, what verification of identity and proof of teaching assignment must be shown?
12. If a staff member lives outside the service area of the library, may he or she obtain a library card without paying a fee if other nonresidents are charged for a library card?
13. Does the library retain library card applications after library cards have been issued? If so, for how long? Where are they stored? Who is responsible for maintaining the files and discarding applications at the appropriate time?
14. If a customer moves to another location within the library service area, how may she or he report the change of address? Is verification of the new address required before the borrower's record will be changed? If so, what constitutes acceptable verification?
15. Must a customer present his or her library card when borrowing items from the library? Under what circumstances, if any, is this regulation waived?
16. If a customer has lost his or her library card, is there a fee to replace it?
17. Do library cards expire? If so, how long is the initial issuance period? What must a customer do to renew his or her card?
18. Are other libraries issued library cards (or assigned barcode numbers) for the purpose of interlibrary loan? Who is responsible for issuing such library cards?
19. Are departments, branches, or other units of the library issued library cards (or assigned barcode numbers) to allow them to perform such work-related tasks as putting items on reserve or tracing items that are missing? Who is responsible for issuing such cards? How does a department, branch, or unit request one?
20. Under what circumstances, if any, will the library acknowledge to a third party that an individual or organization does have a library card?
21. What statistical information does the library collect about library cardholders? For what purposes are such data collected? How is the customer's privacy protected?

LIBRARY CARDS FOR NONRESIDENTS

Policy Questions to Address

1. Does the library issue library cards to nonresidents? If so, why?
2. How does the provision of library cards to nonresidents support the library's goals and objectives?

Definition

What is the definition of a *nonresident?*

Regulations Questions to Address

1. Is there a fee for a nonresident to obtain a library card? If so, is it an annual fee? Will the library issue a card for a shorter period of time on a prorated basis?
2. Do all nonresidents pay the same fee for a library card, or does the amount vary depending on the individual's place of residence or the services he or she wishes to use?
3. Does the library require a nonresident to present verification of identity to obtain a library card? If so, what constitutes acceptable verification?
4. Does the library require a nonresident to present verification of current residence to obtain a library card? If so, what constitutes acceptable verification?
5. What source(s) should staff use to determine whether or not a specific address is outside the service area of the library?
6. May a child who lives outside the library's service area obtain a nonresident library card? Is there a fee? Does the library require a parent's or legal guardian's signature for a child or young adult under a certain age to obtain a library card?
7. Does the library issue a card to a child or young adult when a parent or legal guardian is not present? If so, what verification of identity and current residence must the child or young adult present?
8. Does the library allow a nonresident to register online for a library card? If so,
   a. how and when does the library verify the applicant's identity?
   b. how and when does the library verify the applicant's current residence?
   c. how and when does the applicant receive his or her library card?
   d. is there a delay between the time an applicant applies for a library card and when he or she can use library services that require the use of that card (such as borrowing materials and remote access to electronic databases)?
   e. if there is a fee for the library card, may the applicant pay with a credit card?

(Cont.)

9. Under what circumstances, if any, may an individual use a post office box as a mailing address?
10. If the library has established different borrower types in order to govern circulation policies or gather statistics, what are those categories? What verification of identity, address, or authority to request a library card is required for each borrower type? For example, does the library issue cards to
    a. businesses outside the service area of the library?
    b. institutions or organizations outside the service area of the library?
    c. schools outside the service area of the library?
    d. homebound users outside the service area of the library?
11. If a user lives outside the service area of the library but owns a property or business within the service area, may he or she obtain a library card without paying a fee if other nonresidents are charged for a library card? If so, what verification of identity, property ownership, or payment of taxes must be shown?
12. If a teacher lives outside the service area of the library but teaches in a school within the service area, may he or she obtain a library card without paying a fee if other nonresidents are charged for a library card? If so, what verification of identity and proof of teaching assignment must be shown?
13. If a staff member lives outside the service area of the library, may he or she obtain a library card without paying a fee if other nonresidents are charged for a library card?
14. Does the library retain library card applications for nonresidents after library cards have been issued? If so, for how long? Where are they stored? Who is responsible for maintaining the files and discarding applications at the appropriate time?
15. If a customer moves to another location outside the library service area, how may she or he report the change of address? Is verification of the new address required before the borrower's record will be changed? If so, what constitutes acceptable verification?
16. If a customer who has a nonresident library card moves to a location inside the library service area, is he or she entitled to a partial refund for the nonresident card if he or she paid a fee to obtain it?
17. Must a customer present his or her nonresident library card when wishing to borrow items from the library? Under what circumstances, if any, is this regulation waived?
18. If a customer has lost his or her nonresident library card, is there a fee to replace it?
19. Do nonresident library cards expire? If so, how long is the initial issuance period? What must a customer do to renew an expired nonresident card?
20. Under what circumstances, if any, will the library acknowledge to a third party that an individual or organization does have a library card?
21. What statistical information does the library collect about nonresident library cardholders? For what purposes are such data collected? How is the customer's privacy protected?

LOAN PERIODS AND LOAN LIMITS

Policy Questions to Address

1. Why does the library establish loan periods?
2. Does the library have loan limits? If so, why?
3. How do loan periods and loan limits support the library's goals and objectives?

Definitions

1. What is a *loan period?*
2. What is a *loan limit?*

Regulations Questions to Address

1. What is the loan period for each type of material that the library circulates? If loan periods vary based on the type of material, what is the rationale for the different loan periods?
2. Is there a maximum number of items that a customer may have on loan at any given time?
3. Is there a maximum number of items of one type (such as books, DVDs, or CDs) that a customer may have on loan at any given time?
4. Is there a limit on the number of items on the same subject that a customer may check out at the same time? If so, how is *same subject* defined? Under what circumstances, if any, may the restriction be overridden? May any member of the library staff override the restriction, or may only supervisors or staff with a particular classification override the restriction?
5. May a customer borrower multiple copies of the same title at the same time? If not, under what circumstances, if any, may library staff override the restriction? May any member of the library staff override the restriction, or may only supervisors or staff with a particular classification override the restriction?
6. Under what circumstances, if any, may library staff override the loan period and either shorten or lengthen it? May any member of the library staff override the loan period, or may only supervisors or staff with a particular classification override the loan period?
7. Under what circumstances, if any, may library staff override the loan limits? May any member of the library staff override the loan limits, or may only supervisors or staff with a particular classification override the loan limits?
8. Under what circumstances, if any, may library staff set temporary limits on the number of materials that may be checked out? For example, may staff limit the number of books on science fair projects that any one customer may borrow when there is heavy demand due to a school assignment? Or may staff limit the number of holiday books that a customer may borrow during the holiday season?

CIR-4

RENEWALS

Policy Questions to Address

1. Does the library permit library customers to renew materials? If so, why? If not, why not?
2. How does the library's renewal policy support the library's goals and objectives?

Definition

What is a *renewal?*

Regulations Questions to Address

1. Which circulating materials, if any, are eligible to be renewed?
2. Which circulating materials, if any, are not eligible to be renewed?
3. May an item be renewed if another customer has placed a reserve on the title?
4. Is there a limit on the number of times an item can be renewed? Does this limit vary based on the type of material? Under what circumstances, if any, may library staff override the limit on the number of times an item can be renewed? May any member of the library staff override the limit, or may only supervisors or staff with a particular classification override the restriction?
5. May customers renew items by phone or online? If so, how will the library inform the community that items may be renewed via those means?
6. May a customer renew an item if it is overdue? Must the fine be paid before the item can be renewed?

CIR-5

RESERVES

Policy Questions to Address

1. Does the library permit customers to reserve materials? If so, why? If not, why not?
2. How does the library policy on reserving materials support the library's goals and objectives?

Definition

What is a *reserve?*

Regulations Questions to Address

1. Who may reserve library materials? Are there any borrower types that are not eligible to reserve library materials?
2. May a customer reserve materials if she or he has outstanding fines, overdue materials, or owes other fees? If not, may staff override that restriction under certain circumstances?
3. Are there restrictions on which types of circulating materials may be reserved? For example,
   a. specific issues of circulating magazines?
   b. uncataloged paperbacks?
   c. new books or DVDs?
   d. E-books?
4. May children reserve materials that are in the adult collection?
5. If an item is currently on the shelf at one library location, may a customer request that it be sent to another library location for pickup? If so, is this considered a reserve? If so, is there a charge for this service?
6. Is there a charge to place a reserve on an item? If so,
   a. is the charge the same for all categories of library borrowers? adults? children? seniors? others?
   b. is the charge the same for all types of library materials? books? DVDs? CDs? other?
   c. under what circumstances, if any, is the reserve fee waived?
   d. is the fee due at the time the reserve is placed or when the item is picked up?
   e. other?
7. May customers request that a reserved item be mailed to them when it becomes available? If so, is there a fee for this service?
8. Is there a limit to the number of items that a customer may have on reserve at any one time?
9. May items be placed on reserve via telephone? Via the online catalog?

(Cont.)

10. May a customer designate the
    a. location where she or he would like to pick up the requested material?
    b. date after which she or he no longer needs the item?
    c. date before which she or he does not wish to receive the item?
11. Will each reserve placed have an automatic cancellation date?
12. May customers reserve items that are on order but have not yet been received by the library?
13. May a customer reserve multiple copies of the same title? If not, are there any exceptions to this regulation for teachers, book discussion group leaders, or others?
14. How are customers informed that the material they have reserved is available for pickup? Is the customer's confidentiality maintained during the notification process?
15. Under what circumstances, if any, may a customer pick up a reserve on behalf of another customer?

CLAIMS RETURNED OR CLAIMS NEVER HAD

Policy Questions to Address

1. Why does the library have a policy on items that users claim to have returned or say that they never had?
2. How does the policy to deal with such situations support the library's goals and objectives?

Definitions

1. What does the library mean by the expression *claims returned?*
2. What does the library mean by the expression *claims never had?*

Regulations Questions to Address

Claims Returned

1. What does the library staff do when a customer reports that he or she returned one or more items that the library circulation system indicates are checked out to that customer?
2. Will the library initiate a search for the item(s) that the customer claims was returned? If so,
   a. how will the library staff know to search for the item(s)?
   b. how often and for how long will the library staff search for the item(s)?
   c. how will the results of the search be reported to the customer?
   d. if the item(s) is found by the library staff, is the user responsible for any overdue fines on the item or items?
   e. if the item(s) is found by the customer, is she or he responsible for overdue fines on the item or items? Are fines calculated from the day the item(s) was due, or is the calculation of fines suspended during the search period?
   f. if the item(s) is not found by the library or the customer, does the library consider the item(s) to be lost and bill the customer for it? Is the customer also responsible for overdue fines on the lost item(s)? Is he or she billed for any other charges associated with the lost item(s), such as a processing fee?
3. Are a customer's borrowing privileges restricted while she or he has one or more "claims returned" searches pending?
4. Does the library maintain a cumulative record of how many "claims returned" occurrences a customer has during a given period of time? If so, how is that information used?

(Cont.)

5. Under what circumstances, if any, may a library staff member clear a "claims returned" item from a customer's record even though the item has not been found? May any member of the library staff clear the item, or may only supervisors or staff with a particular classification clear it?

Claims Never Had

1. What does the library staff do when a customer reports that he or she never had (never checked out) one or more items that the circulation system indicates are checked out to that customer?
2. Will the library initiate a search for the item(s) that the customer claims he or she never borrowed? If so,
   a. how will the library staff know to search for the item(s)?
   b. how often and for how long will the library staff search for the item(s)?
   c. how will the results of the search be reported to the customer?
   d. if the item(s) is found by the library staff, is the user responsible for any overdue fines on the item or items?
   e. if the item(s) is found by the customer, is she or he responsible for overdue fines on it? Are fines calculated from the day the item(s) was due, or is the calculation of fines suspended during the search period?
   f. if the item(s) is not found by the library or the customer, does the library consider the item(s) to be lost and bill the customer for it? Is the customer also responsible for overdue fines on the item(s)? Is he or she billed for any other charges associated with the lost item(s), such as a processing fee?
3. Are a customer's borrowing privileges restricted while she or he has one or more "claims never had" searches pending?
4. Under what circumstances, if any, may a library staff member clear the "claims never had" item(s) from a customer's record even though the item(s) has not been found? May any member of the library staff clear the item(s), or may only supervisors or staff with a particular classification clear it?
5. Does the library maintain a cumulative record of how many "claims never had" occurrences a customer has during a given period of time? If so, how is that information used?

LOST OR DAMAGED MATERIALS

Policy Questions to Address

1. Why does the library charge a customer who loses an item belonging to the library?
2. Why does the library charge a customer who damages an item belonging to the library?
3. How does the library policy on lost or damaged items support the library's goals and objectives?

Definitions

1. What is a *lost item?*
2. What is a *damaged item?*

Regulations Questions to Address

Lost Item

1. If a customer loses an item belonging to the library, is he or she expected to pay for it? If so, does the customer pay
   a. a fixed price based on the type of item that was lost?
   b. the price of the item as shown in the library's database?
   c. the current list price of a replacement copy of the item as shown in *Books in Print* or some other published source?
2. If a customer loses an item belonging to the library, is he or she expected to pay a processing fee to defray the library's cost to delete the lost item and purchase a new copy, should the library choose to do so? If so,
   a. is the processing fee the same for all types of lost items?
   b. does the fee vary based on the type of material that was lost? (For example, does the processing fee for a lost book differ from the processing fee for a lost DVD?)
   c. is the processing fee assessed for cataloged and uncataloged items?
3. If a lost item is overdue at the time a customer wishes to pay for it, is the customer also charged an overdue fine?
4. Will a customer be given a receipt if he or she pays any or all of the fees associated with a lost or damaged item?
5. If a customer finds a lost item after he or she has paid all the charges associated with it, is he or she entitled to a full or partial refund of
   a. the item price?
   b. the processing fee, if one was paid?
   c. overdue fines, if any were paid?

(Cont.)

6. Is there a time limit for returning a lost item and requesting a refund? If the customer was given a receipt showing the charges paid, must he or she present the receipt to obtain a full or partial refund?
7. Will the library accept a replacement item in lieu of a lost item? If so, may any member of the library staff determine that the offered item is an acceptable replacement, or may only supervisors or staff with a particular classification determine that the offered item is an acceptable replacement?

Damaged Item

1. Has the library established a standard charge that a customer who damages an item is expected to pay? Does the amount owed depend on the extent of the damage or the type of item that was damaged? If the amount varies based on the extent of the damage, what criteria should the staff use to determine what damage fee to charge?
2. At what point, if any, will the library consider damage to be so extensive that the customer is assessed the full price of the item? Is the customer also assessed a processing fee, if such a fee is collected for items that have been damaged? If a customer pays the full price for a damaged item, may he or she keep the item?
3. If a damaged item is overdue at the time a customer wishes to pay for it, is the customer also charged an overdue fine?
4. Will the library accept a replacement item in lieu of a damaged item? If so, may any member of the library staff determine that the offered item is an acceptable replacement, or may only supervisors or staff with a particular classification determine that the offered item is an acceptable replacement?

CIR-8

FINES AND FEES

Policy Questions to Address

1. Does the library impose any fines or fees? If so, why? If not, why not?
2. How does the imposition of fines support the library's goals and objectives?
3. How does the imposition of fees support the library's goals and objectives?

Definitions

1. What does the library mean by the term *fine?*
2. What does the library mean by the term *fee?*

Regulations Questions to Address

Fines

1. If the library charges overdue fines,
   a. does the fine vary with the type of material borrowed (for example, juvenile books as compared to adult DVDs)?
   b. does the fine vary with the type of borrower (child as compared to adult)?
   c. is the fine charged for days the library is closed?
   d. is there a grace period before the fine begins?
2. Under what circumstances, if any, may staff waive fines (for example, in cases of emergency illness or death in the family)? May any staff member waive a fine, or may only supervisors or staff with a particular classification waive a fine?
3. Is there a maximum overdue fine that is imposed per item if the item is returned in good condition? If so, is the same maximum fine applied to all types of materials, or does it vary based on the type of material?

Fees

1. Does the library charge a fee if a customer wishes to reserve an item? If so, what is the fee? Is that fee imposed on all borrower types, or are some borrower types exempt from the fee? (See Policy CIR-5 for more information on reserves.)
2. Does the library charge a fee if a customer wishes to request an item through interlibrary loan? If so, what is the fee? Is that fee imposed on all borrower types, or are some borrower types exempt from the fee? (See Policy INF-2 for more information on interlibrary loan.)
3. Does the library charge a fee if a customer loses his or her library card? If so, what is the fee? Is that fee imposed on all borrower types, or are

(Cont.)

some borrower types exempt from the fee? (See Policy CIR-1 and CIR-2 for more information on library cards.)

4. Does the library charge a fee if a customer loses library materials? If so, what is the fee? Does the fee vary based on the type or price of material that is lost? Is that fee imposed on all borrower types, or are some borrower types exempt from the fee? (See Policy CIR-7 for more information on lost materials.)
5. Does the library charge a fee if a customer damages library materials? If so, what is the fee? Does the fee vary based on the type or price of material that is damaged? Is that fee imposed on all borrower types, or are some borrower types exempt from the fee? (See Policy CIR-7 for more information on damaged library materials.)
6. Does the library charge a fee if a customer damages the case or packing material used for various circulating materials (such as CD cases, DVD cases, or hang-up bags for media)? If so, what is the fee? Does the fee vary based on the type or price of material that is damaged? Is that fee imposed on all borrower types, or are some borrower types exempt from the fee? (See Policy CIR-7 for more information on damaged library materials.)
7. Does the library charge a fee if a customer wishes to make a copy of library materials? If so, what is the fee? Does the fee vary based on the type of copy made (such as reproduced on a copy machine, printed on a PC, or printed in color)? Is that fee imposed on all borrower types, or are some borrower types exempt from the fee?
8. Does the library charge a fee if a customer wishes to reserve a meeting room? If so, what is the fee? Does the fee vary based on the room reserved, if the library has more than one room available? Is that fee imposed on all borrower types, or are some borrower types exempt from the fee? (See Policy MNG-8 for more information on meeting rooms.)
9. Does the library charge a fee for Internet access? If so, what is the fee? Does the fee vary based on the amount of time the service is used or on some other criteria? Is that fee imposed on all borrower types, or are some borrower types exempt from the fee? (See Policy INF-3 for more information on Internet use.)
10. Does the library charge a fee if a customer wishes to use a PC for word processing or some other purpose? If so, what is the fee? Does the fee vary based on the amount of time the PC is used or on some other criteria? Is that fee imposed on all borrower types, or are some borrower types exempt from the fee? (See Policy INF-4 for more information on PC use.)
11. Does the library charge a fee if a customer wishes to rent library equipment? If so, what is the fee? Does the fee vary based on the type of equipment rented, the amount of time it is used, or some other criteria? Is that fee imposed on all borrower types, or are some borrower types exempt from the fee?
12. Does the library charge a fee if a customer wishes to have an item mailed to his or her home or office? If so, what is the fee? Is there a standard

(Cont.)

charge per item mailed, or does the fee vary based on the type of material that is being mailed? Is that fee imposed on all borrower types, or are some borrower types exempt from the fee?

13. Does the library charge a fee if a customer wishes to receive in-depth information service? If so, what is the fee? Does the fee vary based on the amount of time required to provide the requested service, the type of expertise required to deliver the service, or some other criteria? Is that fee imposed on all borrower types, or are some borrower types exempt from the fee?
14. Does the library charge a fee if a customer wishes to attend certain training sessions or programs offered by the library? If so, what is the fee? Does the fee vary based on the type of training session or program attended?
15. Does the library retain some or all of the fines and fees collected, or does it turn them over to the funding authority (such as the city or county government)?

BORROWING MATERIALS BY STAFF

Policy Questions to Address

1. Are the borrowing rights and privileges extended to library staff the same as those extended to other library users? If so, why? If not, why not?
2. How do the borrowing rights and privileges extended to staff support the library's goals and objectives?

Regulations Questions to Address

1. Must a library staff member who wishes to borrow library materials have a library card? If so, what verification of identity and current residence must a staff member present to obtain a card? (See Policy CIR-1 for more information on library cards.)
2. May a library staff member issue his or her own library card or must it be issued by another staff member?
3. If a staff member lives outside the library service area, may he or she obtain a library card without paying a fee if other nonresidents are charged a fee? (See Policy CIR-2 for more information on library cards for nonresidents.)
4. May a library staff member check out materials to himself or herself, or must another staff member perform the checkout process?
5. Is a library staff member required to present his or her library card when checking out library materials?
6. May a library staff member check in the materials he or she has borrowed, or must another staff member checked them in?
7. Are library staff members subject to the same borrowing limits as other library users? (See Policy CIR-3 for more information on loan limits.)
8. May library staff members borrow library materials before those materials are available for public use?
9. Are library staff members subject to the same loan periods as other library users? (See Policy CIR-3 for more information on loan periods.)
10. If library users are charged a fee to reserve an item, are library staff members charged the same fee to reserve an item? (See Policy CIR-5 for more information on reserves and Policy CIR-8 for more information on fines and fees.)
11. If library users are charged overdue fines, are library staff members charged the same fines if they return materials that are overdue? (See Policy CIR-8 for more information on fines and fees.)
12. If library users are charged fines or fees for other purposes, are library staff members charged the same fines and fees? (See Policy CIR-8 for more information on fines and fees.)

PRIORITIES FOR REFERENCE SERVICE

Policy Questions to Address

1. What is the purpose of identifying priorities for reference service?
2. How does the establishment of priorities for reference service support the library's goals and objectives?

Definition

How does the library define the term *reference service?*

Regulations Questions to Address

1. Who is responsible for providing reference service?
2. Has the library developed guidelines for the provision of reference service? If so, please attach a copy to this policy.
3. Are all library customers eligible to receive reference service on an equal basis, or do the quantity and type of service vary with the age of the customer, his or her residence, or any other factor?
4. Are there limits on the type or quantity of service that is provided if a question is on one of the following topics:
   a. law?
   b. medicine?
   c. genealogy?
   d. finance (such as investments, taxation, and economic analysis)?
   e. appraisals?
   f. other?
5. Will the library answer questions if it is apparent that the customer is requesting the information to participate in a contest?
6. Will the library answer questions if it is apparent that the customer is requesting the information as part of a homework assignment?
7. How are staff to set priorities for requests for service that are received from customers in the building, customers calling on the telephone, and customers who have submitted questions via the mail, e-mail, or fax? Does the type of service or the amount of assistance provided vary depending on how the question was received?
8. How are customers made aware of the availability of reference service provided by the library?
9. Is reference service provided to individuals who live outside the library's service area? If so, does the type of service or the amount of assistance vary from the service or assistance that would be provided to local residents?

(Cont.)

10. Is there a time limit on how long staff will search for the answer to a question or assist a customer with a request? If so, what is that limit?
11. Under what circumstances, if any, is a question referred to another library staff member for resolution?
12. Under what circumstances, if any, is a question referred to another library?
13. How is a customer's confidentiality protected during a reference service transaction? (See Policy MNG-1 for more information on confidentiality.)
14. If a customer wishes to propose a change to the library's reference service policy, to whom should the proposed changes be sent? What process will be followed to evaluate the suggestion? How will the customer be made aware of the library's decision regarding the suggestion?
15. If, for any reason, a customer is dissatisfied with the reference service he or she has received, to whom should he or she express concern? What process will be followed to investigate the concern? How will the customer be informed of the actions, if any, that the library took?
16. How is reference service evaluated? How is the information gained in the evaluation used to improve service?
17. Does the library collect any statistics about the provision of reference service? If so, what information is collected and how are the statistics used?

INF-2

INTERLIBRARY LOAN

Policy Questions to Address

1. Why does the library allow customers to use interlibrary loan to borrow materials from other libraries?
2. How does the provision of interlibrary loan services support the library's goals and objectives?

Definition

What does the library mean by the term *interlibrary loan?*

Regulations Questions to Address

Borrowing Materials from Other Libraries

1. Does the library participate in any local, regional, state, or national programs that facilitate the borrowing or lending of items to other libraries?
2. How are customers made aware that they may borrow items or receive copies of information from other libraries?
3. Are there certain types of materials that the library will not attempt to borrow on interlibrary loan? If so, what?
4. Are all library cardholders eligible for this service, or are only certain borrower types eligible?
5. Is there a fee for the service? If so, what is the fee? (See Policy CIR-8 for more information on fees.)
6. If the library is charged a fee by the lending library (for example, for borrowing or photocopying an item), is the charge passed along to the customer? Is there an additional service fee or processing charge added by the library? (See Policy CIR-8 for more information on fees.)
7. Is there a limit on how many items a customer may request on interlibrary loan at one time?
8. Is there a limit on how many items a customer may have on interlibrary loan at one time?
9. How does a customer request that an item be obtained on interlibrary loan?
10. Which staff members are responsible for processing interlibrary loan requests received from library customers?
11. How is a customer informed that an item he or she has requested on interlibrary loan is available?
12. How is a customer informed of the date by which the item must be returned?

(Cont.)

13. If the customer does not return the item by the due date, is he or she contacted and informed that the item is overdue? If so, is he or she contacted by phone, mail, e-mail, or another way?
14. If a customer returns an interlibrary loan item after the due date, is there an overdue fine? If so, what is the fine? Is there a maximum fine? (See Policy CIR-8 for more information on fines.)
15. If a customer loses an interlibrary loan item, what charges are assessed? Does he or she pay a fixed fee, the replacement cost of the item, or the original purchase price of the item? Does he or she also pay a service charge or processing fee for each lost item? Is there a maximum charge? (See Policy CIR-7 for more information on lost materials.)
16. If a customer damages an interlibrary loan item, does he or she pay a fee? If so, what is the charge? (See Policy CIR-7 for more information on damaged materials.)
17. How is the customer's confidentiality protected during the interlibrary loan process? (See Policy MNG-1 for more information on confidentiality.)

Lending Materials to Other Libraries

1. Which staff members are responsible for processing requests received from other libraries?
2. Are there certain types of materials that the library will not lend on interlibrary loan even though they are available to local library customers?
3. What is the loan period for an item being lent on interlibrary loan? Does the loan period vary based on the type of material that is being lent?
4. Does the library charge a fee when it lends an item to another library? If so, what is the fee? (See Policy CIR-8 for more information on fees.)
5. Does the library charge a fee when it provides a photocopy to another library? If so, what is the charge? (See Policy CIR-8 for more information on fees.)
6. Does the library charge a fee if an item it lent to another library is returned late? If so, what is the fee? (See Policy CIR-8 for more information on fees.)
7. Does the library charge a fee if an item it lent to another library is returned damaged? If so, what is the fee? (See Policy CIR-7 for more information on damaged materials.)
8. Does the library charge a fee if an item it lent to another library is never returned? (See Policy CIR-7 for more information on lost materials.)
9. Under what circumstances, if any, will the library refuse to lend materials to another library or to a specific customer of another library?

INTERNET USE

Policy Questions to Address

1. Does the library offer unfiltered access to the Internet? Why?
2. Does the library offer filtered access to the Internet? Why?
3. What Internet resources may be accessed using library-provided personal computers (PCs)?
4. How does providing access to the Internet support the library's goals and objectives?

Definitions

1. What does the library mean by the term *Internet use?*
2. If the library provides unfiltered access to the Internet, what does the term *unfiltered* mean?
3. If the library provides filtered access to the Internet, what does the term *filtered* mean?

Regulations Questions to Address

1. May any library customer use library-provided PCs to access the Internet? If not, who is eligible to use library-provided PCs for this purpose?
2. How does the library protect the confidentiality of library customers who use a library-provided PC to access the Internet? (See Policy MNG-1 for more information on confidentiality.)
3. Is there a time limit on how long a library customer can use a PC to access the Internet?
4. May library customers use a library-provided PC to access e-mail, participate in discussion groups or chat rooms, play games, access news groups, and so forth?
5. Has the library established guidelines for Internet use that all library customers are expected to observe? If so, please attach a copy to this policy.
6. How are library customers made aware of the guidelines, if any?
7. If a customer wishes to request a change in the library's Internet Use policy, to whom should he or she make that request? What process will the library follow to evaluate the requested change? How will the customer be informed of the library's decision concerning the requested change?
8. If the library allows printing from library-provided PCs, is there a per-page charge for printing information from an Internet resource? If so, what is the charge? How and when is it collected? (See Policy CIR-8 for more information on fees.)
9. What should a staff member do if he or she notices a library customer not observing the Internet Use policy?

(Cont.)

10. What should a staff member do if a library customer reports that another library customer is not observing the Internet Use policy?
11. What should a staff member do if a library customer reports that he or she is offended or bothered by the Internet use of another library customer?
12. What assistance should staff provide for customers who are unfamiliar with how to access Internet resources?

USE OF LIBRARY-PROVIDED PERSONAL COMPUTERS

Policy Questions to Address

1. For what purposes, other than accessing library information or the Internet, may library customers use library-provided personal computers (PCs)? Why?
2. How does the provision of PCs for public use support the library's goals and objectives?

Regulations Questions to Address

1. May any library customer use library-provided PCs? If not, who is eligible to use them?
2. Are there guidelines for the use of library-provided PCs? If so, please attach a copy to this policy.
3. What should a staff member do if he or she sees a library customer not observing the PC use policy?
4. Is there a charge to use a library-provided PC? If so, what is the charge? How and when is it collected? (See Policy CIR-8 for more information on fees.)
5. Is there a time limit on how long an individual may use a library-provided PC at one time? On one day? During any other period of time?
6. If there is a time limit, does the time limit vary based on the intended use of the PC? If so, what time periods are associated with what activities?
7. Must library customers sign up to use a PC? If so, how is this accomplished?
8. May a library customer reserve a PC at a designated location for a specific time period? If so, how is that accomplished?
9. What assistance, if any, will staff provide with basic start-up operations?
10. What assistance, if any, will staff provide with software applications?
11. Are there restrictions on the types of things that customers may do on a library-provided PC? For example,
    a. may customers store files on the computer's hard drive?
    b. may customers load software onto the library's PCs?
    c. may customers download free software to the library's PCs?
    d. may customers use programs that make sounds that might be heard by other library customers?
12. How are library customers made aware of restrictions on PC use?
13. What should a staff member do if he or she sees a library customer not observing the restrictions on PC use?
14. Does the library allow customers to print from library-provided PCs?
    a. If the library allows printing from library-provided PCs, is there a per-page charge for printing? If so, what is the charge? How and when is it collected?

(Cont.)

   b. If the library allows printing, may customers supply their own paper? If there is a charge for printing, is the charge lower or eliminated if customers provide their own paper?

15. Is it possible for customers to save their work on a CD or floppy disk? If so, will the library provide or sell disks to customers who need them?
16. How may a customer request that additional software be made available on library-provided PCs? What process will the library follow to evaluate the request?
17. If the library provides PCs at more than one facility or at more than one location within the library, are different regulations observed? (For example, are the PCs in the children's room to be used only by children and their caregivers? Or does the time limit on PC use vary from branch to branch depending on the number of PCs that are available?)

GSV-1

PROGRAMS IN THE LIBRARY

Policy Questions to Address

1. What is the purpose of offering programs in the library?
2. Do some types of programs have a higher priority than other types of programs? If so, why?
3. How does the offering of programs in the library support the library's goals and objectives?

Definition

A *program* is a planned public activity (other than a tour or training session) for two or more people that takes place at the library and is presented or sponsored by library staff. A program can be a storytime, lecture, workshop, discussion group, performance, reading, booktalk, puppet show, demonstration, or panel discussion. Programs are presented for adults, young adults, and children.

Regulations Questions to Address

1. Who may present programs in the library?
   a. Only staff?
   b. Only certain classifications of library staff?
   c. Volunteers?
2. What types of programs does the library offer?
3. If volunteers are authorized to present programs in the library, are they required to complete a training program or orientation to qualify as program presenters? Are there restrictions on the types of programs that volunteers can present?
4. Who is responsible for determining the mix of programs (how many of each type) the library will offer?
5. Who is responsible for scheduling programs in the library?
6. Will programs be offered on a regularly scheduled basis? If so,
   a. on what schedule?
   b. who will present the programs?
   c. how will the library inform the community of the programs being offered?
7. Are there guidelines for the presentation of programs in the library that should be followed by all program presenters? If so, please attach a copy to this policy.
8. Is there a minimum or maximum number of anticipated attendees for programs offered in the library? Does that number vary based on the type of program being offered? What is the maximum number of people allowed in the meeting room or other areas of the library according to the fire department occupancy regulations?

(Cont.)

9. Is registration required for any library programs? If so, under what circumstances? How is registration accomplished?
10. May groups (such as school classes, day-care groups, and community organizations) attend regularly scheduled library programs? If so, is prior permission required?
11. Will the library present programs in the library and restrict attendance to the members of a certain group (such as a school class, a day-care center, or a community organization)? If so,
    a. how does the group request a program?
    b. how far in advance must the request be made?
    c. who will present the program?
    d. how many times in a given time period may a group request a program?
12. Will program attendees be given any printed information about the library during the program? If so, what?
13. Will a display of library materials related to the topic of the program be created to enhance the program?
14. Under what circumstances, if any, will the library accept financial support or donations of goods or services to help defray the cost of library programs? If the library is willing to accept such support, how will it recognize contributions?
15. What statistics, if any, will be kept about programs presented in the library? If statistics are kept,
    a. how are they reported?
    b. to whom are they reported?
    c. how frequently are they reported?
16. Will staff be asked to evaluate the programs? If so,
    a. what criteria will be used to evaluate the programs?
    b. how will evaluations be conducted?
    c. to whom will completed evaluations be given?
    d. when are evaluations to be submitted?
    e. how will the results of evaluations be used?
17. Will participants be asked to evaluate the program? If so,
    a. how will the evaluation be conducted?
    b. to whom will the completed evaluations be given?
    c. how will the results of the evaluations be used?

GSV-2

CO-SPONSORED PROGRAMS IN THE LIBRARY

Policy Questions to Address

1. What is the purpose of co-sponsoring programs?
2. Do some programs have a higher priority for co-sponsorship than others?
3. How does co-sponsoring programs support the library's goals and objectives?

Regulations Questions to Address

1. What constitutes co-sponsorship? Is it some or all of the following:
   a. use of a library facility?
   b. staff involvement in the planning or presentation of a program?
   c. displays of library materials related to a program?
   d. promotion of a program by the library on its web page, in printed flyers, and so forth?
   e. financial support
   f. other?
2. With whom will the library co-sponsor programs?
   a. Local, state, or federal governments?
   b. Educational institutions? Public schools? Private schools?
   c. Non-profit organizations?
   d. Friends of the Library? The library foundation? Other library organizations or associations?
   e. Community organizations and clubs?
   f. For-profit companies?
   g. Individuals offering a service?
   h. Other?
3. Do different regulations apply depending on the organization that is requesting the co-sponsorship? If so, which regulations apply?
4. Who is authorized to commit the library to co-sponsor a program?
5. What criteria will be used to determine whether or not the library will co-sponsor a program?
6. Will the library expect a written agreement that outlines the terms, conditions, and responsibilities for each of the partners involved in a co-sponsored program?
7. Will the library co-sponsor programs that are offered outside the library? If so, do additional regulations apply? If so, what are they?
8. Will event partners be allowed to use a co-sponsored program to solicit business?
9. What are the library's expectations about the publicity for a co-sponsored event?
10. Will the library co-sponsor an event if participants must pay a fee to attend the program?

(Cont.)

11. What statistics, if any, will be kept about co-sponsored programs? If statistics are kept,
    a. how are they to be reported?
    b. to whom are they reported?
    c. how frequently are they reported?
12. Will staff be asked to evaluate co-sponsored programs? If so,
    a. what criteria will be used to evaluate a co-sponsored program?
    b. how will the evaluations be conducted?
    c. to whom will the completed evaluations be given?
    d. when are the evaluations to be submitted?
    e. how will the results of the evaluations be used?
13. Will the library's program partners be asked to evaluate co-sponsored programs? If so,
    a. How will the evaluations be conducted?
    b. How will the library be informed of the results of the evaluations?
14. Will participants be asked to evaluate the co-sponsored program? If so,
    a. how will the evaluation be conducted?
    b. to whom will the completed evaluations be given?
    c. how will the results of the evaluations be used?

GSV-3

COMMUNITY PRESENTATIONS

Policy Questions to Address

1. What is the purpose of a community presentation?
2. Do some types of community presentations have a higher priority than other types of community presentations?
3. How does the offering of community presentations support the library's goals and objectives?

Definition

A *community presentation* is a planned activity that takes place outside the library and is presented or sponsored by library staff for two or more people. A community presentation may take place in such diverse locations as a school, a park, a hospital, a nursing home, a convention center, or a religious or community center. A community presentation may be a storytime, booktalk, library talk, library exhibit, performance, demonstration, or discussion group. Community presentations are presented to adults, young adults, or children.

Regulations Questions to Address

1. Who may deliver community presentations?
   a. Only staff?
   b. Only certain classifications of library staff?
   c. Volunteers?
2. If volunteers are authorized to offer community presentations, are they required to complete a training program or orientation?
3. Who is responsible for scheduling community presentations?
4. Are there guidelines for community presentations that should be followed by everyone who offers such presentations? If so, please attach a copy to this policy.
5. Is there a minimum or maximum number of anticipated attendees for a community presentation?
6. How will the library inform the community that it offers community presentations?
7. How does an organization request a community presentation?
8. Is there a form that must be completed by the requesting organization or the library that contains the pertinent information about the community presentation (such as name of group, size of group, date and requested time of presentation, and areas of interest to the group)?
9. Will the attendees be given any printed information about the library during the presentation? If so, what?

(Cont.)

10. Under what circumstances, if any, will the library accept financial support or donations of goods or services to help defray the cost of community presentations? If the library is willing to accept such support, how will it recognize contributions?
11. What statistics, if any, will be kept about the community presentations made by the library? If statistics will be kept,
    a. how are they to be reported?
    b. to whom are they reported?
    c. how frequently are they reported? (See Policy MNG-2 for more information on statistics.)
12. Will staff be asked to evaluate community presentations? If so,
    a. what criteria will be used to evaluate community presentations?
    b. how will the evaluations be conducted?
    c. to whom will the completed evaluations be given?
    d. when are the evaluations to be submitted?
    e. how will the results of the evaluations be used?
13. Will attendees be asked to evaluate the community presentation? If so,
    a. how will the evaluation be conducted?
    b. to whom will the completed evaluations be given?
    c. how will the results of the evaluations be used?

SPECIAL EVENTS

Policy Questions to Address

1. What is the purpose of participating in special events?
2. How does participation in special events support the library's goals and objectives?

Definition

What does the library mean by the term *special event?*

Regulations Questions to Address

1. How does an organization or institution request that the library participate in a special event?
2. How does a staff member propose that the library participate in a special event?
3. What criteria will the library use to determine if a request to participate in a special event will be approved?
4. Under what circumstances, if any, will the library participate in a special event if there is a fee to participate?
5. Who is responsible for determining whether or not the library will participate in a special event?
6. How is the decision on whether or not the library will participate in a special event communicated to the organization, institution, or staff member that proposed the library's participation?
7. If a library participates in a special event, will it authorize
   a. staff time to participate?
   b. use of library equipment?
   c. promotional materials about the event to be distributed in the library if the materials were produced by another organization or institution?
   d. promotion of the event in library-produced publicity materials?
   e. purchase of goods or services to support the event?
   f. other?
8. Who is responsible for the authorization of items 7a through 7f?
9. Are the library and the library staff covered by the library's insurance policy during special events? Under what circumstances, if any, does the library need to acquire additional insurance to provide coverage for a special event?
10. If a special event occurs outside of normal working hours, will staff receive overtime pay for their participation?

TOURS

Policy Questions to Address

1. What is the purpose of a tour?
2. Do some types of tours have a higher priority than other types of tours?
3. How does the offering of tours support the library's goals and objectives?

Definition

A *tour* is a guided presentation of a library facility or department by a staff member or volunteer given to two or more people. A tour can be a general orientation to a building or department, an architectural walk-through, or an introduction to special collections or information services. Tour groups may include adults, young adults, or children.

Regulations Questions to Address

1. Who may present tours?
   a. Only staff?
   b. Only certain classifications of library staff?
   c. Volunteers?
2. If volunteers are authorized to give tours, are they required to complete an orientation to qualify as tour guides?
3. Who is responsible for scheduling tours?
4. Will tours be offered on a regularly scheduled basis? If so,
   a. on what schedule?
   b. who will conduct the tours?
   c. how will the library inform the community that regularly scheduled tours will be offered?
5. Are there guidelines that should be followed by everyone who gives tours of the library? If so, please attach a copy to this policy.
6. Must tours be scheduled in advance? If so, how far in advance?
7. Is there a minimum or maximum number of participants in a tour group? Does the number vary based on the age of the tour participants?
8. How will the library inform community residents that they can request a tour of the library?
9. How do organizations request a tour?
10. Is there a form that must be completed by the requesting organization or the library that contains the pertinent information about the requested tour (such as name of group, size of group, requested date and time of tour, and areas of interest to the group)?

(Cont.)

11. Will customized tours be developed for a group? If so,
    a. under what conditions?
    b. how much lead time is required?
12. Will tour attendees be given any printed information about the library during a tour? If so, what?
13. Under what circumstances, if any, will the library accept financial support or donations of goods or services to help defray the cost of library tours? If the library is willing to accept such support, how will it recognize contributions?
14. What statistics, if any, will be kept about the tours conducted by the library? If statistics will be kept,
    a. how are they to be reported?
    b. to whom are they reported?
    c. how frequently are they reported?
15. Will staff be asked to evaluate tours? If so,
    a. how will the evaluations be conducted?
    b. to whom will the completed evaluations be given?
    c. when are the evaluations to be submitted?
    d. how will the results of the evaluations be used?
16. Will tour participants be asked to evaluate the tour? If so,
    a. how will the evaluation be conducted?
    b. to whom will the completed evaluations be given?
    c. how will the results of the evaluations be used?

COMPUTER TRAINING FOR THE PUBLIC

Policy Questions to Address

1. Why does the library offer computer training for the public?
2. Do some types of computer training have a higher priority than other types of computer training?
3. How does the offering of computer training for the public support the library's goals and objectives?

Regulations Questions to Address

1. What types of computer training will be offered?
2. What is the maximum number of attendees that will be accepted in each class?
3. Who will offer computer training for the public?
   a. Only staff?
   b. Only certain classifications of library staff?
   c. Volunteers?
   d. For-profit contractors?
4. If volunteers are authorized to present computer training, are they required to complete a training program or orientation to qualify as computer trainers?
5. Who is responsible for designing computer training and producing any related materials that will be used in the classes? Will attendees be given workbooks or handouts that they can take home with them?
6. Will all computer trainers be expected to present a standard curriculum for each type of computer training that the library offers?
7. Is there a fee to attend computer training? Under what circumstances, if any, will the fee be waived?
8. If there is a fee, when must it be paid (for example, at the time of registration or prior to the start of the class)? (See Policy CIR-8 for more information on fees.)
9. Are there restrictions on who can attend the training? If so, are they based on
   a. age?
   b. residence?
   c. prior attendance?
10. Is registration required to attend computer training? If so, how does a person register?
11. If registration is required, who is responsible for
   a. registering attendees?
   b. notifying attendees that they have been registered?
   c. determining and publicizing that a session is filled?

(Cont.)

12. Who is responsible for scheduling computer training sessions?
13. Where will computer training be offered?
14. Will attendees be given any printed information about the library during training sessions? If so, what?
15. Under what circumstances, if any, will the library accept financial support or donations of goods or services to help defray the cost of computer training programs? If the library is willing to accept such support, how will it recognize contributions?
16. What statistics, if any, will be kept about computer training sessions presented in the library? If statistics will be kept,
    a. how are they to be reported?
    b. to whom are they reported?
    c. how frequently are they reported?
17. Will staff be asked to evaluate the training? If so,
    a. what criteria will be used to evaluate the training?
    b. how will the evaluations be conducted?
    c. to whom will the completed evaluations be given?
    d. when are the evaluations to be submitted?
    e. how will the results of the evaluations be used?
18. Will participants be asked to evaluate the training? If so,
    a. how will the evaluation be conducted?
    b. to whom will the completed evaluations be given?
    c. how will the results of the evaluations be used?

Appendix B

Instructions and Workforms

WORKFORM 1
Contents of the Library Policy Manual

Purpose of Workform 1

Use this workform to record the current official library policies included in the library policy manual.

Who Should Complete Workform 1

This workform should be completed by the chairperson of the Policy Audit Advisory Committee and sent to the staff for additions or corrections.

Factors to Consider When Completing Workform 1

1. All official policy elements have been approved by the board or the library director. Anything that has not been officially approved is a practice.
2. Complete a separate copy of Workform 1 for each category of policies under review.
3. It is important to include the date of the latest revision of the policy or policy element.
4. This workform is most useful for libraries that issue individual policies. If the official policy manual in your library is in a narrative format, you probably won't want to use this workform.
5. This workform should be distributed to staff at the same time as Workform 2.
6. This workform should be distributed as an attachment to a full explanation of the policy audit process. See figure 9 in chapter 2 for a sample memorandum.

To Complete Workform 1

1. Enter the name of the policy category on the first line.
2. **Column A** Enter the number of the policy, if it has been previously numbered. If it has not been numbered, leave this column blank
3. **Column B** Enter the subject or title of the policy.
4. **Column C** Enter the date the policy was originally issued or the date it was revised.
5. **Column D** Enter the name of the person or group who approved it.

Factors to Consider When Reviewing Workform 1

1. Be sure that policies included in the official library policy manual are recorded on this form. Use Workform 2 for other official policy elements.
2. Be sure that you list the most recent revision of each policy in the manual.

WORKFORM 1

Contents of the Library Policy Manual

Policy Category ______________________________

A. No.	**B. Subject**	**C. Date Issued/Revised**	**D. Approved By**

Prepared by ______________________________ Date ______________

WORKFORM 2
Other Policy Statements, Regulations, Procedures, and Guidelines

Purpose of Workform 2

Use this workform to create a summary of any policy statements, regulations, procedures, or guidelines that the chairperson of the Policy Audit Advisory Committee knows have been created but have not been incorporated into the library's official policy manual.

Who Should Complete Workform 2

This workform should be completed by the chairperson of the Policy Audit Advisory Committee and sent to the staff for additions or corrections.

Factors to Consider When Completing Workform 2

1. This form is to include policy elements that the chairperson of the Policy Audit Advisory Committee *knows* about but have not been incorporated into the official policy manual. It is very possible that the chairperson will not have any information about such policy elements. To gain the needed information, the chairperson should distribute a blank copy of the workform to the staff.
2. This workform is most useful for libraries that issue individual policies. If the official policy manual in your library is in a narrative format, you probably won't want to use this workform.
3. This workform should be distributed to staff at the same time as Workform 1.
4. This workform should be distributed as an attachment to a full explanation of the policy audit process. See figure 9 in chapter 2 for a sample memorandum.

To Complete Workform 2

1. **Column A** Enter the number of the policy element, if it has a number. If it does not have a number, leave this column blank.
2. **Column B** Enter the category of the policy element.
3. **Column C** Enter the policy element: policy statement, regulations, procedures, or guidelines.
4. **Column D** Enter the subject of the policy element.
5. **Column E** Enter the date the policy element was originally issued or the date it was revised.
6. **Column F** Enter the name of the library unit that issued the document.
7. **Column G** Enter the name of the person or group who approved the element.

Factors to Consider When Reviewing Workform 2

1. The information on this workform is more likely to come from staff than from the chairperson of the Policy Audit Advisory Committee.
2. The policy elements reported on this form are likely to have been developed and approved at the unit level of the library.

WORKFORM 2

Other Policy Statements, Regulations, Procedures, and Guidelines

A. No.	B. Category	C. Element	D. Subject	E. Date Issued/ Revised	F. Unit	G. Approved By

Prepared by ______________________ Date ______________

WORKFORM 3
Policy Audit Inventory Log

Purpose of Workform 3

Use this workform to keep track of the policy-related documents received from staff during the policy audit inventory.

Who Should Complete Workform 3

This workform should be completed by the chairperson of the Policy Audit Advisory Committee.

Factors to Consider When Completing Workform 3

1. The chairperson of the Policy Audit Advisory Committee is probably going to receive multiple copies of the same documents from various staff members. This form will help the chairperson identify duplicates.
2. Complete as many columns on the form as possible. The information will be needed later in the process.
3. Assign and write the log number (column A) on each document as it is logged.
4. Three-hole punch documents after they have been logged and place them in numerical order in a notebook.
5. Check apparent duplicate documents carefully to ensure that they are in fact exact duplicates. If they are exact duplicates, discard one of them. If there are differences in two copies of a document, log them both, using the log number plus the letter A for the first version that was received and the same log number plus the letter B for the second version.

To Complete Workform 3

1. **Column A** Assign a log number to each document as it is received and enter the log number in this column.
2. **Column B** Enter the name of the library unit that submitted the document.
3. **Column C** Enter policy element: policy statement, regulations, procedures, or guidelines.
4. **Column D** Enter the subject of the policy element.

Factors to Consider When Reviewing Workform 3

Be sure that Workform 3 includes all of the policy elements received.

WORKFORM 3
Policy Audit Inventory Log

A. Log No.	B. Received From	C. Element	D. Subject

Prepared by ________________________ Date ______________

Policy Audit Inventory Results

Purpose of Workform 4

Use this workform to record the results of the review of each policy element collected during the policy audit inventory.

Who Should Complete Workform 4

This workform should be completed by the chairperson of the Policy Audit Advisory Committee.

Factors to Consider When Completing Workform 4

1. Carefully review Workform 3, Policy Audit Inventory Log, and identify and collect any items in the log that apply to the category under review.
2. Analyze each document carefully to determine what elements it contains. Use the definitions of *policy statement, regulation, procedure,* and *guideline* from chapter 1 as the basis for your review and analysis.
3. As you make your decisions about the elements in each document, note them in the margin. For example, write "policy statement" by the part of the document that appears to be a policy statement, "regulation" by each regulation, "procedure" by each procedure, and so. Remember, your decisions may differ from the current labels.
4. If some documents appear to belong in this category but are not covered in the master category list developed in Step 3.1 of chapter 2, list them on Part 2 of the workform, in the "Other Documents in This Category" section. Chapter 3 explains how to evaluate them further.
5. If the current library policy manual is a narrative document, this is going to be a more difficult process. See chapter 2 for help in deconstructing a narrative policy manual.

To Complete Workform 4

1. Enter the name of the policy category on the first line.
2. Complete the "Documents in the Master Category" section (Part 1).
   a. **Column A** Enter the number that has been assigned to the subject in the master category list.
   b. **Column B** Enter the subject of the policy from the master category list.
   c. **Column C** Indicate whether or not the policy contains a policy statement by placing an X in the Yes or No column.
   d. **Column D** Indicate whether or not the policy contains regulations by placing an X in the Yes or No column.
   e. **Column E** Indicate whether or not the policy contains procedures by placing an X in the Yes or No column.
   f. **Column F** Indicate whether or not the policy contains guidelines by placing an X in the Yes or No column.
3. Complete the "Other Documents in This Category" section (Part 2). Begin by collecting all of the policy elements that appear to belong in the category under review but were not included in the master category list. Workforms 2 and 3 should provide this information.
   a. **Column A** Leave this column blank.
   b. **Column B** Enter the subject of any other documents that seem to belong in this category but were not included in the master category list.
   c. **Column C** Indicate whether or not the policy contains a policy statement by placing an X in the Yes or No column.
   d. **Column D** Indicate whether or not the policy contains regulations by placing an X in the Yes or No column.
   e. **Column E** Indicate whether or not the policy contains procedures by placing an X in the Yes or No column.
   f. **Column F** Indicate whether or not the policy contains guidelines by placing an X in the Yes or No column.

Factors to Consider When Reviewing Workform 4

Be sure that you understand the differences among the four policy elements and have correctly identified each element. Workform 5 provides a way to test your understanding of the definitions of the policy elements.

Policy Audit Inventory Results

Policy Category ______________________________

Part 1: Documents in the Master Category

A. No.	B. Subject	C. Policy Statement		D. Regulations		E. Procedures		F. Guidelines	
		Yes	No	Yes	No	Yes	No	Yes	No

Prepared by ______________________________ Date ______________

Policy Audit Inventory Results

Part 2: Other Documents in This Category

A. No.	B. Subject	C. Policy Statement		D. Regulations		E. Procedures		F. Guidelines	
		Yes	No	Yes	No	Yes	No	Yes	No

Prepared by ______________________________ Date ______________

WORKFORM 5
Defining Policy Elements

Purpose of Workform 5

Use this workform to test your understanding of the definitions of the four policy elements.

Who Should Complete Workform 5

This workform should be completed by everyone involved in the policy audit and the development of revised or new policies.

Factors to Consider When Completing Workform 5

1. Each item is an example of one of the four policy elements.
2. Carefully read the definitions of the four policy elements presented in chapter 1 before beginning Workform 5.
3. If you have trouble identifying one of the examples in Workform 5, refer again to the definitions of the four policy elements in chapter 1.

To Complete Workform 5

1. Enter your name on the first line.
2. Read each numbered statement in column A and determine whether it is a policy statement, a regulation, a procedure, or a guideline.
3. Write your decision in column B.

Factors to Consider When Reviewing Workform 5

1. Compare your answers with those on the answer sheet.
2. Discuss any questions or issues that arose as you identified the policy elements on the workform.
3. If necessary, refer again to the definitions of the four policy elements in chapter 1.

WORKFORM 5
Defining Policy Elements

Name ______________________________

A. Example	B. Element
1. A user may not have more than 25 items on loan at any given time.	
2. After the application to use the meeting room has been completed, a. file the white copy in the meeting room notebook. b. give the yellow copy to the individual reserving the meeting room. c. place the green copy in the mailbox designated Custodial Services in the staff room.	
3. The XXX Public Library must maintain an accurate and current record of user addresses. An applicant for a library card must, therefore, present valid verification of identity and residence to obtain a library card. The proof of address is particularly important to support the library's efforts to encourage the return of borrowed county property.	
4. Meeting rooms will be available for use only during the hours the library is open to the public. Exceptions may be made by the library director.	
5. Search the patron database to establish that the applicant is indeed a new borrower.	
6. Successful Preschool Storytimes • When planning a storytime, keep the age of your intended audience in mind. • Select books that you enjoy. • Practice a few days before the presentation. • Greet the children as they enter the storytime area. Let them know that you are really glad to see them. • Hold the book in such a way that the children can see the pictures.	
7. A library user who has forgotten or temporarily misplaced his or her library card may charge up to ten items if he or she can show valid proof of identity and current address.	
8. Processing fees will not be charged for damaged uncataloged items.	
9. The XXX Public Library is the community living room of XXX County. Therefore, the library provides meeting rooms in all of its facilities to enable community residents to share ideas and to learn from one another.	
10. Send the completed Request for Reconsideration form to the Collection Development Department in the next interagency delivery.	
11. Tours are presented by staff members or volunteers who have completed the tour guide training offered by the library volunteer coordinator.	

(Cont.)

A. Example	B. Element
12. Customer Behavior Expectations • Courteous behavior toward other library customers and staff members is expected. • The library is not responsible for unattended children and expects that children under eight years of age will be accompanied by a parent or an adult responsible for them. • Customers are requested to turn off their cell phones and pagers or place them on vibrate when in the reference area of the library.	
13. To renew an item that a customer has brought to the library, the circulation clerk will a. choose the renew function from the circulation menu. b. scan the barcode on the borrower's library card. c. scan the barcode on the item the customer wishes to renew. d. stamp the new due date on the item. e. inform the customer of the new due date. f. return the item to the borrower.	
14. Library users will be limited to one hour of computer use if others are waiting to use the PCs.	
15. The XXX Public Library supports access to basic services and materials, without individual charge, whenever possible. The Library Board of Trustees annually establishes fees and fines for the XXX Public Library. These charges are intended to ensure maximum availability of library materials and to support the board's philosophy of charging for value-added services.	
16. Each morning maintenance staff will check all meeting rooms to be sure that tables and chairs have been stored appropriately and that the rooms are clean and ready for use.	
17. Library DVDs have a loan period of seven days.	
18. The reference interview is the most important part of the reference process. The reference interview starts when you greet the library user.	

Defining Policy Elements

ANSWER SHEET

A. Example	**B. Element**
1. A user may not have more than 25 items on loan at any given time.	*Regulation*
2. After the application to use the meeting room has been completed, a. file the white copy in the meeting room notebook. b. give the yellow copy to the individual reserving the meeting room. c. place the green copy in the mailbox designated Custodial Services in the staff room.	*Procedure*
3. The XXX Public Library must maintain an accurate and current record of user addresses. An applicant for a library card must, therefore, present valid verification of identity and residence to obtain a library card. The proof of address is particularly important to support the library's efforts to encourage the return of borrowed county property.	*Policy Statement*
4. Meeting rooms will be available for use only during the hours the library is open to the public. Exceptions may be made by the library director.	*Regulation*
5. Search the patron database to establish that the applicant is indeed a new borrower.	*Procedure*
6. Successful Preschool Storytimes • When planning a storytime, keep the age of your intended audience in mind. • Select books that you enjoy. • Practice a few days before the presentation. • Greet the children as they enter the storytime area. Let them know that you are really glad to see them. • Hold the book in such a way that the children can see the pictures.	*Guideline*
7. A library user who has forgotten or temporarily misplaced his or her library card may charge up to ten items if he or she can show valid proof of identity and current address.	*Regulation*
8. Processing fees will not be charged for damaged uncataloged items.	*Regulation*
9. The XXX Public Library is the community living room of XXX County. Therefore, the library provides meeting rooms in all of its facilities to enable community residents to share ideas and to learn from one another.	*Policy Statement*
10. Send the completed Request for Reconsideration form to the Collection Development Department in the next interagency delivery.	*Procedure*
11. Tours are presented by staff members or volunteers who have completed the tour guide training offered by the library volunteer coordinator.	*Regulation*

(Cont.)

ANSWER SHEET

A. Example	B. Element
12. Customer Behavior Expectations • Courteous behavior toward other library customers and staff members is expected. • The library is not responsible for unattended children and expects that children under eight years of age will be accompanied by a parent or an adult responsible for them. • Customers are requested to turn off their cell phones and pagers or place them on vibrate when in the reference area of the library.	*Guideline*
13. To renew an item that a customer has brought to the library, the circulation clerk will a. choose the renew function from the circulation menu. b. scan the barcode on the borrower's library card. c. scan the barcode on the item the customer wishes to renew. d. stamp the new due date on the item. e. inform the customer of the new due date. f. return the item to the borrower.	*Procedure*
14. Library users will be limited to one hour of computer use if others are waiting to use the PCs.	*Regulation*
15. The XXX Public Library supports access to basic services and materials, without individual charge, whenever possible. The Library Board of Trustees annually establishes fees and fines for the XXX Public Library. These charges are intended to ensure maximum availability of library materials and to support the board's philosophy of charging for value-added services.	*Policy Statement*
16. Each morning maintenance staff will check all meeting rooms to be sure that tables and chairs have been stored appropriately and that the rooms are clean and ready for use.	*Procedure*
17. Library DVDs have a loan period of seven days.	*Regulation*
18. The reference interview is the most important part of the reference process. The reference interview starts when you greet the library user.	*Guideline*

Purpose of Workform 6
Use this workform to record the evaluation criteria developed for each policy element.

Who Should Complete Workform 6

This workform should be completed by the members of the Policy Audit Advisory Committee.

Factors to Consider When Completing Workform 6

A. Criteria for Policy Statements

Policy Statement: A *policy statement* is a brief written statement that describes *why* the library does something. Policy statements are written from the customer's point of view and approved by the library's governing authority.

Obviously, an effective and well-written policy statement is one that meets this definition. But how do you know if the policy statements in your library meet the definition? How do you develop criteria to evaluate policy statements? The best place to begin is to deconstruct the definition of a policy statement into declarative sentences and insert a value-laden word such as *good* or *excellent* or *effective* in the appropriate place in the sentence. The result is a list of four core evaluation criteria for policy statements.

- An excellent policy statement is brief.
- An effective policy statement describes why the library does something.
- An excellent policy statement is written from the customer's point of view.
- An excellent policy statement has been approved by the library's governing authority.

Now you need to consider if there are additional criteria that are important in your library. One way to do this is to read some of the library's policy statements. As you read them, ask yourself the following questions:

1. Is the policy statement written in language that the typical library user would understand? Is it clear what is meant by the terms used in the policy statement? Are the definitions clear?
2. Does the policy statement indicate how the policy supports the library's goals and objectives?
3. When the policy statement is implemented, does it actually support the library's goals and objectives or does it hinder them?
4. Does all of the information included in the policy statement actually belong in the policy statement, or should some of it be deleted or moved to another element of the policy?
5. Does the policy statement refer to any state laws or local regulations that relate to the policy topic?
6. Will the policy statement be one that the typical library user and the library staff can support?

If the answers to these questions are an unqualified yes, then you probably have a good policy statement. Think for a few moments about what caused you to answer yes to each of the questions. The reasons you answered yes can often be transformed into criteria to evaluate other policy statements.

If the answer is no or not really, then you probably have a policy statement that needs some revision. Look at the policy statements again. What was wrong with the policy statements that caused you to answer no? What would need to be done to them before you could answer yes? The answers to those questions can also be transformed into criteria that you can use to evaluate other policy statements.

For example, you might add the following elements to your list of criteria:

- An excellent library policy is easily understood by both the staff and the public.
- An effective policy statement is one that supports the library's goals and objectives.
- An excellent policy statement is one that is up-to-date and reflects the library's current environment.

As noted earlier, this is a somewhat intuitive process. The foregoing questions are not intended to be all-inclusive. They provide a starting point for discussion. As the members of the group responsible for creating the evaluation criteria consider the library's existing policies, there is little doubt that additional questions will be identified.

B. Criteria for Regulations

Regulation: A *regulation* is a specific, written rule that further defines policy, describing *what* must be done to support the policy. Regulations are normally approved by the library's governing authority.

Begin by deconstructing the definition and stating each of its components as a declarative sentence. Once again, use a value-laden word such as *effective* or *excellent* to convey quality. Doing so leads to the following six core evaluation criteria:

- An effective regulation is one that derives from the policy statement and is supportive of the library's goals and objectives.
- An excellent regulation is specific.
- An effective regulation further defines the policy.
- An excellent regulation supports the policy statement.

(Cont.)

- An effective regulation tells what must be done to support the policy.
- An excellent regulation has been approved by the library's governing authority.

When you have reviewed and made any necessary revisions in the core criteria, select two of the library's current regulations to review, compare, and contrast. Since regulations are not written in a vacuum, you'll also have to read the policy statement associated with the regulations. The comparison will be most useful if you can locate two policies in the same category with regulations that differ in number or depth. For example, you might select a circulation policy that has more than a dozen regulations and a circulation policy that has two or three regulations.

Read each policy statement and its associated regulations and ask yourself the following questions:

1. Does each of the regulations logically flow from the policy statement?
2. Does each of the regulations support the policy statement?
3. Is each of the regulations specific? When appropriate, do they state
    a. how many? ("A borrower may have a maximum of five videotapes on loan at one time.")
    b. how long? ("A library user may reserve the meeting room six weeks in advance of the desired date of use.")
    c. if there is a fee, how much it is? ("Library users will be charged $.10 for each page they print when using the library PCs.")
    d. where the service is provided? ("Computer training classes will be held in the training lab at the central library.")
    e. what classification of staff will provide the service or complete the task? ("The branch manager at each location is responsible for submitting the statistical report to library administration by the third working day after the end of each month.")
    f. to whom do the regulations apply? ("An individual who owns property in Tree County is eligible for a free library card even if his or her primary residence is outside the county limits.")
    g. under what circumstances, if any, exceptions may be made? ("Library customers may use the microfilm reader for more than the one-hour limit if no other users are waiting to use the machine.")
    h. which staff members have the authority to make exceptions? ("Reference librarians may allow noncirculating items from the reference collection to be borrowed overnight.")
    i. other information, where specified?
4. Does all of the information actually belong in the regulations, or should some of it be deleted or moved to another section of the policy?
5. Do the regulations address all of the situations that the staff are likely to encounter when implementing the policy? In other words, by reading the regulations, will the staff know what they are supposed to do (but not how to do it)?
6. Are the regulations written in a language that the typical library staff member can understand?
7. Are the regulations reasonable? Can the typical library user and the typical library staff member support them?

Compare your answers to the questions above for the regulations supporting the two policies that you reviewed. You may find that the more regulations the policy had, the easier it was for you to answer yes to many of the questions, but that is certainly not always the case. It is the quality of the regulations, not the quantity, that is important. Did you answer yes more often for the regulations that supported one policy rather than the other? If so, what made the difference? What factors led you to answer no to more questions about the regulations for the other policy?

Remember, too, that the preceding list of questions is just a starting point. As you review and discuss the regulations, you and the rest of the committee will undoubtedly identify additional questions you need to ask. Use the answers to all of your questions to expand the list of criteria you will use to evaluate regulations. For example, you might add the following criteria to your list:

- An excellent regulation supports the policy to which it refers.
- An excellent regulation is specific.
- An excellent regulation is written in lay terms that the public can understand.
- An effective regulation would be considered reasonable by the typical library user.

C. Criteria for Procedures

Procedure: A *procedure* is a written, step-by-step description of *how* the staff will carry out the policy and regulations. Procedures are more flexible than regulations and will change as the tools available to staff change. Frontline staff may be allowed to modify procedures in certain circumstances. Procedures are developed by staff and approved by library man-

(Cont.)

agers. They are not reviewed by or approved by the library's governing authority.

Most library staff members are familiar with procedures and understand exactly what purpose they serve. They know how to create an outline and use it to describe a linear process. Therefore committee members will probably find that criteria for evaluating procedures are easier to develop than criteria for evaluating policy statements and regulations.

The process begins by deconstructing the definition of a procedure and stating each of the components of the definition as a declarative sentence, adding a value-laden word such as *effective* or *excellent* to convey quality. For example:

- An excellent procedure is a step-by-step description of how the staff will carry out the policy and regulations.
- An effective procedure may be modified by staff under certain circumstances.
- An effective procedure has been developed by staff who are familiar with the task to be performed.
- An excellent procedure has been approved by library managers.

Once you have reviewed and revised the core criteria, select two of the library's current procedures to review, compare, and contrast. Since procedures shouldn't exist unless they are connected to a policy statement and regulations, you'll also have to read those related elements. The comparison will be most useful if one policy has a long, detailed set of procedures and the other policy has a very brief set of procedures. As you read the two policies (the policy statement, regulations, and procedures), ask yourself the following questions:

1. Do the procedures provide a step-by-step description of how to carry out the policy and regulations?
2. Are the procedures complete? Have all steps been included and have all situations been addressed?
3. Does all of the information actually belong in the procedures, or should some of it be deleted or moved to another section of the policy?
4. Are the procedures presented in sufficient detail that a new staff member or a staff member who is unfamiliar with the task could complete it by following the procedures?
5. Do the procedures support the regulations and the policy statement?
6. Are the procedures presented in a logical order?
7. Are the procedures written in a style and vocabulary that the typical library staff member can understand?
8. Are the procedures up-to-date? Do they accurately reflect the forms, computer software, practices, and so forth that staff are expected to use or observe?
9. If a form is mentioned in the procedure, has a copy of the form been included with the policy? Have instructions been provided on how to complete the form?
10. Do the procedures indicate when staff may modify them?
11. Have the procedures been approved by library management?

Compare your answers for the two policies that you reviewed. Are the more detailed procedures easier to follow than the less detailed ones? Did you answer yes more often for the procedures that supported one policy rather than the other? If so, what made the difference? What factors led you to answer no to more questions about the procedures that supported the other policy? As you compare and discuss the two sets of procedures, make note of any additional questions you identify. The answers to those questions should also be included in your criteria. For example, you might decide to add the following two criteria to your list:

- An excellent procedure accurately reflects the current functionality of the library's automation system.
- An effective procedure provides samples of forms as well as instructions about how to complete them.

D. Criteria for Guidelines

Guideline: A *guideline* is a description of best practices that provides suggestions for staff on the most efficient ways to implement policy statements, regulations, and procedures. Guidelines are more philosophical than policy statements, regulations, or procedures and often are developed by staff committees. Guidelines are always approved by the library director but are rarely reviewed by the library's governing authority.

By definition, every policy should include a policy statement, regulations, and procedures. However, every policy will not include guidelines. In fact, you many find that few of your policies need guidelines. The policies for which guidelines are appropriate are apt to relate to customer services, information services, and group services.

(Cont.)

Follow the same process you used to develop the previous evaluation criteria. Begin by deconstructing the definition and stating each of its components as a declarative sentence that contains a value-laden word to denote quality. For example,

- An effective guideline describes best practice.
- An excellent guideline provides suggestions for staff on the most efficient ways to implement policy statements, regulations, and procedures.

If your library does not currently have any guidelines, then the basic criteria derived from the definition will probably be used to evaluate any new guidelines that are developed in chapter 4.

If the library currently has one or more sets of guidelines, select one or two of them to review. Remember, you will also have to review the policy statement, regulations, and procedures that the guidelines support. If one or more of those components are missing, then review all that are available. Once you have completed the review, ask yourself the following questions:

1. Do the guidelines describe best practice?
2. Do the guidelines provide suggestions for staff on how to implement policy statements, regulations, and procedures?
3. Does all of the information actually belong in the guidelines, or should some of it be deleted or moved to another section of the policy?
4. Are the guidelines sufficiently detailed to address the majority of situations that a staff member might encounter?
5. Are the guidelines sufficiently detailed to answer the majority of questions the staff might ask?
6. Do the guidelines provide new staff with concrete examples of how the policy should be implemented?
7. Are the guidelines written in a style and vocabulary that the typical library staff member can understand?
8. Are the guidelines up-to-date? Do they accurately reflect how staff members are currently expected to implement the policy?
9. Have the guidelines been approved by the library director?

If you had more than one set of guidelines to consider when you answered the preceding questions, you can compare the sets of answers as you did when examining your policy statements, regulations, and procedures. If you answered yes more often for one set of guidelines than another, what made the difference? Why did you answer no to more questions for the other set of guidelines? If you reviewed only one set of guidelines, what would have made those guidelines better? If other questions arose during your review, make note of both those questions and their answers.

Based on your review of the existing guidelines, develop the additional criteria that your library will use to evaluate the existing guidelines and any future guidelines. For example:

- An effective guideline supports the policy statement and the regulations.
- An effective guideline, when observed by staff, will help the library achieve its goals and objectives.
- An excellent guideline is written in a style that is clear, concise, and comprehensible.

To Complete Workform 6

1. Indicate any changes that have been made to the preprinted evaluation criteria for the policy element that is being discussed.
2. Enter the locally developed evaluation criteria for the policy element that is being discussed. Remember that each evaluation criterion must be stated as a value-laden declarative sentence.

Factors to Consider When Reviewing Workform 6

1. If these criteria are followed, will they lead to excellent and effective policy elements?
2. Are any of the criteria unclear?
3. Do any of the criteria conflict with the others?

WORKFORM 6
Evaluation Criteria

A. Criteria for Policy Statements

1. An excellent policy statement is brief.
2. An effective policy statement describes why the library does something.
3. An excellent policy statement is written from the customer's point of view.
4. An excellent policy statement has been approved by the library's governing authority.
5. ______________________________

   ____

   ____
6. ______________________________

   ____

   ____
7. ______________________________

   ____

   ____
8. ______________________________

   ____

   ____
9. ______________________________

   ____

   ____
10. ______________________________

    ____

    ____

Prepared by ______________________________ Date ______________

Evaluation Criteria

B. Criteria for Regulations

1. An effective regulation is one that derives from the policy statement and is supportive of the library's goals and objectives.
2. An excellent regulation is specific.
3. An effective regulation further defines the policy.
4. An excellent regulation supports the policy statement.
5. An effective regulation tells what must be done to support the policy.
6. An excellent regulation has been approved by the library's governing authority.
7. ______________________________

   ____

   ____
8. ______________________________

   ____

   ____
9. ______________________________

   ____

   ____
10. ______________________________

    ____

    ____

Prepared by ______________________________ Date ______________

Evaluation Criteria

C. Criteria for Procedures

1. An excellent procedure is a step-by-step description of how the staff will carry out the policy and regulations.
2. An effective procedure may be modified by staff under certain circumstances.
3. An effective procedure has been developed by staff who are familiar with the task to be performed.
4. An excellent procedure has been approved by library managers.
5. ______________________________

____

____

6. ______________________________

____

____

7. ______________________________

____

____

8. ______________________________

____

____

9. ______________________________

____

____

10. ______________________________

____

____

Prepared by ______________________________ Date ______________

Evaluation Criteria

D. Criteria for Guidelines

1. An effective guideline describes best practice.
2. An excellent guideline provides suggestions for staff on the most efficient ways to implement policy statements, regulations, and procedures.
3. ______________________________
4. ______________________________
5. ______________________________
6. ______________________________
7. ______________________________
8. ______________________________
9. ______________________________
10. ______________________________

Prepared by ______________________________ Date ______________

Policy Element Review Summary

Purpose of Workform 7

Use this workform to record the evaluation of each policy under review.

Who Should Complete Workform 7

The people assigned to evaluate the policies complete one copy of this workform for each policy they review.

Factors to Consider When Completing Workform 7

1. You will use the information on Workform 4, Policy Audit Inventory Results, and Workform 6, Evaluation Criteria, as you complete this workform.
2. Review the rating scale at the end of the form carefully before beginning.
3. Remember that you are only evaluating the policy and indicating the level and types of revision needed. New or revised wording for the policy will be developed later, in a separate process.

To Complete Workform 7

1. Enter the policy category as shown on Workform 4.
2. Enter the subject of the policy as shown on Workform 4.
3. Enter your name.
4. Read the policy statement and compare it to the evaluation criteria that your library developed and recorded on Workform 6.
   a. **Column A, row 1** Record your observations about the policy statement, paying special attention to the areas in which the policy statement does not meet the established criteria. Be as specific as possible because your observations will be used during the policy-revision process described in chapter 4.
   b. **Column B, row 1** Record the level of revision, if any, required for the policy statement to comply with the criteria.
5. Read the regulations and compare them to the evaluation criteria that your library developed and recorded on Workform 6.
   a. **Column A, row 2** Record your observations about the regulations, paying special attention to the areas in which the regulations do not meet the established criteria. Be as specific as possible because your observations will be used during the policy-revision process described in chapter 4.
   b. **Column B, row 2** Record the level of revision, if any, required for the regulations to comply with the criteria.
6. Read the procedures and compare them to the evaluation criteria that your library developed and recorded on Workform 6.
   a. **Column A, row 3** Record your observations about the procedures, paying special attention to the areas in which the procedures do not meet the established criteria. Be as specific as possible because your observations will be used during the policy-revision process described in chapter 4.
   b. **Column B, row 3** Record the level of revision, if any, required for the procedures to comply with the criteria.
7. Read the guidelines, if they exist, and compare them to the evaluation criteria that your library developed and recorded on Workform 6. If guidelines do not exist and are not necessary, write "NA" in column B.
   a. **Column A, row 4** Record your observations about the guidelines, if any, paying special attention to the areas in which the guidelines do not meet the established criteria. Be as specific as possible because your observations will be used during the policy-revision process described in chapter 4. If guidelines do not exist, but are necessary, note that as well.
   b. **Column B, row 4** Record the level of revision, if any, required for the guidelines to comply with the criteria.

Factor to Consider When Reviewing Workform 7

Someone should review all of the completed copies of Workform 7 to ensure that the reviewers were consistent in their use of the ranking scale.

WORKFORM 7

Policy Element Review Summary

Policy Category ______________________________

Subject ______________________ **Evaluated by** ______________________

A. Element	**B. Revision Level Required***
1. Policy Statement *Observations:*	
2. Regulations *Observations:*	
3. Procedures *Observations:*	
4. Guidelines *Observations:*	

***Use the following scale to identify the level of revision required for each element of a policy:**

Level of Revision Required for an Element	
0	No revision needed to meet criteria
1	Minor revision needed to meet criteria
2	Moderate rewrite necessary to meet criteria
3	Total rewrite necessary to meet criteria
4	Does not exist—needs to be written
NA	Not applicable—refers only to guidelines

Prepared by ______________________ Date ______________

WORKFORM 8 **Policy Revision and Development Summary**

Purpose of Workform 8

Use this workform to organize the work to be done and to track assignments and deadlines.

Who Should Complete Workform 8

1. Columns A and B are completed by the chairperson of the Policy Audit Advisory Committee.
2. Columns C, D, E, and F are completed by a small team of managers appointed by the library director.

Factors to Consider When Completing Workform 8

1. You will be considering the individual elements of a policy when you complete columns E and F of Workform 8.
2. The level of effort required to complete a policy is affected by a number of factors, including the amount of revision required, the need for board action, the extent to which a given policy relates to other policies, the complexity of the issues addressed in the element, the amount of controversy expected, legal issues, the amount of staff time required to develop and review the policy, and the necessity for training staff. Those issues are discussed in detail in chapter 4.
3. Use the following scale to determine the level of effort needed:
   - 0 No revision necessary—policy meets or exceeds all criteria.
   - 1 Very minimal effort—a knowledgeable staff member could quickly make the few minor changes needed to meet all criteria. Necessary changes are elaborations or clarifications and are noncontroversial.
   - 2 Minimal effort—a knowledgeable staff member could make the changes needed to meet all criteria or create the new element. Subject is neither complex nor controversial.
   - 3 Moderate effort—a few staff with expertise related to the subject could make the changes needed to meet all criteria or create the new element. Subject is noncontroversial but may be complex.
   - 4 Significant effort—a staff task force is required to identify options and make recommendations. Subject is complex and affects other policies. May require governing authority to choose between proposed options related to policy statement or regulations.
   - 5 Extensive effort—the library administration and library board are required to establish policy and regulations. Subject is potentially controversial, and proposed changes may require public comment or legal review.
4. You will need to create your own scale to indicate priority. You can use whatever scale you normally use in your library. See chapter 4 for more information on assigning priorities.
5. It is recommended that no more than three or four levels of priority be used in the priority scale.

To Complete Workform 8

1. Enter the name of the policy category on the first line.
2. **Column A** Record the number of the policy.
3. **Column B** Record the subject of the policy.
4. **Column C** Record the level of effort required to complete the policy.
5. **Column D** Record the priority of the policy.
6. **Column E** Record the name of the chairperson of the committee assigned to develop each element of the policy.
7. **Column F** Record the date by which the members of each committee are expected to have finished their work.

Factors to Consider When Reviewing Workform 8

1. You will want to review and update this workform regularly to ensure that you always have a current record of the process. Changes will occur throughout the time you are developing policies, and this workform will enable you to keep track of those changes.
2. As policy elements are completed and approved, note the dates in the margin of the workform.
3. Periodically send the entire staff an update about the progress being made on the policy manual. Workform 8 will supply the information you need to make sure that the appropriate people are acknowledged for their contributions to the process.

WORKFORM 8

Policy Revision and Development Summary

Policy Category ______________________________

A. No.	B. Subject	C. Level of Effort	D. Priority	E. Assigned To		F. Due Date
				Policy/Regulations		
				Procedures		
				Guidelines		
				Policy/Regulations		
				Procedures		
				Guidelines		
				Policy/Regulations		
				Procedures		
				Guidelines		
				Policy/Regulations		
				Procedures		
				Guidelines		
				Policy/Regulations		
				Procedures		
				Guidelines		
				Policy/Regulations		
				Procedures		
				Guidelines		
				Policy/Regulations		
				Procedures		
				Guidelines		
				Policy/Regulations		
				Procedures		
				Guidelines		

Level of Revision Required for an Element	
0	No revision necessary
1	Very minimal effort
2	Minimal effort
3	Moderate effort
4	Significant effort
5	Extensive effort

Prepared by ______________________________ Date ______________________

WORKFORM 9
Master Schedule

Purpose of Workform 9

Use this workform to schedule the development of your revised and new policies.

Who Should Complete Workform 9

The small team of managers appointed by the library director to complete columns C, D, E, and F of Workform 8 should complete Workform 9.

Factors to Consider When Completing Workform 9

1. You will be scheduling the elements of a policy individually.
2. Schedule all of the policies with the highest priority to be completed first. Then schedule the policies in the next level of priority, and so on.
3. The person who reviewed a policy determined the level of revision required for each element and recorded that level on Workform 7, Policy Element Review Summary. Refer to that level of revision to help estimate how long it will take to complete a given element.
4. Schedule interconnected policies for completion at the same time.
5. Be sure to include time to review and approve each element.
6. Remember that procedures are normally not scheduled to be developed until policy statements and regulations have been approved.
7. Determine when you plan to develop any needed guidelines. You may choose to defer the development of guidelines until all of the policies in a category have been completed.
8. Most library staff members believe that they already have more to do than they ever can accomplish. Use the master schedule to ensure that no staff member or group of staff members will be asked to do an unreasonable amount of work in an unreasonable amount of time.

To Complete Workform 9

1. **Column A, row 1** List the number and name of the first policy you intend to develop.
2. **Column A, row 1a** Determine the date you intend to start developing the policy statement and regulations and place a small X on that date. Then determine the date you intend for the policy statement and regulations to be completed and place a small X on that date. Now connect the two Xs with a line that represents the time required to complete the two elements.
3. **Column A, row 1b** Determine the date you intend to start developing the procedures for this policy and place a small X on that date. Then determine the date you intend for the procedures to be complete and place a small X on that date. Now connect the two Xs with a line that represents the time required to complete the element.
4. **Column A, row 1c** If you have decided not to develop guidelines at this time, draw a line through the word guidelines. If you intend to develop guidelines, determine the starting date and place a small X on that date. Then determine the date you intend for the guidelines to be complete and place a small X on that date. Now connect the two Xs with a line that represents the time required to complete the element.
5. **Column A, row 1d** Place a star on the date you intend to implement the completed policy.
6. If you use more than one page to schedule all of your policies, number each page of the master schedule at the bottom.

Factors to Consider When Reviewing Workform 9

1. Does the workload seem reasonable?
2. Have you considered holiday schedules and special events in your schedule?
3. Have you checked to ensure that each individual's responsibilities have been scheduled sequentially rather than simultaneously?

WORKFORM 9

Master Schedule

A. Policy/Activity	Jan.	Feb.	Mar.	Apr.	May	June	July	Aug.	Sept.	Oct.	Nov.	Dec.
1. a. Policy Statement and Regulations b. Procedures c. Guidelines d. Implementation												
2. a. Policy Statement and Regulations b. Procedures c. Guidelines d. Implementation												
3. a. Policy Statement and Regulations b. Procedures c. Guidelines d. Implementation												
4. a. Policy Statement and Regulations b. Procedures c. Guidelines d. Implementation												
5. a. Policy Statement and Regulations b. Procedures c. Guidelines d. Implementation												

Page ______ of ______

Prepared by ______________________________ Date ______________

Glossary of Policy Terms

This glossary contains all of the definitions presented at the beginning of each chapter of *Creating Policies for Results.* The chapter in which a term is first defined is noted in parentheses at the end of the definition.

Approved By The person or board that formally approved the policy statement, regulation, procedure, or guideline. If someone with the authority to do so hasn't approved the policy statement, regulation, procedure, or guideline, it is simply a written description of a practice. (chapter 2)

Best Practice Management practices and work processes that produce highly effective and efficient library services. (chapter 4)

Degree of Revision A numeric indicator of the extent of the revision required to bring a policy element into compliance with the evaluation criteria for that element. (chapter 3)

Evaluation Criteria The value-laden declarative statements that describe the characteristics of effective library policy statements, regulations, procedures, and guidelines. These criteria provide the framework for the assessment phase of the policy audit. (chapter 3)

External Audience Residents of the library service area, elected officials, members of the media, and others who are not library employees or members of support groups. (chapter 5)

Guideline A description of best practice that provides suggestions for staff on the most efficient ways to implement policy statements, regulations, and procedures. Guidelines are more philosophical than policy statements, regulations, or procedures and often are developed by staff committees. Guidelines are always approved by the library director but are rarely reviewed by the library's governing authority. Typical guidelines include reference guidelines and guidelines for serving people with special needs. (chapter 1)

Internal Audience Library staff members and volunteers. (chapter 5)

Level of Effort The amount of staff time and energy required to develop a new policy or revise an existing policy. (4)

Library Support Groups Members of library boards, friends groups, and foundations. (chapter 5)

Master Category List A complete list of the policy categories within a given policy type and an enumeration of the specific policies included in each category. See figure 5 for an example of a master category list. (chapter 2)

Policy The generic term used for the policy statement, regulations, procedures, and guidelines (if any) that apply to a specific issue. (chapter 1)

Policy Audit The methodical collection, examination, and review of the library's existing policy statements, regulations, procedures, and guidelines. Policy audits have two parts:

> **Inventory** The process of identifying, collecting, and organizing the library's existing policy statements, regulations, procedures, and guidelines.
>
> **Assessment** The process of evaluating the library's existing policy statements, regulations, procedures, and guidelines. (chapter 2)

Policy Category Subdivisions of types of policies. Six policy categories have been used in this book to classify public service policy statements and the regulations, procedures, and guidelines that support those policy statements. The categories are listed below and described in more detail in figure 5:

- governance and organizational structure
- management policies
- customer services
- circulation services
- information services
- group services (chapter 2)

Policy Element One of the four components of a policy: a policy statement, regulation, procedure, or guideline. (chapter 1)

Policy Manual A collection of library policy statements. Policy manuals may include regulations, procedures, and guidelines. Policy manuals are normally available in print format and may be available electronically as well. (chapter 1)

Policy Statement A brief, written statement that describes *why* the library does something. Policy statements are written from the customer point of view and approved by the library's governing authority. See figure 3 for a sample policy statement. (chapter 1)

Policy Type General groupings of library policies. Public libraries typically have at least five types of policies: public service, technical service, personnel, financial, and collection development. (chapter 2)

Practice The way things are actually done in your library. Practice may or may not be supported by policy statements, regulations, and procedures. Practice is generally conveyed via oral tradition as a part of a new staff member's orientation, and it can become very subjective. (chapter 1)

Priority The relative importance of each policy being developed.

Procedure A written, step-by-step description of *how* the staff will carry out a policy and regulations. Procedures are more flexible than regulations and will change as the tools available to staff change. Frontline staff may be allowed to modify procedures in certain circumstances. Procedures are developed by staff and approved by library managers. They are not reviewed by or approved by the library's governing authority. (chapter 1)

Regulation A specific, written rule that further defines a policy, describing *what* must be done to support the policy. They are normally approved by the library's governing authority. See figure 3 for a sample list of regulations. (chapter 1)

Index

Q

R

S

T

U

V

W